GUIDE TO NORTHEAST OREGON

Robert Dreisbach

ENTROPY CONSERVATIONISTS
SEATTLE

Abbreviations: I = Interstate Highway; SR = State Highway; CR = County Road; US = Federal Highway; MP = Mile Post; RT = Round trip; ' = feet; ' gain = total feet of elevation gain; store = grocery store; stores = groceries and other supplies, food = restaurant.

Notes: All telephone numbers are area code (503). Populations are from the 1990 census. The directions for hikes and bicycle tours assume that users will have the US National Forest map for the area, a compass, and a road map. A map produced by the Oregon Department of Transportation is available free at any tourist information. All compass directions are true (not magnetic). Distance and elevation gain are given for the round trip. Where a National Forest map is not available, the 1-100,000 scale BLM map is recommended. All references to USGS maps are to the 7-1/2 minute topographic series quadrangles. Some public libraries have files of these maps. A five letter map designation (in parenthesis with the USGS map) refers to a map available from National Forest or National Recreation Area offices. Only one of these maps doesn't give the topography. These maps are listed on page 156.

The covered wagon on the cover is used by permission of The Oregon Trail Motel, 211 Bridge Street, Baker City OR, 97814.

Copyright © 1995 Robert H. Dreisbach

Library of Congress Catalog Card Number 94-62219

ISBN 0-942153-14-6

ENTROPY CONSERVATIONISTS
20123–60th Ave. NE
Seattle WA 98155-1933

Contents

I–84

The Oregon Trail Route:
Ontario to Boardman

ONTARIO REST AREA–OREGON TRAIL, 2200', MP-378 (USGS Payette). This rest area, west of the Snake River after crossing the bridge from Idaho, presents the general history of the Oregon Trail migration to the crossing of the Snake River south of here, relationships with the Indians, and indicates the local sites worth visiting. Facilities and activities: picnicking, rest rooms, maps and local information, sanitary disposal station.

ONTARIO, 2240', population 9,392, area population 12,195, Exits 374 and 376 (USGS Payette). Ontario, in an area of intense agriculture irrigated by water from eight reservoirs and the Snake River, is a major business center for southeastern Oregon. The region produces onions, potatoes, sugar beets, corn, peppermint, dairy products, beef, wheat, alfalfa, and several seed crops, ranking second in agricultural production in the state of Oregon. The town was first settled in the 1880's when the Oregon Shortline Railroad laid tracks into the area, providing passenger service and a shipping point for beef cattle.

Ontario Convention and Visitor's Bureau, 88 Southwest 3rd Ave., 97914, tel. 889-8012, has maps and information.

Events: Malheur County Fair, mid-August; **Japanese Obon Festival**, mid-July; **Fourth of July Parade**; **Winter Wonderland Parade**, mid-December; tel. 889-8012 for information.

Recreational Activities: fishing for catfish in the Snake River, golf course, aquatic center, boating on the Snake River.

Camping and RV Parks:

Ontario Fair Grounds, 795 NW 9th St., 97914, tel. 889-3431. Facilities and activities: parking for recreational vehicles of any size, tents, showers, water, seasonal. Fee.

Westgate Mobil Village, 2511 SW 4th Ave., 97914, tel. 889-4068. Facilities and activities: pull throughs and full hookups for recreational vehicles of any size, tent area, showers. Fee.

River Village, 3200 N Oregon St., 97914, tel. 889-1544. Facilities and activities: pull throughs and full hookups for recreational vehicles of any size, tent area, showers. Fee.

Country Campground, two miles west of Ontario Airport on US-20, tel. 889-6042. Facilities and activities: pull throughs and full hookups for

recreational vehicles of any size, tent area, showers. Fee.
Idle Wheels, 198 SE 5th St., 97914, tel. 889-8433. Facilities and activities: pull throughs and full hookups for recreational vehicles of any size, tent area, showers. Fee.

ONTARIO STATE PARK, 2200' (USGS Payette). From Exit 374, drive east to the park. Facilities and activities: picnicking, boating, boat launch, water, no camping. The Washoe Ferry, located north of the mouth of the Malheur River nearby, began operation in 1864.

PAYETTE JUNCTION, 2141', area population 1,472 (USGS Payette). From Exit 374 on I-84, drive six miles north on SR-201. A store is located two miles west on SR-201 (MP-17).

TERRACE GRAVELS, MP-373 (USGS Payette, Malheur Butte). These deposits of gravel remain from Lake Idaho.

LAKE IDAHO SEDIMENTS, MP-362 to MP-359 (USGS Malheur Butte, Moores Hollow, Tub Mountain). The stratified soil seen to the east of I-84 developed from sediments deposited from a great sea known as Lake Idaho, which covered much of the inland area of Oregon and Idaho from 7 million to 2 million years ago. The lake eventually drained into the area that became Hell's Canyon as tectonic forces tilted the land to connect this large inland region with the Snake River. These lake sediments are best seen from SR-201 at MP-8 where parking is possible and the sedimentary layers can be examined on foot. Leave I-84 at MP-356.

DEER FLAT NATIONAL WILDLIFE REFUGE, 2086' (USGS Olds Ferry). From Exit 356 on I-84, drive east on SR-201. SR-201 follows the Snake River for four miles along the Wildlife Refuge. In August, pelicans, Canada geese, seagulls, and deer were visible from the highway. Facilities and activities: picnicking, Snake River access, primitive camping, boat launch ramp.

OASIS CAMPGROUND, 2100' (USGS Olds Ferry). Drive three miles east on SR-201 from MP-356 on I-84. Facilities and activities: full hookups, tent area, boat launch ramp, fishing, bait, ice, open April to October. Fee. Address: Huntington 97907, tel. 262-3365.

FAREWELL BEND, 2100', Exit 353 (USGS Olds Ferry, BLM Brogan). Facilities: food, gas, camping, lodging.

SAND DUNES, MP-353 (USGS Olds Ferry). The white banks of sand in these actively moving dunes across the Snake River in Idaho accumulated from flood deposits left as the glaciers receded 14,000 years ago.

TILTED COLUMBIA BASALTS, MP-353 (USGS Olds Ferry). The tilted layers of basalt on the ridge northeast of Farewell Bend State Park illustrate the tectonic forces that have been active in this region in the last 15 million years. The lava flows were originally nearly level.

OREGON TRAIL, high point 2400', 20 miles RT, 500' gain (USGS Olds Ferry, Huntington, McCarthy Ridge, BLM Brogan). **Mt. Bicycle Route.** The Oregon Trail route, after passing west of Tub Mountain (see p. 33) coming from Vale, went north into the valley west of Love Reservoir, then turned northeast to pass through the area now occupied by Love Reservoir to reach the Snake River at Birch Creek. From the west side of I-84 at Exit 353, ride six miles southwest on a gravel road following the Oregon Trail route past Love Reservoir to Willow Springs, an emigrant campsite beside a 2586' summit. Turn south and ride along the Oregon Trail route toward the Tub Mountain crossing.

BIRCH CREEK–OREGON TRAIL, 2100' (USGS Olds Ferry). Drive two miles west of I-84 from Exit 353 on a gravel road to this interpretive exhibit on the route of the Oregon Trail. Markers indicate the route emigrants took from here to the Snake River. A path allows access to the ruts left by the travellers.

FAREWELL BEND STATE PARK–OREGON TRAIL, 2080' (USGS Olds Ferry). From Exit 353 on I-84, drive north on US-30 one mile to the park. The park is located at the beginning of Brownlee Reservoir where the current is slow. Nearby on the Snake River is the location of Olds Ferry, which carried early travelers across the Snake River until 1922. Facilities and activities: electrical hookups for recreational vehicles up to maximum 56', picnicking, swimming, boating, boat launch ramp, sanitary disposal. Open all year. Fee. Tel. 869-2365.

HUNTINGTON, 2108', population 522, area population 694 (USGS Huntington). If westbound on I-84, take Exit 353 and drive northwest five miles. If eastbound, take Exit 345 from I-84 and drive southeast. The city park in the middle of town between US-30 and the railroad tracks has picnic tables, water, and restrooms in summer. Facilities and activities: food, stores, lodging, gas.

SPRING RECREATION AREA, 2050' (USGS Olds Ferry Northwest). Drive four miles northeast of Huntington on the Burnt River road to this campground maintained by the Bureau of Land Management. Facilities and activities: tent area, pull throughs and full hookups for recreational vehicles of any size, showers, launch ramp, dock, fishing, boating, swimming, picnicking. Fee.

RYE VALLEY LOOP, high point 4500', 40 miles RT, 2800' gain (USGS Huntington, Birch Creek Meadow, Rye Valley, Lime, BLM Brogan). **Mt. Bicycle Route.** From Huntington, ride west on Durbin Creek road, taking a left fork (west) at five miles from Huntington into Birch Creek

Meadows. At 14 miles from Huntington, 1.5 miles west of the Birch Creek bridge, turn north across the west shoulder of Cinder Butte. Leave bicycle at the highest point of the road, 4300', and hike east to the summit of Cinder Butte, 4838', for a general view to the west and south of this high plateau country. Cinder Butte is a volcanic vent that was active during the time the Columbia Basalts were being emitted. Return to bicycle and continue northwest to descend to Dixie Creek, taking the north or northwest fork at road junctions. On reaching Dixie Creek, cross the creek, and turn right (northeast) downstream to Rye Valley, an area which saw mining activity before 1900, now cattle ranches. Continue east down the valley of Dixie Creek to I-84 and the Burnt River valley. Turn south on I-84 or on parallel roads to return to the starting point.

TABLE ROCK, 4738', 30 miles RT, 2800' gain (USGS Huntington, Birch Creek Meadow, Rye Valley, BLM Brogan). **Mt. Bicycle Route.** Ride as above from Huntington west up Durbin Creek. At a road junction five miles from Huntington, continue northwest up Durbin Creek to the saddle between Durbin Creek and Beaver Creek. Turn right (northeast) to ascend toward Table Rock. Where the road begins to descend, leave bicycle and hike east to the summit and a view east to the hill country on both sides of the Snake River.

LIME, 2250' (USGS Lime). If westbound, take Exit 345 and drive north on US-30, or if eastbound, take Exit 342. Here, the decaying remains of a cement plant stand beside the highway. The cliffs west of the highway were the quarry where the rock was excavated for use in making the cement.

DIXIE CREEK LOOP, high point 5100', 50 miles RT, 3000' gain (USGS Lime, Rye Valley, Mormon Basin, Lost Basin, Durkee, Big Lookout Mountain, BLM Brogan, BLM Baker City). **Mt. Bicycle Route.** Park on the west side of the Rye Valley Exit from I-84 (Exit 340). Ride west up the Dixie Creek valley, reaching Rye valley at 10 miles. Continue northwest up the north fork of Dixie Creek for nine miles. Where Dixie Creek bends to the southwest, continue northwest over the saddle, 5100', into the drainage of Reagan Creek. Descend northwest into the valley of the Burnt River, turning right (east) down the river to Durkee and I-84. Ride southeast along or on I-84 to return to the Rye Valley Exit starting point.

JUNIPER MOUNTAIN LOOP, high point 5275', 35 miles RT, 3300' gain (USGS Lime, Rye Valley, Durkee, Big Lookout Mountain, BLM Brogan, BLM Baker City). **Mt. Bicycle Route.** Ride west from the Rye Valley Exit (Exit 340), 2319', up Dixie Creek into Rye Valley. At 12 miles from I-84, turn northeast and ascend to a saddle, 4348'. In the saddle turn southeast and ride a road that bends east to the summit of Juniper Mountain, 5275'. From the summit, return to saddle and descend northeast along Shirttail Creek to reach I-84 near the Ash Grove Cement Plant (Exit 330).

Turn southeast on I-84 to the starting point.

DIXIE CREEK–BURNT RIVER LOOP, high point 5700', 75 miles RT, 3000' gain (USGS Lime, Rye Valley, Mormon Basin, Bridgeport, French Gulch, Lost Basin, Durkee, Big Lookout Mountain, BLM Brogan, BLM Baker City). **Mt. Bicycle Route.** Park on the south side of I-84 at the Rye Valley Exit (Exit 340). Ride west up Dixie Creek into Rye Valley. At 10 miles from I-84, turn southwest to continue up the south fork of Dixie Creek. At 20 miles from I-84, continue following the south fork of Dixie Creek as it turns north. Cross a saddle, 5700', into the Burnt River drainage and descend northwest through Devil's Canyon to Cottonwood Creek. Continue down Cottonwood as it joins Clarks Creek, riding through the sites of Clarksville and China Town, ghost towns from the mining era. Reach the Burnt River in the Bridgeport Valley, 35 miles from I-84 at the Dixie Creek Exit. Turn east and ride down the Burnt River to reach Durkee. Ride south on US-30 to MP-330 then on I-84 to reach the starting point at the Rye Valley Exit. The Burnt River canyon is noted as a source of jasper agate.

MORGAN MOUNTAIN, 5063', 15 miles RT, 2800' gain (USGS Lime, BLM Baker City). **Mt. Bicycle Route.** From Exit 338, ride northeast on the Jordan Creek Road for three miles. At a "Y" road junction, keep to the right (northeast). Where the road turns east to meet a four-way intersection, five miles from I-84, go right (south) and ascend to the summit of Morgan Mountain, a viewpoint into the Snake River.

SUGARLOAF MOUNTAIN, 6136', 32 miles RT, 3500' gain (USGS Big Lookout Mountain, Connor Creek). **Mt. Bicycle Route.** Park at the Jordan Creek Exit (Exit 338), 2400'. Ride northeast and north on the road up the ridge east of Jordan Creek to 5900'. Leave bicycle 15 miles from I-84 and hike east to the broad summit of Sugarloaf Mountain.

BASSER DIGGINS CAMPGROUND, 6700' (USGS Big Lookout Mountain). From the Jordan Creek Exit (Exit 338), drive north and northeast on the Lookout Mountain Road to the campground, located just off the road to the summit of Big Lookout Mountain. Facilities and activities: water, tent area, tables. No fee.

WEATHERBY REST AREA–OREGON TRAIL, 2400', MP-335 (USGS Lime). The interpretive display here tells of the difficulties encountered while travelling through the Burnt River canyon, which took the emigrants several days. To bypass the narrow gorge of the Burnt River between Weatherby and Nelson, the route of the Oregon Trail left the Burnt River Canyon south of Weatherby to travel northeast up Sisley Canyon three miles, then turned north to cross into Swayze Creek and descend back to the Burnt River Canyon. Facilities and activities: picnicking, restrooms, water. To view the Oregon Trail route, drive west from the rest area on the north side of I-84 into the Sisley Creek road. At one mile from I-84, a concrete post Oregon Trail marker stands on the left side (west) of the road and a plastic Oregon Trail marker is 0.1 mile farther. At 1.5 miles from I-84, a miners shack is built into the side of the hill.

GOLD HILL, 4136', 10 miles RT, 2000' gain (USGS Durkee, Lime). From the north side of I-84, at Exit 335, the Weatherby Exit, drive one mile west and northwest on the road up Sisley Creek past a cattle guard. BLM land begins at the cattle guard and continues to the west. To stay in BLM land, hike west to the summit of the first hill (3220'). Turn north to cross Pearce Gulch (2700'). Go west for one mile, then turn northwest for 1.5 miles to reach the summit of Gold Hill, passing several mines and prospects and Gold Hill Spring. This area is under study as a site for in-place cyanide leaching to recover the gold in this low grade deposit.

CONNOR CREEK FAULT, MP-335 to MP-334. This fault, trending northeast and southwest where it crosses I-84, marks the southern boundary of the Blue Mountains Gold Belt and the Baker Terrane. The rocks north of the fault are sea floor and ocean islands pushed into the continent by sea floor spreading and continental movement. The rocks south of the fault accumulated as sediments eroding from the rising land into a basin between the descending sea floor and the continent.

ASH GROVE CEMENT WEST, 2400', MP-330 (USGS Lime). This industrial complex on the south side of the highway makes cement and other industrial products using limestone from the Nelson Marble formation, a 240 million year old bit of sea-floor that was pushed into the North American continent by plate tectonic forces. This limestone-marble formation is also exposed north of I-84 between MP-331 and MP-332.

OREGON TRAIL (USGS Durkee). From Exit 330, drive west on Piano Road up Swayze Creek. At three miles from I-84, find a concrete post north of the road marking the route of the Oregon Trail. Two more markers of the Oregon Trail route are within the next 0.3 mile. No ruts are visible.

TERRACE GRAVELS, 2600' (USGS Durkee). South of Durkee, terrace gravels remain after Lake Idaho drained into what is now the Snake River two million years ago.

DURKEE, 2657', MP-327 (USGS Durkee). The Durkee valley was a favorite camping place for the Oregon Trail emigrants and, later, a stage coach stop and relay station on the Umatilla to Boise route. The Oregon Trail route here is just east of I-84. Graves of Oregon Trail emigrants are on the bluff one mile north. Facilities and activities: store, gas. **Express Ranch RV Park.** Located off US-30 on the south side of I-84 2.5 miles west of Exit 330 or two miles east of Exit 328. Facilities and activities: hookups, tent area. Fee. PO Box 257, Durkee, 97905, tel. 877-2457.

BIG LOOKOUT MOUNTAIN, 7120', 30 miles RT, 4500' gain (USGS Durkee, Big Lookout Mountain, BLM Baker City). **Mt. Bicycle Route.** Park on the east side of I-84 at the Durkee exit (Exit 327) or begin at the RV Park. Ride southeast parallel to I-84 for one mile then turn east into the Manning Creek valley. On reaching Manning Creek, cross the creek and continue northeast up Manning Creek, turning east to a saddle, 5300'. Leave bicycle and hike south cross country to the summit.

IRON MOUNTAIN, 3716', 10 miles RT, 1000' gain (USGS Durkee, Lawrence Creek, BLM Baker City). **Mt. Bicycle Route.** From the east side of I-84 at the Durkee Exit (Exit 327), 2700', ride northeast three miles up Durkee Creek on Vandecar Road to a road fork. Turn northwest and ride toward Iron Mountain, ascending to the northeast shoulder. Leave bicycle and hike to the summit of a volcanic vent that was active during the time the Columbia Basalt lava flows were being emitted.

IRON MOUNTAIN, 3716', 12 miles RT, 1000' gain (USGS Durkee, BLM Baker City). **Mt. Bicycle Route.** From the center of Durkee, ride west on US-30 for 1.5 miles to the junction with the road to Bridgeport. Turn right (north) and ride on a gravel road, crossing the railroad tracks and passing under I-84. After 0.7 mile, turn right (north) and ascend into the hills. At the shoulder of Iron Mountain, leave bicycle and ascend on BLM land to the summit.

LITTLE LOOKOUT MOUNTAIN, 6674', 30 miles RT, 3000' gain (USGS Durkee, Lawrence Creek, Little Lookout Mountain, BLM Baker City). **Mt. Bicycle Route.** Park on the north side of I-84 at the Durkee Exit, MP-327. Ride northeast up Durkee Creek, taking a left fork at four miles from I-84 to remain in the valley of Durkee Creek. At 4600', eight miles from I-84, turn north to 5800' on the south flank of the mountain. Leave bicycle and hike eastnortheast to the summit.

ENCINA SUMMIT, 3998', MP-315 (USGS Encina). The gentle ridge here separates the drainages of the Burnt River on the south and the Powder River on the north. From this summit, the Elkhorn Range of the Blue Mountains, from the Dooley Mountains in the south to Elkhorn Peak to the northwest, form the western backdrop to the Powder River valley.

BEAVER MOUNTAIN, 6400', 25 miles RT, 2500' gain (USGS Encina, French Gulch, Dooley Mountain). **Mt. Bicycle Route.** If westbound, leave I-84 at Exit 317 and drive two miles west. If eastbound, leave the freeway at Exit 313 and drive two miles southeast on US-30. Park and ride across the railroad tracks, continuing south on Ebell Creek road which becomes FS-11, taking a right fork (west) at the crest of the ridge after eight miles to reach the summit, the highest point of Bald Ridge. On the return, take the first road to the left (east) down a branch of Sutton Creek to make a loop.

BAKER CITY, 3449', population 9,140, area population 10,024, MP-304 (USGS Baker). Seat of Baker County (population 15,317, area 3,089 square miles). The first settlement at the site of what is now Baker City served Oregon Trail emigrants and predated the discovery of gold five miles to the southwest in Griffin Gulch. Travel to this point, a popular ford on the Powder River as it emerged from the hills to the south, from the Oregon Trail in the Burnt River Canyon, was facilitated by construction of a toll road. Baker City became the county seat in 1868 and the railroad arrived in 1884. The city has been a center of supply for mining, agriculture, and logging since the beginning. The city and the county are named for Col. Edward Baker, the first U.S. Senator from Oregon, who was killed in the Civil War.

Baker County Visitor & Convention Information Center, 490 Campbell St., 97814, tel. 800-523-1235 or 523-3356, and located one block west of I-84 at Exit 304, has a large selection of free maps and information about the area. The **Oregon Trail Traveler**, a descriptive newspaper, is available here.

Oregon Trail Regional Museum, 2490 Grove Street. Hours: 9am to 4pm, May to October. The museum contains artifacts from the regional schools and the local mines, farms, ranches, logging industry, and Native Americans. The building was erected in 1920 to house a swimming pool fed by natural hot water from a local mineral spring. An outstanding collection of rocks, minerals, gems, and fossils provided by the Cavin family and others gives visitors an opportunity to see the local rocks identified.

Baker City Historic Walking Tour. Begin at the Oregon Trail Regional Museum. Walk west on Campbell street, passing the Geiser-Pollman City Park on the east shore of Powder River and the Baker County Library on the west shore. The library has a history room with much information about the county and the region. Continue west one block to Main Street. Turn south and walk to the business district, which has many buildings dating from before 1900, including the First National Bank building and the Geiser-Grand Hotel, at opposite corners of the intersection of Main and Washington. The imposing brick Ison residence, now used by the Bank of America, is one block east of Main Street on Washington Avenue. The U.S. Bank, across from the Geiser-Grand Hotel, has the largest display of gold in the state, including a facsimile of the 80.4 ounce Armstrong Nugget, discovered in 1913 by miners in the Susanville area. The gray rock of which many of the buildings are constructed is a locally quarried volcanic tuff.

Continue south on Main Street then turn west one block on Auburn

Avenue to the City Hall, built in 1903, and the Carnegie Library building, now used as an arts and drama center. Go west on Auburn Avenue to 3rd St. Turn north two blocks to the Baker County Courthouse. Turn east to Second Street and continue north across Broadway to Church Street and St. Francis Cathedral, again of the local volcanic tuff. (A descriptive folder of a walking tour is available from the Visitor Center).

Activities: Samo-O-Swim Center, east end of Broadway Avenue. The swimming pool is supplied by water from a nearby hot spring. **Oregon Trail Theater**, in Basche-Sage Place on Main Street, has performances Wed and Fri at 7 PM from Mid-June to Mid-September.

Camping and RV Parks:

Mountain View RV Park, 2845 Hughes Lane, tel. 523-4824, at the north city limits and US-30. Facilities and activities: pull throughs and full hookups for recreational vehicles of any size, showers, tent area, swimming pool, laundry. Fee. **Oregon Trails West RV Park**, one block west of I-84 at Exit 302, tel. 523-3236. Facilities and activities: pull throughs and full hookups for recreational vehicles of any size, tent area, showers, laundry. Fee. **Lariat RV Park**, 880 Elm Street (north of Oregon Trail Regional Museum), tel. 523-6381. Facilities and activities: pull throughs and full hookups for recreational vehicles of any size, tent area, showers, laundry. Fee.

Trips and Tours: HCA Raft offers float trips on the Snake River and elsewhere. Address: PO Box 663, 97814, tel. 523-6580. **Eastern Oregon Tours.** Tours by van of ghost towns, fossil country, and wildlife. Address: Route 1, Box 133, 97814, tel. 523-7109. **Oregon Trail Trolley:** Horse-drawn tours of Baker City and tours of elk-feeding stations. Address: PO Box 223, Haines 97833, tel. 800-523-1235 or 856-3356. **Mid-Columbia Bus Company** has day excursions. Tel. 800-574-3424, or 523-7712.

SALMON CREEK PLACER MINE, 3600' (USGS Wingville). In Baker City, drive to the north city limits on US-30. Turn west for seven miles on Pocahontas Road. After the paved road turns north, five miles from US-30, turn left (west) on a gravel road for 1.3 miles. Walk south a few feet across a dry ditch to a viewpoint overlooking the pit, now filled with water, that was dug by streams of water from monitor nozzles to wash the dirt and gravel with the gold into sluice boxes.

MARBLE POINT, 7931', 10 miles RT, 3500' gain (USGS Wingville, Elkhorn Peak). **Mt. Bicycle Route.** From Baker City, drive north on US-30 to Hughes Lane, then west on Pocahontas Road to the junction of the Marble Creek road, eight miles from US-30. Where the paved road turns right (north), park and ride west on a gravel road, taking the first left (south) fork after 100 yards. Ride southwest up the Marble Creek canyon, passing the Marble Creek Picnic Area in two miles and the inactive Chemical Lime Company quarry after three miles, to the crest of the ridge. Leave bicycle and hike south to the summit of Marble Point (see p. 59).

POCAHONTAS, 3670' (USGS Wingville). From Baker City, drive north on US-30 to the north city limits, then west on Pocahontas Road. At 8.5 miles, 0.5 mile north of the intersection with the Marble Creek Road, the road passes the location of Pocahontas, where nothing remains. Pine City, located about three miles northwest on Pine Creek, was originally settled by the Chandler Wagon Train in 1862. Later, the community moved to the site of Pocahontas. Descendants of the Chandlers still live in the Powder River valley.

PINE CREEK RESERVOIR, 6552', 16 miles RT, 2500' gain (USGS Elkhorn Peak, Wingville). **Mt. Bicycle Route.** From Baker City, drive north on US-30 to the city limits, then west on Pocahontas Road for nine miles from US-30 to an intersection with Pine Creek Road. Drive left (west) on Pine Creek Road for 1.5 miles, bending right (north) at a corner in the paved road for one-fourth mile, to the intersection with a gravel road. Park off the pavement and ride west in the Pine Creek valley, passing the site of Pine City (see above under Pocahontas) about where the road joins Pine Creek. A gate on the gravel road 0.5 mile from the pavement may be closed but bicycles are permitted. Continue west along Pine Creek to ascend the valley. The road gradually bends southwest to reach the reservoir. A road and trail continue west past the reservoir to the ridge leading to Rock Creek Lake.

HUNT MOUNTAIN, 8225', 12 miles RT, 4300' gain (USGS Elkhorn Peak, Wingville). Drive as above for Pine Creek Reservoir. Park at the end of the pavement and hike west and northwest in the canyon of Pine Creek on a rough gravel road. A gate on the road may be closed, but hiking is permitted. At three miles from the pavement, reach concrete foundations left from the operation of the lower Baisley-Elkhorn mine, two houses and a road junction. Take the branch road north away from Pine Creek and ascend north on switchbacks to a saddle, 6000', next to a hill to the east with the canyon of the North Fork of Pine Creek dropping to the north. Continue ascending toward the west on switchbacks to a road junction, 6200'. Take the right fork (north) and contour north to the location of the Middle Camp of the Baisley-Elkhorn Mine just above the North Fork of Pine Creek. Continue contouring on the road past remains of a structure remaining from operation of the mine, climbing over a landslide that has filled the road to reach the North Fork of Pine Creek where the mine was located, now hidden by collapse of the entrance. Cross the creek and continue on the road 0.5 mile as it contours past two more creek gullies.

Where the road turns to the east after passing the North Fork of Pine Creek and the two more gullies, leave the road and ascend at first north, then slightly east of north, keeping just to the east of a rocky subsidiary ridge that descends from the crest toward Pine Creek. On reaching the crest of the ridge and the summit plateau, turn northwest to the highest summit. The rocks of the summit are quartz diorite of the Bald Mountain batholith.

WINGVILLE, 3400' (USGS Wingville). From Baker City, drive north four miles on US-30 from the junction of Hughes Lane and Pocahontas Road with US-30, then turn west on Wingville Road. The area is a center of wheat and hay farming. The cemetery has gravestones dating from the 1870's.

HAINES, 3331', population 405, area population 1,642 (USGS Haines). This town is 9 miles north of Baker City on US-30. Facilities and activities: food, stores, lodging, gas. Several log houses, a mine replica, and stamp mill are located in a park at the south edge of town on US-30.

Eastern Oregon Museum. At 3rd and School streets east of US-30. Open daily April 15 to October 15, hours 9am to 5pm. The museum has an enormous collection of artifacts, clothing and items from the regional farming and mining. The museum is in the old Haines Railroad Depot that was moved to the present location. Tel. 856-3233, 856-3366.

Events: Old fashioned **Fourth of July** celebration with rodeo.

Oldest Cowhand. At the 4th of July Celebration, Haines has a competition to determine the oldest working cowhand in the west. Address: Olds Hands Committee, Box 1, 97833, tel. 856-3777.

KILLAMACUE LAKE, 7137', 12 miles RT, 3000' gain (USGS Rock Creek, Anthony Lakes). **Mt. Bicycle Route.** From US-30 at Haines, drive west on CR-1146, turning south one-fourth mile at the first intersection to continue west on Rock Creek Road. At five miles from US-30, the paved road bends right (north) for 0.5 mile then continues west. Park near the Rock Creek Power House, six miles from US-30. Ride west on the road, which soon deteriorates, four miles to the trailhead. Leave bicycle and hike northwest to the lake.

RED MOUNTAIN, 8928', 15 miles RT, 4500' gain (USGS Rock Creek, Anthony Lake). **Mt. Bicycle Route.** Drive, ride, and hike as for Killamacue Lake (see above). Where the road turns southeast 0.5 mile before reaching the lake, 7000', leave the road and hike northwest cross country up a subsidiary ridge to the summit.

ROCK CREEK LAKE, 7680', 18 miles RT, 3500' gain (USGS Bourne, Rock Creek, Elkhorn Peak). **Mt. Bicycle Route.** Drive and ride as above for Killamacue Lake. Continue past the Killamacue Lake trailhead for 2.5 miles to the Rock Creek Lake trailhead. Leave bicycle and hike 3.5 miles south to the lake, the most beautiful lake in the Elkhorn Range.

NORTH POWDER RIVER, high point 6000', 12 miles RT, 4000' gain (USGS Rock Creek, Anthony Lakes). **Mt. Bicycle Route.** From US-30 in Haines, drive west and north, following the Elkhorn Scenic Byway. At a road junction four miles from US-30 where the Elkhorn Scenic Byway turns north, continue west on the Muddy Creek road to the site of the Muddy Creek school, seven miles from US-30. Turn right (north) for one mile, leaving the paved road. Park and ride west on a gravel road, FS-7301, into the canyon of the North Powder River to the junction with the North Powder River road at five miles. See page 79 (Road Log FS-73) for trips in the North Powder River canyon.

OREGON TRAIL, 2350' (USGS Baker). Leave I-84 at Exit 298. Drive 1.3 miles east on SR-203 to an Oregon Trail crossing at the intersection of Linley Lane and SR-203. Return west under I-84 and immediately turn north on a road parallel to I-84. At 1.5 miles from the I-84 interchange, cross the route of the Oregon Trail. From here, the route of the Oregon Trail bends to the northeast to avoid swamps and marsh, then again turns northwest to intersect the frontage road again 2.5 miles from I-84 at the Exit 298 interchange. The route of the Oregon Trail continues northwest, intersecting I-84 at MP-292. From this intersection with I-84, the Oregon Trail goes north for two miles before turning northwest to pass through what is now the town of North Powder.

POWDER RIVER REST AREA–OREGON TRAIL, 2400', MP-295 (USGS Magpie Peak). The theme of the Oregon Trail information display is the history of the lone Pine tree which served as a landmark for early travellers until cut down by someone travelling the Oregon Trail. Facilities: sanitary disposal station.

NORTH POWDER, 3256', population 448 (USGS North Powder). Leave I-84 at Exit 285. North Powder was settled before 1900 to serve the needs of the local agriculture, hay and cattle raising. The Oregon Trail came directly through the town, along what is now "E" St. Several buildings along "E" St. date from around 1900. For one week in August, North Powder hosts a flea market. Telephone 800-848-9969. **Tours: Thee Farm**, which keeps a herd of yaks, has tours all year. Address: Route 1, Box 45, North Powder, 97867, tel. 898-2848.

DORION HISTORICAL MARKER, 3200' (USGS North Powder). Drive northeast from North Powder for two miles on SR-237/US-30. A marker relates the history of Marie Dorion, the Indian wife of Pierre Dorion, Jr. She accompanied her husband and two children while pregnant when he was serving as guide and interpreter for John Jacob Astor's Overland Expedition of 1811 with Wilson Price Hunt as the leader. Her child was born on December 29th of that year.

THIEF VALLEY RESERVOIR CAMPGROUND, 3150' (USGS Telocaset).

From North Powder, drive northeast five miles on SR-237/US-30, then southeast for nine miles on a gravel road to the reservoir, 14 miles from North Powder. Facilities and activities: tents, trailers to 30', fishing, swimming, board sailing, boating. No fee.

WOLF CREEK RESERVOIR CAMPGROUND, 3704' (USGS Tucker Flat).

From Exit 283 on I-84, drive west four miles to the campground on the reservoir. Facilities and activities: tents, trailers, fishing, swimming, boat launch. No fee.

OREGON TRAIL (USGS North Powder, Craig Mt., Glass Hill, La Grande SE).

From North Powder to La Grande the Oregon Trail route parallels I-84, usually east of I-84 and up to one-fourth mile distant. At MP-279, seven miles from North Powder, a clump of willow trees west of I-84 mark an early stage stop and spring known as "Sixteen Mile House". At MP-274, where the canyon narrows, the Oregon Trail route goes north across the hills then descends sharply to the Grande Ronde valley near the Charles Reynolds Rest Area.

GLASS HILL, 5391', 6 miles RT, 2000' gain (USGS Glass Hill).

From eastbound I-84 at Exit 270, drive two miles southwest up Ladd Creek Road. Park at 3500' where a road forks to the right (north). Hike north on this branch road for 100' to a "Y". Turn left (west) to a corral. Go northwest up the ridge, keeping north of a fence line. When the fence line veers west, continue northwest in open woods to the summit ridge. Go north to the summit tower.

CHARLES REYNOLDS REST AREA–OREGON TRAIL, 2850' (USGS Glass Hill).

At MP-269, enter the rest area. The Oregon Trail route is one-fourth mile east, coming down the steep slope just east of Ladd Canyon. Informative displays give the history of the travelers in this area. After 1852, many Oregon Trail travellers turned to the west, near the foothills, to avoid the swamps and soft ground surrounding the rest area in the valley bottom. Facilities and activities: picnicking, playground, sanitary disposal.

LADD MARSH NATURE TRAIL AND VIEWING AREA, 2760',

One mile RT, no gain (USGS La Grande SE, Glass Hill, Conley, Craig Mt.). From I-84 at Exit 268, drive east 0.1 mile then north 0.4 mile to the trailhead at the Ladd Marsh, 0.5 miles from the I-84 exit. For the viewing area, return west under I-84 at exit 268 to Foothills Road. Turn left (north) on Foothills Road for two miles to the entrance to the viewing area on the east side of Foothills Road.

HOT LAKE RV RESORT, 2700' (USGS Craig Mt.). 65182 Hot Lake

Lane, La Grande 97850, tel. 963-5253. From Exit 268, drive east two miles. Facilities and activities: pull throughs and full hookups for recreational vehicles of any size, showers, swimming, nature walk, hiking, hot mineral springs and lake, tent area. Fee. Seasonal.

LA GRANDE, 2770', population 11,766, area population 15,310, Exits 259, 261, 265 (USGS La Grande SE). La Grande, the seat of Union County (population 26,300, area 2,038 square miles) was first settled in 1861 as a supply point for Oregon Trail travellers. A stone building dating from the earliest settlement still stands near "C" and Cedar Streets. The area around Birnie Park was a favorite resting spot for early travelers before they began the arduous climb over the Blue Mountains to the west. From Birnie Park, the Oregon Trail route continued west where "B" Avenue is now located, ascending to the west up Table Mountain. Since it took up to 20 oxen to pull each wagon up the hill, many days elapsed before a large party had regrouped at the top and were ready to continue on to the west. The first permanent buildings were located in the area around Birnie Park, then in 1884, when the railroad came to this area, buildings began to grouped around the tracks.

La Grande–Union County Tourist Information, 2111 Adams Ave., 97850, tel. 963-8588, 800-848-9969, has maps and travel information on weekdays.

Oregon Trail Tour. Begin at Exit 265 from I-84. Go west 0.5 mile on SR-203/US-30 to McAlister Lane, a gravel road, then turn south for one mile. From LaGrande, drive south on SR-203/US-30 five miles to McAlister road. Drive south on McAlister Road one mile. Where McAlister road bends west, the Oregon Trail route comes directly under the bend from the southeast (160°) and continues northwest parallel to Foothill Road, bending west where Foothill Road meets Gekeler Lane. The Oregon Trail valley route and the Oregon Trail foothill route joined near the junction of Foothill Road and Gekeler Lane. Drive west on McAlister to Foothill Road. Turn northeast along this road toward La Grande. At the first cross street, Gekeler Lane, turn left (west) and proceed one mile to "B" Avenue and park at Birnie Park. These streets overlie the Oregon Trail route. Remember that the actual trail in these flat valley lands was one hundred yards or more wide. Birnie Park has several displays.

Eastern Oregon State College, 9th St. and K Ave., has an art gallery, a museum with local and regional artifacts, and a performing arts center with a year-around schedule of cultural events. A schedule of events can be obtained by calling 800-452-8639 or 962-3393.

Riverside Park. From I-84, Exit 261, drive two miles west on Island Ave. Turn right (northwest) on Monroe and immediately north on Spruce. The park lies on the shore of the Grande Ronde river. Facilities and activities: restrooms in summer, shelter, tables, playground, river access.

Pioneer Park. At the north edge of La Grande coming from I-84 (Exit 259) on US-30, turn left (north) on Oak to the park. Facilities and activities: restrooms, picnic tables, play fields. A trail leads west to an Oregon Trail wayside on US-30.

Events: Winter Carnival is held in February. **Blue Mountain Days** with parade, rodeo, and motorcycle rally is held in June. The **Fourth of July** is celebrated with a parade and fireworks. **Union County Fair** is held in July at the fairgrounds in La Grande. **Oregon Trail Days** celebration is held in mid-August each year. For information about the above events, call 800-848-9969. **Oktoberfest** is held in October, tel. 962-3740.

Trips and Tours. Little Creek Outfitters, Box 2935, 97850, tel. 963-7878. Fishing and float trips. **Oregon Trail Adventures.** Fishing and float trips, 66716 Oregon Highway 237, 97850, tel. 800-527-8787, 963-2583, 534-5393.

Camping and RV Parks:

Broken Arrow RV Park, 2215 Adams Ave., 97850, tel. 963-7116. Facilities and activities: showers, laundry, pull throughs and full hookups for recreational vehicles of any size. Fee. **Quail Run RV Park,** 2400 Adams Ave., 97850, tel. 963-3400. Facilities and activities: showers, laundry, pull throughs and full hookups for recreational vehicles of any size. Fee. **Sundowner RV Park,** 1806 26th St., 97850, tel. 963-2648. Facilities and activities: showers, laundry, pull throughs and full hookups for recreational vehicles of any size. Fee. **Wendel's Corner RV Park,** Adams at "H", tel. 963-2757. Facilities and activities: No tents, hookups for self-contained recreational vehicles only. Fee. **Morgan Lake Recreation Area and Campground,** 4154' (USGS Hilgard). From Birnie Park in La Grande, drive west on "B" Avenue to the intersection with Walnut St. Turn left (south) on Morgan Lake Road to reach the lake and campground three miles from Birnie Park. Facilities and activities: tents, trailers, swimming, fishing, summer only. No fee.

GLASS HILL, 5391', 30 miles RT, 2600' gain (USGS La Grande SE, Glass Hill). **Mt. Bicycle Route.** From Birnie Park in La Grande (see above), ride east to 12th St., then go south on 12th St. into Bushnell Lane, ascending along Taylor Creek. At a saddle after five miles, 4500', take the right fork (northwest) and ascend to the plateau of Glass Hill. Continue south, taking the uphill or south fork at road junctions to the lookout at the summit of Glass Hill. On the return from the lookout, ride northwest on the west side of the ridge for four miles then descend north into the Mill Creek valley to the Morgan Lake Road. Turn northeast to return to "B" avenue. Turn right (east) to the starting point.

MORGAN LAKE LOOP, high point 4200', 25 miles RT, 1500' gain (USGS La Grande, Hilgard). **Mt. Bicycle Route.** From Birnie Park (see under La Grande above), ride west on "B" Ave. to Walnut. Turn south on Morgan Lake road and ascend toward Morgan Lake. At the junction to Morgan Lake, continue west, crossing the canyons of Rock Creek, Little Rock Creek, Graves Creek and Little Graves Creek. At a "T" junction, three miles past the Morgan Lake junction, where a road goes north and south on the rim of Whiskey Gulch, turn north, descending to SR-204. Turn right (north) to Hilgard State Park (water and restrooms). Continue on SR-204 into I-84 to return to La Grande. On entering La Grande, turn south to return to Birnie Park and the starting point.

MOUNT EMILY LOOP, 6110', 30 miles RT, 3500' gain (USGS La Grande SE, Summerville, Drumhill Ridge, Hilgard). **Mt. Bicycle Route.** From the center of La Grande, drive west on Spruce St. and park at Riverside Park. Ride north on Spruce St. then west on Blackhawk Trail to the Owsley Canyon Road. Ride north on Owsley Canyon Road taking the north or the uphill fork at junctions, staying on the Mt. Emily Road. Reach the summit in 12 miles. From the summit return south two miles then turn right (west) into Fox Hill Road. Descend south to Black Hawk Trail to return east to the starting point.

COVE, 3002', population 507, area population 1,880 (USGS Cove). Drive 15 miles east of La Grande on SR-237 to Cove, nestled at the base of Mt. Fanny, 7132', in the midst of orchards. The Calvary Baptist Church, more than one hundred years old, is across from the high school. Facilities and activities: store, food, gas. **Cove Warm Springs Swimming Pool.** Owned privately, the hot spring fed pool is open to the public from the end of May to September. Picnicking area. **Moss Springs Packing** has pack trips into the Eagle Cap wilderness, PO Box 104, Cove 97824, tel. 568-4823.

MOSS SPRING CAMPGROUND, 5842' (USGS Mount Fanny). From Cove (see above), drive southeast on Mill Creek road for 10 miles to the campground at the summit of the ridge. Facilities and activities: tents, trailers, horse ramp, horse stalls, hiking, backpacking, picnicking.

RED'S HORSE RANCH, 3600', 18 miles RT, 2300' gain (USGS Mount Fanny). From the trailhead near Moss Springs campground, hike northeast to this guest ranch on the Minam River (see p. 100).

POINT PROMINENCE, 6745', 40 miles RT, 4500' gain (USGS Cove, Mt. Fanny, Mt. Moriah, Gassett Bluff, WWLGT). **Mt. Bicycle Route.** From Cove (see above), ride southeast and east on Mill Creek road to Moss Springs campground. Turn north on the ridge road past Mt. Fanny Spring, Dunn's Bluff, and Pine Butte to Point Prominence Lookout, a viewpoint into the Minam River valley and 10 miles from Moss Springs campground. From the lookout, continue north, turning left (west) at the first junction onto road FS-62. After the first mile, FS-62 bends north for two miles, then again turns west over Grey Mountain, 4660', before descending to the paved road. Turn south on the pavement to the starting point at Cove.

MOUNT FANNY, 7155', 30 miles RT, 4200' gain (USGS Mt. Fanny, Cove). **Mt. Bicycle Route.** From Cove, ride southeast and east to Moss Springs campground on the Mill Creek Road. Turn north on the ridge road for five miles to a road junction. Turn west two miles to the summit with its towers.

MOUNT FANNY, 7155', 7 miles RT, 3600' gain (USGS Mt. Fanny, Cove). From Cove at the church, drive east on the Mill Creek road for four miles to the second cattle guard near the National Forest boundary, 3500'. The pavement ends at two miles. Park and hike north, staying east of the fence line. Join a road at 4000'. Follow the road east until it turns back to the northwest. Leave the road and hike north in open woods, crossing an overgrown road at 4700'. At the next road, 4800', a well-used logging road, follow the road north and northeast until it begins to turn east and descend, 5200'. Leave the road and ascend diagonally northeast to a crossing of the North Fork of Bridge Creek at 5900' at a gap in the brush along the creek. After crossing the creek, continue ascending diagonally northeast, staying below the rocky outcrops to a ramp that gives access to the summit plateau. Turn west on the plateau to the summit with its transmitter towers.

SR-203

UNION, 2792', population 1,847, area population 3,034 (USGS Union). From La Grande, drive southeast 14 miles on SR-203/US-30. Union is noted for its collection of Victorian homes, one dating from 1869. A self-guided tour of these homes begins at the corner of Brian and Main Streets at the north end of Union as SR-203 enters from La Grande. The tour begins with the Miller House, built in 1869, on the east side of Main at Brian. Next, at 475 N. Main St., is the Octagonal Tower House, built in 1873 and the Eaton House at 464 N. Main St., built in 1904. After passing the Eaton House, turn left (east) on Ash St. to the Wright House at 429 N. Bellwood, built in 1882. The Townley and Gale Houses, built in the 1890's, are west of Main Street at 782-5th and west of 5th on Delta. An informative folder on these houses is available at the museum (see below) or at the Tourist Information Office in La Grande. The Catholic Church (originally Methodist) dates from 1873.

> **Union County Museum**, 311 S. Main St., hours 1pm to 5pm Thursday through Monday, tel. 562-5197 or 562-6003, is open early May to October. The museum has a wide variety of local and regional artifacts ranging from Indian to mining.

> **Events: Eastern Oregon Livestock Show**, a six-day event with rodeo and

livestock judging is held in June, tel. 800-848-9969. **Main Street Madness**, a fair and flea market, is held each August, tel. 800-848-9969. A **Junior Rodeo** is held in mid-July at the Eastern Oregon Livestock Show stadium, tel. 800-848-9969.

CATHERINE CREEK STATE PARK, 3218' (USGS Little Catherine Creek). Drive eight miles southeast of Union on SR-203. Facilities and activities: swimming, fishing, tents, trailers, picnicking, water, barrier-free restrooms. Fee.

BALD MOUNTAIN, 6823', 20 miles RT, 3800' gain (USGS Little Catherine Creek, WWLGT). **Mt. Bicycle Route**. From Catherine Creek State Park (see above), ride southeast one-half mile on SR-203, then east and north on road FS-2036 on the east side of Little Catherine Creek, taking the north fork at road junction for 12 miles from SR-203 to a junction. Turn east on road FS-400 and follow the road northeast and east for one mile. Where the road turns southeast, leave bicycle and hike east cross country 0.5 mile to the summit.

NORTH FORK CATHERINE CREEK PICNIC AREA, 4000' (USGS China Cap). Drive 11 miles southeast of Union on SR-203 then five miles east and northeast on road FS-7785. Facilities and activities: fishing, picnicking, hiking.

NORTH FORK CATHERINE CREEK CAMPGROUND, 4200' (USGS China Cap). Drive 11 miles southeast of Union on SR-203 then six miles east and northeast on road FS-7785. Facilities and activities: tents, trailers to 25', fishing, swimming, hiking. No fee.

MEADOW MOUNTAIN, 7821', 16 miles RT, 4200' gain (USGS China Cap, WWLGT). From the North Fork Catherine Creek campground (see above), hike north on trail FS-1905 along the north fork of Catherine Creek for five miles to Catherine Creek Meadow. At a trail junction in the meadow, turn right (east) on trail FS-1906 and ascend to Meadow Mountain.

CHINA CAP, 8656', 8 miles RT, 3300' gain (USGS China Cap, WWLGT). Eleven miles southeast of Union on SR-203, drive east on road FS-7785 for 4.3 miles, passing a road to the right at three miles. Turn right (east) on road FS-7787. At eight miles from SR-203, turn left on road FS-140 for 0.3 miles to the trailhead, 5500', signed Buck Creek Trail. From here, Elk Creek is seven miles, Diamond Lake is nine miles, and the Minam River is 11 miles. Hike three miles east on trail FS-1944 to a trail junction, 7600'. Take the right fork (east and south), trail FS-1906, 0.7 mile to the saddle south of China Cap, 7840'. Leave the trail and hike north cross country up the ridge 0.5 mile to the summit of China Cap.

BURGER BUTTE, 8400', 8 miles RT, 3100' gain (USGS China Cap, WWLGT). Drive and hike as above for China Cap to the trail junction at 7600'. Turn right (east and south) on trail FS-1906 and ascend in one mile to the northeast shoulder of Burger Butte at Burger Pass. Leave trail and hike southwest to the summit.

HIGH HAT BUTTE, 8160', 12 miles RT, 3500' gain (USGS China Cap, WWLGT). From the trailhead as for China Cap (see above), hike at first north then east on a old road for one mile. Turn north on trail FS-1944 to cross the Middle Fork of Catherine Creek and reach the Squaw Creek Trail, FS-1951. Go at first northeast then north on the trail up Squaw Creek to an intersection with trail FS-1906 at 7400'. Turn right (southeast) on the trail up the ridge for one mile. Leave the trail at 7850' and hike northeast cross country up the ridge to High Hat Butte.

SQUAW BUTTE, 7840', 12 miles RT, 3300' gain (USGS China Cap, WWLGT). Hike as above toward High Hat Butte. At the junction with trail FS-1906, 7400', leave trail and hike southwest on the ridge to the summit.

MULE PEAK LOOKOUT, 8560', 10 miles RT, 3400' gain (USGS Flagstaff Butte, China Cap, WWLGT). From the intersection of SR-203 and FS-77 near MP-14 southeast of Union on SR-203, drive east on road FS-77 for ten miles, then northwest on road FS-600 for three miles to the south fork of Catherine Creek. Turn right one mile on FS-650 to the trailhead at the junction of the South Fork of Catherine Creek with Collins Creek at 5200' and 15 miles from SR-203. Hike northeast on trail FS-1924 to the summit of Mule Peak, passing the Sand Pass-Burger Pass trail, FS-1912, after two miles.

GRANITE BUTTE, 8679', 12 miles RT, 3500' (USGS Flagstaff Butte, China Cap). Drive and hike as above on trail FS-1924 for Mule Peak Lookout to the junction of trail FS-1912, two miles northeast of the trailhead. Turn north and ascend on the ridge between Pole Creek and Sand Pass Creek to Sand Pass, an area of decomposed granite. From Sand Pass, hike east on trail FS-1924 to the summit.

FLAGSTAFF BUTTE LOOKOUT, 6511', 30 miles RT, 3200' gain (USGS Medical Springs, Flagstaff Butte). **Mt. Bicycle Route.** Drive SR-203 14 miles southeast of Union to the junction with road FS-77, 3400'. Park and ride 12 miles east on road FS-77, the Eagle Creek Road, to the crest of the ridge 0.5 mile south of the lookout. Turn north to the lookout. Returning from the lookout, ride west two miles to an intersection, then south on road FS-6730 to road FS-67. Turn west on FS-67 into FS-71 and continue northwest to Medical Springs. Ride northwest on SR-203 to the starting point.

I-84

HILGARD STATE PARK–OREGON TRAIL, 3003' (USGS Hilgard). Leave I-84 at Exit 252 to the park on the south side of I-84. This camping place was frequently used by the Indians as well as the Oregon Trail emigrants. The crossing from the Grande Ronde valley to this point was one of the steepest parts of the entire route. The Oregon Trail exhibit here tells some of the methods used to get up and down these steep slopes. Facilities and activities: tents, trailers to maximum 30', open all year. Fee.

RED BRIDGE STATE PARK, 3160' (USGS Kamela SE). From Exit 252 on I-84, drive 7 miles west on SR-244 to the park on the Grande Ronde river. Facilities and activities: picnicking, fishing, no camping.

STARKEY, 3400', area population 115 (USGS Marley Creek, McIntyre Creek). From Exit 252 on I-84, drive southwest on SR-244 for 10 miles then one mile south on FS-51 to the Starkey Store. Facilities and activities: store. Agate nodules have been found in this region and in the gravels of the Grande Ronde river.

STARKEY EXPERIMENTAL FOREST, see p. 141. Drive west 20 miles on SR-244 from Exit 252 on I-84.

LEHMAN SPRINGS CAMPGROUND, see p. 140. Drive west 30 miles on SR-244 from Exit 252 on I-84.

BLUE MOUNTAIN CROSSING INTERPRETIVE CENTER, 3960' (USGS Huron). Take Exit 248 from I-84. Turn north and northwest toward Kamela for 0.6 miles. Turn right (northeast) into road FS-1843, passing under I-84 and the railroad track to reach the interpretive center, three miles from I-84. Displays explain the story of the Oregon Trail emigrants. Barrier-free trails give access to the actual ruts of the Oregon Trail. Volunteers in period costume at times add to the realism of a visit to this center.

INDIAN ROCK, 5668', 40 miles RT, 1800' gain (USGS Huron, Summerville, Drumhill Ridge). Mt. Bicycle Route. Park at Exit 243 on I-84. Ride east and northeast on gravel road FS-31, the Mt. Emily road. Where this road turns briefly northeast, nine miles from the starting point, the road is near the Marcus Whitman route of 1836 (see below). From the junction with road FS-3109, continue 12 miles east to Grandview road, FS-3120. Turn south three miles on Grandview road to the Indian Rock viewpoint, which has a view east to the Grande Ronde Valley and the Wallowa Mountains.

WHITMAN INTERPRETIVE CENTER. The Forest Service has established an information center on road FS-3109. The Marcus Whitman group of 1836, travelling on horseback, went from the La Grande area to

Meacham Creek on their way to the Walla Walla area, taking a more direct route to Walla Walla than that followed by the Oregon Trail emigrants. Leave I-84 at Exit 243. Drive east on road FS-31 (gravel) for nine miles. At the junction with road FS-3109, turn left (north) on road FS-3109 for two miles to the Whitman Overlook and interpretive sign (restrooms, no camping). Trails give access to two overlooks and Sacajawea Spring. The Whitman route travels northeast near FS-3109 for two miles as far as Sacajawea Spring, which might have been used by the early travelers.

MEACHAM, 3678' (USGS Meacham). From Exit 238 on I-84, drive northwest on US-30 to Meacham. Facilities and activities: food, store. The Union Pacific railroad turns east here to descend into Meacham Creek canyon to reach the Umatilla River. An informative marker relates the early history of the area. It was first known as Lees's Camp after Major H. A. G. Lee. Later Harvey Meacham ran a hotel here

TIP TOP LOOKOUT, 4574', 15 miles RT, 1000' gain (USGS Meacham Lake). Leave I-84 at Exit 238 (the South Meacham exit). **Mt. Bicycle Route.** Park near the exit and ride southwest on US-30, the frontage road, for five miles to Kamela. Cross the railroad tracks and ride west for two miles on the Tip Top Lookout road. Turn north 0.5 miles to the lookout. Return to the county road and continue northwest to Little Beaver Creek. Bend northeast to pass south of Meacham Lake, continuing east to reach US-30 at Meacham. Turn south on US-30 to return to the starting point.

JOHNSON RIDGE LOOP, high point 4800', 50 miles RT, 2800' gain (USGS Meacham Lake, McIntyre Creek, Bassey Creek, Meacham). **Mt. Bicycle Route.** Leave I-84 at Exit 238 (Meacham). Park near the interchange and ride south on US-30, the frontage road, to Kamela. Cross the railroad tracks west, then ride southwest seven miles over Salmonback Ridge on FS-400 and FS-2135. At a road junction, 4659', turn right (northwest) on FS-2136, which becomes CR-7, the Johnson Tower Road, to go over Johnson Ridge to pass the high point. Continue northwest, descending into the canyon of Little Johnson Creek to join McKay Creek. At 2150', three miles after the road turns west, turn right (northwest) up Rail Creek, turning left for one mile after riding six miles from McKay Creek, to join Ross road. Continue east into Meacham. Turn south on US-30 to the starting point.

EMIGRANT SPRINGS STATE PARK–OREGON TRAIL, 3800' (USGS Meacham). From Exit 234 on I-84 follow signs to this state park on the south side of I-84. Facilities and activities: tents, trailers to maximum length 60', full hookups, showers, lodge and log cabin to rent, hiking, skiing, bicycling, tel. 983-2277. Fee. Open mid-May to October. The spring, which made this a favorite camping and rest stop for the Oregon Trail emigrants, is west of the campground under a small building. The Oregon Trail exhibit describes some of the problems encountered: lost livestock and encounters with Indians. To get here from the Grande Ronde Valley took several days, a distance that we now cover in a few minutes. Ezra Meeker, one of the leaders, spent many years retracing the Oregon Trail route and establishing markers.

SQUAW CREEK OVERLOOK, 3747' (USGS Meacham). If westbound, leave I-84 at Exit 234 and drive north on the east side of I-84 for two miles to this overlook east into the Umatilla Indian Reservation. If eastbound, drive south from Exit 228. The Marcus Whitman route of 1836 travelled west on the second ridge to the east of this overlook. From the overlook, continue either direction on the frontage road to return to I-84.

DEADMAN PASS REST AREA—OREGON TRAIL, 3600' (USGS Cabbage Hill). Leave I-84 at Exit 228 to the rest areas. The name comes from deaths near here in the Bannock Indian War of 1878. The theme of the information display at the rest area tells of the feelings of the Oregon Trail emigrants who by this point were beyond most of the difficulties, the steep slopes and possible snow storms to the east. Here they had only 200 miles to travel to reach the Willamette river. The Oregon Trail from here travels northwest into the Umatilla River valley, now only six miles distant. Facilities: picnicking, restrooms, sanitary disposal.

VIEWPOINT. Located at MP-221 eastbound and MP-223 westbound, these parking areas off I-84 give a comprehensive view over the rolling hills west of Pendleton, all underlain by Columbia Basalt lava flows.

PENDLETON, 1068', population 15,126, area population 18,032, Exits 207, 209, 210, 213 (USGS Pendleton). The town, founded in 1868, and the seat of Umatilla County (population 59,249, area 3,218 square miles), grew rapidly as a major supply center for this agricultural region. For many years, wheat was the principle crop, but now, with widespread irrigation from nearby reservoirs, many other crops are grown, ranging from peas to corn.

Pendleton Chamber of Commerce, 25 SE Dorion, 97801, tel. 276-7411, has maps and information.

Umatilla County Historical Museum, located at 8 SW Fraser St. in the former Union Pacific Railroad depot, built 1910, displays a collection of artifacts from the local Indians and early settlers.

Pendleton Round-up is held for a week in mid-September of each year (call 800-457-6336 for information and tickets). Included in the show are: Happy Canyon Days, the Westward Ho! historical parade through downtown Pendleton with many horse-drawn vehicles and other animals (no motors), a junior Indian Beauty contest, a Main Street cowboy show, a tribal ceremonial dancing contest, and many displays. Several Indian tribes participate in the pageant and activities. A Roundup Hall-Of-Fame exhibit is open all year in the Roundup Stadium on weekdays.

Pendleton Woolen Mills, 1307 SE Court Place, has tours Monday through Friday until 3pm. The tour shows the process for converting the wool that arrives at the mill already cleaned and sorted, through the operations of carding, spinning, dyeing, spooling, and weaving to produce blankets and cloth for sports apparel.

Pendleton Underground Tours at 37 SW Emigrant, tel. 276-0730, has a walking tour in the basements under the old part of town and through some of the entertainment places of the frontier days.

Hanley's Western Store at 30 SE Court Ave. has a display of saddlemaking and a gallery of native American art.

Vert Memorial Museum devoted to native American culture, early settler artifacts, minerals, and rocks is at SW 4th and Dorion Sts. Call 276-8100 for hours.

Downtown Walking Tour. Begin at the Umatilla County Museum (see above). Bowman Hotel, 1905, 17 SW Frazer; Matlock-Brownfield, 1904, 413 S Main; Masonic, 1887, 403 S Main; Hendricks, 1897, 369 S Main; Empire, 1907, 21 SW Emigrant; Postoffice, 1916, 104 SW Dorion; Medernach, 1898, 333 S Main; Frazier, 1889, 343 S Main; Griggs and Tryon, 1896, 349 S Main; Rivoli, 1900, 355 S Main; Temple, 1900, 370 S Main; Temple-Martin, 1890, 342 S Main; Columbia, 1900, 322 S Main; Bond, 1905, 308 S Main; Berkeley, 1900, 304 S Main; City Hall, 1908, 34 SE Dorion; Oak, 1904, 327 SE 1st; State, 1905, 40 SE Emigrant; Ferguson, 1903, 412 S Main. A descriptive folder is available at the Chamber of Commerce.

Home Tour. Fell, 1902, 319 NE 1st; Judd, 1902, 3 NE Ellis; Livermore, 1885, 203 NW Ellis; Burroughs, 1895, 215 NW Ellis; McCormmach, 1907, 313 NW Ellis; Potwine, 1880's, 503 NW 4th; Sturgis, 1907, 215 NW Furnish; Jackson, 1900, 505 NW Desplain; Murphy, 1895, 215 NW 7th; Kupers, 1909, 301 NW 9th; Best, 1900's, 811 SE Goodwin; Fee, 1900's, 906 SE Frazier; Kirkpatrick, 1907, 525 SE 8th; Dickson, 1880's, 807 S. Main; Vaughan, 1877, 615 SW 13th; Temple, 1900, 523 SE Byers; Smith, 1894, 520 SE Byers; McComas, 1900's, 602 SE Byers; Mumm, 1903, 613 SE Byers; Ellis, 1877, 711 SE Byers; Swinburne, pre-1900, 714 SE Byers; Temple, 1900, SE 8th & Byers; Peringer, 1900, 916 SE Byers; Brownfield, 1893, 1206 SE Court. A descriptive pamphlet is available at the Chamber of Commerce.

Parks: Roy Raley, off Court Ave. east of the Roundup Stadium; **Rice-Blakey,** drive east of US-395 on Perkins and 24th; **Community Park,** drive west of US-395 on Montee Drive and 37th.

Trips: Living Heritage Tours: Oregon Trail, Umatilla Indian Reservation,

Adams. PO Box 1314, 97801, 239 SE Court, tel. 278-2446.

Camping and RV Parks:

Brooke RV Court, 5 NE 8th St., tel. 276-5353. Located on the river. Facilities and activities: pull throughs and full hookups for recreational vehicles of any size, showers, pets ok, laundry, no tents. Fee. **Emigrant Trailer Court,** 300 SW 22nd, tel. 276-2482. Facilities and activities: hookups, showers, laundry. Fee. **Riverview Terrace Mobile Home,** 2712 NE Riverside, tel. 276-7632. Facilities and activities: hookups, tent area, showers, laundry. Fee. **Shadeview RV Park,** 1417 SW 37th, tel. 276-0688. Facilities and activities: hookups, tent area in summer, showers, laundry. Fee. **Stotlars RV Park,** 15 SE 11th, tel. 276-0734. Facilities and activities: hookups, no tents, restrooms open summer only. Fee. **Oregon Trail RV Park,** one mile east on Mission Highway, tel. 276-4957. Facilities and activities: hookups, self-contained only. Fee.

CR-900. Umatilla River Road.

UMATILLA INDIAN RESERVATION, 1237' (USGS Mission). From Pendleton, drive east up the Umatilla River for seven miles on CR-900 to the Indian Reservation Headquarters. An Indian Interpretive Center is in the planning stage.

GIBBON, 1754', (USGS Gibbon). Drive 23 miles east of Pendleton on CR-900. The Union Pacific railroad turns south here to ascend over the Blue Mountains.

BAR M RANCH, 2161' (USGS Bingham Springs). Drive 30 miles east of Pendleton on CR-900 along the Umatilla River. Facilities and activities: lodging, food, riding, hiking, fishing. Address: Route 1, Adams 97810, tel. 566-3381.

CORPORATION FOREST SERVICE STATION, 2200' (USGS Bingham Springs). Located 32 miles east of Pendleton on the Umatilla River road, CR-900. Maps and information are available here during the summer.

BOBSLED RIDGE TRAIL, high point 4760', 10 miles RT, 2200' gain (USGS Bingham Springs). Park near the Corporation Forest Service Station. From the Umatilla National Forest sign, walk a road toward the river. The trail is across the river beginning at a signboard. The junction with the Bobsled Creek Trail is three miles and the junction with the Bobsled Ridge Road is five miles, near the high point.

LICK CREEK TRAIL, high point 4400', 8 miles RT, 2200' gain (USGS Bingham Springs, Blalock Mountain). From the entrance to the Corporation Forest Service Station, go 0.1 mile east along the road to the trailhead or find a connecting trail going north from the Corporation Forest Service

Station. The trail ascends one-fourth mile east to a trail junction. Turn left and ascend north to a road connecting in three miles to SR-204.

GROUSE MOUNTAIN, 4121', 6 miles RT, 2000' gain (USGS Bingham Springs). Begin at the Lick Creek Trail trailhead (see above). Follow the trail about one mile past the water tower above the ranger station. Where the trail comes into the open after passing a gully, leave the trail and descend cross country to Lick Creek. Cross the creek bed, and ascend north on a subsidiary ridge to the summit. The best views are just before entering the trees that surround the summit.

UMATILLA FORKS CAMPGROUND, 2360' (USGS Bingham Springs). Drive 34 miles east of Pendleton on CR-900 up the Umatilla River. The last four miles is narrow and gravel, not suitable for trailers. Facilities and activities: tents and small recreational vehicles, hiking, fishing. No fee.

BUCK MOUNTAIN TRAIL, high point 4651', 8 miles RT, 2600' gain (USGS Bingham Springs, Andies Prairie). From Umatilla Forks Campground, hike southeast 0.3 miles to the trailhead, off the South Fork road. Hike south on the Buck Mountain trail to Whitman Springs, named for the Whitman emigrant party.

BUCK CREEK TRAIL, high point 4000', 8 miles RT, 2000' gain (USGS Bingham Springs, Andies Prairie). The trailhead is 0.3 miles southeast of the Umatilla Forks Campground. The trail follows the course of Buck Creek to the junction with Lake Creek, then turns east to the Wilderness Boundary.

NINE MILE RIDGE TRAIL, high point 5100', 15 miles RT, 3000' gain (USGS Bingham Springs, Andies Prairie). The trailhead is one-fourth mile south of the Umatilla Forks Campground. Ascend away from the North Fork of the Umatilla River in open timber and grassland to the Wilderness Boundary at Shamrock Spring and road FS-330.

UMATILLA RIVER TRAIL, high point 5000', 15 miles RT, 3000' gain (USGS Bingham Springs, Andies Prairie). From the Umatilla Forks campground, hike east on the trail along the Umatilla River, crossing Coyote Creek at 2.5 miles and leaving the river at four miles. The trail then ascends north to a trailhead on a road that leads in three miles to SR-204 near Tollgate.

SR-11

ADAMS, 1526', population 223 (USGS Adams). Drive 11 miles northeast of Pendleton on SR-11. Facilities and activities: food, stores, gas, several buildings from the 1900's.

ATHENA, 1739', population 997, area population 1,662 (USGS Athena). From Pendleton, drive 16 miles north on SR-11. Facilities and activities: food, stores, lodging, gas, city park with water, picnicking, restrooms. The Caledonian Festival the second weekend in July has Scottish dancing, games, and barbecue (tel. 566-3880).

WESTON, 1838', population 606, area population 1,019 (USGS Athena). At MP-17 on SR-11, drive three miles east. The town, founded in 1865, is one of the oldest in the area. Facilities and activities: food, stores, lodging, gas, city park, museum. Many buildings were constructed of locally made bricks between the years 1879 and 1910. The city hall is located in a building that was originally a bank, built around the vault in 1884, and now restored with the original ceiling and decorations. Ask to see the vault and the Bank President's office, which has an escape door if the president didn't wish to see a customer.

Events and Activities:

Pioneer Picnic on Memorial Day with a parade of participants in period costumes, barbeque, games, dance.

Potato Show last Saturday in October with craft exhibits, 4-H exhibits, fair, tel. 566-2075.

Smith Frozen Foods has tours of a frozen food processing plant for groups (tel. 566-3515).

Lamb-Weston has tours of a food processing plant for groups (tel. 566-3511).

TOLLGATE RECREATION AREA. Drive east from Weston 20 miles on SR-204. See pages 95 to 97.

MILTON-FREEWATER, 1,033', population 5,533, area population 8,923 (USGS Milton-Freewater). Drive northeast on SR-11 for 30 miles from Pendleton. Facilities and activities: food, stores, lodging, gas.

Chamber of Commerce, 505 Ward St., 97862, tel. 938-5563, has maps and information.

Yantis Park. Drive west on SW 6th Ave. from Main St. to find a park with picnicking, playground, water, swimming pool, restrooms, and a hiking trail to a viewpoint.

Dorion Park, with a memorial to Marie Dorion (see p. 12), located one mile southeast off the Walla Walla river on Couse Creek road, has picnicking, a playground, and a stairway to the memorial, built in 1913, with names of early and later settlers inscribed in the steps. The earliest date is 1832.

Frazier Farmstead Museum, 1403 Chestnut St., tel. 938-4636, at the south end of the town near the Walla Walla River, open April through December, Th-Sa 10am to 4pm, Su 1pm to 4pm, has a collection of farm implements and household items used by the pioneers.

City Hall, at Main St. and 7th, has an Oregon Trail information marker.

Events: August, **Muddy Frogwater Days,** tel. 938-5563. October, **Frazier Farmstead Festival,** tel. 938-4636.

Back Country Trips: Anderson River Adventures, Snake and Grande Ronde Rivers, Rt. 2 Box 192-H, 97862, tel. 558-3629.

HARRIS PARK, 2000' (USGS Blalock Mountain). Drive 12 miles southeast from Milton-Freewater on the South Fork of the Walla Walla River. Facilities and activities: tents, trailers, water, swimming, fishing, hiking, bicycling, tel. 938-4237, usually opens May 1st. Fee.

WALLA WALLA RIVER PARK, a BLM facility near Harris Park, has access to the river for fishing. No camping.

BLALOCK MOUNTAIN, high point 4500', 35 miles RT, 2600' gain (USGS Blalock Mountain, Tollgate, Big Meadows, Peterson Ridge). **Mt. Bicycle Route.** From Harris Park (see above), ride southeast up the south fork of the Walla Walla river, turning northeast after two miles. At six miles from the campground, turn north up Bear Creek to the saddle between the north and south forks of the Walla Walla river. At the saddle, turn west on the plateau of Blalock Mountain.

UMAPINE, 680', area population 796 (USGS Milton- Freewater). From Milton-Freewater, drive seven miles west. Facilities and activities: food, store. Near the epicenter of the most damaging earthquake in Oregon's history (1936), the area lies on the Olympic-Wallowa Lineament (see p. 150).

I-84

ECHO, 700', population 499 (USGS Echo). Off I-84 at Exit 188, this community has the following facilities and activities: food, stores, gas. The Echo Museum is housed in the glazed brick Bank of Echo building, dating from 1905. Hours: Sa-Su 1-5, mid-April to mid-October.

Corral Springs Oregon Trail Site. Drive five miles southeast of Echo on old US-30. Just east of MP-6, find the marker on the highway. In the field east of the highway, one-half mile of visible Oregon Trail ruts come from the east and turn up the hill to the north. In places, up to three sets of ruts are visible. The Oregon Trail emigrants camped near the spring, which was located near the trees on the west side of the road. A cairn of basalt boulders one hundred yards east of the highway and located near the ruts may have held a signpost. The land on which these ruts are located has been in the same family for more than a century.

David Koontz Grave, an Oregon Trail emigrant who died in 1852, is located at the east edge of Echo on old US-30.

Fort Henrietta RV Park. On west edge of Echo on the banks of the Umatilla River. Facilities and activities: recreational vehicle and tent camping, full hookups, restroom, shower, blockhouse replica, Oregon Trail and Echo information with walking tour guide available here. Fee.

Events: Fort Henrietta Days, September, PO Box 9, 97826, tel. 376-8411.

Utilla Indian Agency–Fort Henrietta Archeological Site. From Fort Henrietta Park, go west across the Umatilla river to the first street. Turn left (south) to the Catholic Church. Turn east 100 yards on the north side of the Church to the archeological site, which has several explanatory signs and replica artifacts. The Indian Agency was occupied from 1851 to 1855 and the fort was built in 1855.

Oregon Trail Marker. Drive west on SR-320 for one-half mile from the Umatilla River bridge to the Westland Main Canal. Walk south on the east bank of the canal to the beginning of the Allen Canal. A concrete post at the edge of the field marks the location of the Oregon Trail. No ruts.

Oregon Trail Ruts. From the Umatilla River bridge at Echo, drive 2.7 miles west on SR-320. Park at an intersection with a gravel road. Walk north 200 yards to the first set of ruts crossing from east to west. A second set of ruts is 100 feet farther north. These ruts are on private land.

Echo Meadows Oregon Trail (USGS Echo, Service Buttes). From Echo, drive six miles west (MP-29.3) on SR-320 from the Umatilla River bridge. Turn north 0.5 mile on a narrow, rough, gravel road to the entrance to the BLM Oregon Trail site, which has explanatory signs. Hike one mile north to view an unspoiled section of Oregon Trail ruts. No camping, no fires, no vehicles on trails.

Oregon Trail Marker. From Echo, drive west on SR-320 to the intersection with SR-207. Turn north one mile to the marker (MP-17). The Oregon Trail crossed to the west here to reach Butter Creek and an emigrant camping place.

Back Country Trips: Wapiti Outfitters, hunting trips, HC 70, Box 114, 97826, tel. 558-3629.

HINKLE, 619', (USGS Hermiston). Turn north from I-84 at Exit 182. Facilities and activities: Amtrak station, sorting yards for the Union Pacific railroad.

BUTTERCREEK GAS AND RV PARK, 553', (USGS Hermiston). On the north side of I-84 at Exit 182. Facilities and activities: food, store, gas, full hookups for recreational vehicles of any size, tent area, showers, tel. 564-9272. Fee.

UMATILLA ORDNANCE DEPOT (USGS Ordnance). North of I-84 from MP-179 to MP-173 is an ammunition storage depot with 1,000 storage igloos of which 90 are used to store chemical weapons.

UMATILLA WILDLIFE AREA, 300' (USGS Irrigon). From I-84 at Exit 168, drive four miles northeast on US-730. Turn north two miles to a parking area with restrooms and water. Access to the Columbia River.

IRRIGON FISH HATCHERY, 300' (USGS Irrigon). From I-84 at Exit 168, drive five miles northeast on US-730.

IRRIGON, 300' (USGS Irrigon). From I-84 at Exit 168, drive northeast for eight miles on US-730. Facilities and activities: food, stores, gas, lodging, park with picnicking and restrooms. Overnight vehicle camping is allowed in the park. No fee. For information, call 922-3047.

BOARDMAN, 300', population 1,387, area population 4,444 (USGS Boardman). Take Exit 164 from I-84. Facilities and activities: food, stores, lodging, gas, city park with picnicking, water, restrooms, playground, information at the Chamber of Commerce office on the central square, tel. 481-3014. **Boardman County Park** on the Columbia River has the following facilities and activities: boat launching ramp, dock, camping, swimming, sanitary disposal, showers, pull throughs and full hookups for recreational vehicles of any size, mooring, sailboard beach. Fee. PO Box 8, 97818, tel. 481-7217.

Events and Tours: Harvest Festival is held in September. **Portland General Electric** has a coal-fired generating station in Boardman. Call 481-9351 for tours at 10am, 1pm and 3pm.

BOARDMAN REST AREA. Find the rest area at MP-161 on I-84. Facilities and activities: picnicking, restrooms.

US–26, SR–19

Nyssa To Kimberly

NYSSA, 2177', population 2,629, area population 3,999 (USGS Nyssa). Facilities and activities: food, stores, lodging, gas.
Nyssa Chamber of Commerce and Agriculture. 112 Main St., 97813, tel. 372-3091, has maps and information.
Events: Thunderegg Days. Tours to rock gathering areas and theatrical performances, mid-July, PO Box 2397, 97913, tel. 372-3715. **Night Rodeo.** Late June, tel. 372-3091.
Nyssa Agricultural Museum features sheepherder wagons and other farming equipment. Special events throughout the year. Schedule of events available from the Chamber of Commerce (see above).
Nyssa Historic Walking Tour, beginning at Good St. and First St., passes a turn of the century hotel, saloons, and blacksmith shop. Map available at the Chamber of Commerce.

OREGON TRAIL (USGS Owyhee, Mitchell Butte, Cairo, Vale East). Drive south from Nyssa five miles on SR-201 to a interpretive overlook east to an Oregon Trail crossing of the Snake River. Interpretive signs describe the problems of crossing the Snake River from Fort Boise, directly across the river, and gives a brief history of Fort Boise. By the end of the 1840's, Fort Boise was already in serious decline as a result of decimation of the local beaver population, the mainstay of the fur-trading industry. After reading the signs, drive north on SR-201 to MP-3. Where SR-201 turns north, continue east 0.5 mile to the bank of the Snake River to consider the problems faced by the emigrants trying to cross the river here. The volume of flow in late summer is not much different than it was during the Oregon Trail emigration.

OREGON TRAIL–KEENEY PASS. From the Interpretive Display at MP-5 on SR-201, drive west on SR-201 for one mile. Where SR-201 turns south, continue west one block to stop sign. Turn north on Fairview Drive for one mile, crossing an unmarked Oregon Trail intercept at 0.5 miles. At the next intersection, 1.1 miles from SR-201, turn west on Grand Avenue. At 2.1 miles from SR-201, at the intersection with Heritage Drive, cross the line of the Oregon Trail again as it heads toward Keeney Pass. Continue west on Grand Avenue to Lytle Avenue, four miles from SR-201. Turn north on Lytle Avenue. Where Lytle Avenue bends northwest, 1.3 miles from Grand Avenue, the road overlies the Oregon Trail. From this point on, markers indicate the route of the Oregon Trail, under or on either side of Lytle Avenue nearly all the way to Vale through Keeney Pass.

An interpretive display provided by the Bureau of Land Management in Keeney Pass, ten miles from SR-201 or six miles from Vale, is near the four to five visible wagon tracks left by the Oregon Trail travelers. Some of the ruts are three feet deep. Walk a trail one-third mile to the Keeney Pass Overlook with a view southeast to the Snake River near Fort Boise and north to the fields along the Malheur River, a distance that was travelled in one day by the emigrants. Keeney pass was named for Captain Jonathan Keeney, a noted frontiersman who operated the ferry near Ontario for a short time.

Continue toward Vale on Lytle Boulevard. Five miles north of Keeney Pass, turn left (west) off Lytle Boulevard. Park and walk north on a gravel road parallel to Lytle Boulevard past a gate. Below a bluff, find the grave of John D. Henderson who is reported to have died of thirst here in view of the Malheur River in 1852. He, with a companion, was attempting to cross from the Snake River near Fort Boise to Farewell Bend on foot without pack animals. They had lost their horses to the Indians.

Reach the Malheur River at six miles from Keeney Pass.

MALHEUR BUTTE, 2661' (USGS Malheur Butte). A viewpoint at MP-254 on US-26 overlooks this ancient volcano that erupted during some of the time that the Columbia Basalts were emitted. No access.

VALE, 2242', population 1,491, area population 3,579 (USGS Vale East, Vale West). Vale is the seat of Malheur county, population 27,400, area 9,926 square miles. Situated at the junction of US-20 and US-26 on the Malheur River, the town has the following facilities and activities: food, stores, lodging, gas.

Vale Chamber of Commerce, at 272 North Main Street, 97918, tel. 473-3800 has maps and information and a display of barbed wire.

Oregon Trail. An interpretive sign placed off westbound US-20, US-26 at the eastern edge of Vale tells some of the history of the Oregon Trail travellers in this region. A stone marker placed by Ezra Meeker, one of the leaders of Oregon Trail emigrant groups, is at the northeast corner of the courthouse lawn on "B" Street. The Meek Cutoff Marker, located in the East Entrance Park on US-20, relates the history of the ill-fated attempt by a party led by Stephen Meek to take a route directly west from Vale.

Vale Name Marker can be found in the West Entrance Park on US-20. The Bureau of Land Management office at 100 Oregon St. supplies maps and information.

Walking Tour. A cluster of buildings on Main St. and "A" St. date from around and before 1900, including The Stone House from 1872. A map is available at the Chamber of Commerce (see above).

Vale Hot Springs. The Oregon Trail travellers rested and washed at the hot springs, which were located near the Malheur River at what is now the eastern edge of Vale. The Oregon Trail Mushroom Company uses water from the springs for heat. Tours: PO Box 400, 97918, tel. 473-3103.
Back Country Trips: High Lonesome Hunts, 4733 John Day Hwy., 97918, tel. 473-2916.

Camping and RV Parks:

Prospector RV Park, 511 N 11th St., 97918, tel. 473-3879. Pull throughs and full hookups for recreational vehicles of any size, tent area, showers. Fee. **Westerner RV Park,** 350 A St., 97918, tel. 473-3617. Pull throughs and full hookups for recreational vehicles of any size, showers. Fee.

BULLY CREEK PARK, 2530' (USGS Hope Butte). Address: 2475 Bully Creek Road, Vale, 97918, tel. 473-2969. Drive west five miles from Vale then four miles northwest to the dam and campground. Facilities and activities: pull throughs and electrical hookups for recreational vehicles of any size, tents, fishing, boat launch, hiking bicycling, swimming, showers, disposal. Fee.

HOPE BUTTE–SUGARLOAF BUTTE LOOP, 3640', 20 miles RT, 1600' gain (USGS Hope Butte, BLM Brogan). **Mt. Bicycle Route.** From the campground at Bully Creek Reservoir, ride northwest one mile on the road circling the lake on the north side. Turn north on a road that ascends a valley northwest for three miles to a junction, 3000'. Turn left (southwest) to the summit, six miles from the campground. Return to the last junction and ride northwest another mile. Turn left (west) and ride southwest across the north shoulder of Hope Butte toward Sugarloaf Butte. At a "T" road junction, leave bicycle and hike southwest to the summit of Sugarloaf Butte, 3780'. Return to bicycle and ride southeast, passing east of Sugarloaf Butte. The road bends south, then passes Coyote Spring one mile before joining the road along Cottonwood Creek. Turn left (east) to return to the campground. Opalized wood and cinnabar have been found in the area around Hope Butte and the area is now under study for possible in place cyanide leaching to recover gold from a low-grade deposit.

COTTONWOOD MOUNTAIN, 6482', 45 miles RT, 4200' gain (USGS Hope Butte, Swede Flat, Brogan, Brady Creek, BLM Brogan). **Mt. Bicycle Route.** From Bully Creek Reservoir campground, ride northwest along Cottonwood Creek, passing along the north side of the reservoir and reaching farm buildings five miles from the campground and the road to Sugarloaf Butte and Hope Butte six miles from the campground. Precipitous basalt lava flows line the canyon beyond the reservoir. The highest of these flows has been oxidized by exposure to a deep red color. Where

Cottonwood Creek bends west, turn northwest to ascend the road on the ridge between Cottonwood Creek and Rock Cabin Creek, heading for the tower on the highest point. An alternative route follows Cottonwood Creek two more miles, then ascends a road along NG Creek (see BLM map).

OREGON TRAIL–TUB MOUNTAIN, high point 3447', 26 miles RT, 1000' gain (USGS Willow Creek, McCarthy Ridge, Tub Mountain, BLM Brogan). **Mt. Bicycle Route.** This route is possible only in dry weather. Six miles northwest of Vale on US-26, and just east of MP-272, park at the junction of US-26 and Fifth Avenue E. Ride east one mile, crossing branches of the Owyhee Canal, then turn north, bending to the east after four miles for two miles in Alkali Gulch to pass Alkali Springs, an occasional emigrant campground where the Bureau of Land Management maintains an interpretive sign. Continue north to the shoulder west of Tub Mountain, 10 miles from US-26 and 2927'. Leave bicycle and hike east to the summit for a general view of the Oregon Trail route from Vale and the Snake River valley to the east. The roads after leaving US-26 are near or over the Oregon Trail route. Return to bicycle and continue north one mile to the McCarthy Ridge–Moore's Hollow road junction, 13 miles from US-26. The Oregon Trail is under this intersection and this route continues north to rejoin the Snake River near Farewell Bend. The deep depression of the road in the dusty soil of this upland region was started by the Oregon Trail travellers. From the McCarthy Ridge–Moore's Hollow road junction, return to the starting point.

WILLOW CREEK, 2413', MP-267 (USGS Willow Creek). Facilities and activities: food, store.

JAMIESON, 2490', MP-261 (USGS Jamieson). Facilities and activities: store.

BROGAN, 2610', area population 392, MP-254 (USGS Brogan, Decker Creek). Facilities and activities: food, stores, lodging, gas, bicycling. **Brogan Trailer Park.** Pull throughs and full hookups for recreational vehicles of any size, showers, tent area, PO Box 23, 97903, tel. 473-2002. Fee.

BROGAN CANYON. Drive two miles northwest on US-26 then four miles north into Brogan Canyon, a favorite nesting area for eagles and hawks.

MALHEUR RESERVOIR LOOP, high point 4100', 40 miles RT, 500' gain (USGS Cow Valley East, Cow Valley West, Wendt Butte, Bridgeport, Becker Creek, BLM Brogan). **Mt. Bicycle Route.** From Brogan, ride northwest on US-26 for two miles. Turn right and ride north to Willow Creek. Turn northwest, passing Huntington Junction, nine miles from US-26. Continue west to go north of Malheur Reservoir and reach Indian Creek Road. Turn south to US-26. Turn left (east) to return to Brogan.

BROGAN HILL SUMMIT, 3983', MP-246 (USGS Becker Creek, Cow Valley East). From this gentle summit ridge on US-26, broad Cow Valley is west and inaccessible Juniper Mountain is southwest.

MALHEUR CITY–ELDORADO LOOP, high point 4200', 28 miles RT, 1800' gain (USGS Cow Valley West, Cow Valley East, Bridgeport, Wendt Butte). **Mt. Bicycle Route.** Park at the junction of Indian Creek Road, MP-240 on US-26. Ride north to Willow Creek passing west of Cow Valley Butte, then turn east (right) down Willow Creek for two miles to a road junction. At this junction, turn north three miles to the site of Malheur City, an abandoned mining community with only a cemetery remaining. The site of Eldorado and a crossing of the Eldorado Ditch is two miles further north on the road to Bridgeport. From the site of Malheur City, ride east two miles then turn south down Birch Creek toward Willow Creek Reservoir. At the first road junction on approaching the reservoir, turn right (west) to the reservoir. Continue northwest to a junction with Indian Creek road, then south on Indian Creek Road to return to the starting point.

BONITA, 4000', 10 miles RT, 500' gain (USGS Cow Valley West). **Mt. Bicycle Route.** At MP-238, two miles west of the Indian Creek road, park and ride south for 2.5 miles. Turn west one mile, then again south one-half mile to the site of Bonita, an old farming community. No services.

IRONSIDE JUNCTION, 3844', MP-232 (USGS Ironside). A once-active farming community is now only a crossroad.

WILLOW CREEK–INDIAN CREEK LOOP, high point 4000', 30 miles RT, 500' gain (USGS Ironside, Cow Valley West, BLM Brogan). **Mt. Bicycle Route.** Park near Ironside Junction, MP-232. Ride north and northeast down the road along Willow Creek toward Malheur Reservoir. After 12 miles, turn right (south) on the Indian Creek Road, passing north of Cow Valley Butte, to return to US-26. Turn right (west) to the starting point.

ELDORADO PASS, 4387', MP-223 (USGS Eldorado Pass). This broad saddle separates the Burnt River drainage to the north and the Willow Creek drainage flowing into the Malheur River to the south. The remains of the Eldorado Ditch crosses exactly at the pass. Park on the north side of the pass and walk to the top of the highway cut on the east side of the highway to see traces of the ditch continuing off to the east.

ELDORADO CAMPGROUND, 4400' (USGS Eldorado Pass, Rastus Mountain). At MP-222 on US-26, drive southwest on narrow, paved FS-16 for two miles. Facilities and activities: tents, recreational vehicles to 25', trailers not recommended, water from creek, hiking. No fee. The Eldorado Ditch is 100 yards up the hill to the south. Explore west along the ditch for one mile to where the ditch crosses FS-16 and continues to the north. Separating corrals for an annual cattle roundup are nearby.

ELDORADO DITCH, 4600' (USGS Rastus Mountain). The Eldorado Ditch crosses FS-16 one mile west of the Eldorado campground. An interpretive sign at the crossing tells the history of this ditch that was completed in 1874 after ten years work by Chinese laborers and abandoned before 1900 as a result of controversy over the use of the water between the miners and the farmers. This ditch, more than one hundred miles long and built to supply a stamp mill for the mines around the mining communities of Eldorado and Malheur City, crosses US-26 at Eldorado Pass, 1.5 mile southwest of Murray Reservoir, then goes northwest along US-26, turning away northeast two miles north of Murray Reservoir. It carried water from the headwaters of the Burnt River, beginning at Chance Creek, two miles northwest on FS-2640 above Mammoth Spring Campground, to Malheur City. Much of the route of the ditch can be traced on the Wallowa-Whitman National Forest map, edition 1990.

RASTUS MOUNTAIN, 6810', 6 miles RT, 2000' gain (USGS Rastus Mountain, WWURD). Drive five miles south from US-26 on FS-16, three miles past the Eldorado campground, and 0.2 mile south of a fence and cattle guard. Park (4950') and ascend west on a logging track, FS-850, to the summit.

MURRAY HILL, 6559', 6 miles RT, 1800' gain (USGS Rastus Mountain, WWURD). Park one-half mile beyond the logging track to Rastus Mountain (see above) at a logging track that follows Camp Creek (FS-920). Ascend along the creek for one mile then leave the logging track and ascend in open woods to the open, grassy summit with broad views of Ironside Mountain to the south.

SQUAW BUTTE, 6908', 3 miles RT, 900' gain (USGS Rastus Mountain, SMMRW, WWURD). Drive nine miles south of US-26 on FS-16 to the saddle between East Camp Creek on the north and Squaw Creek on the south, 6088'. Hike the gravel road that goes west from the pass on the south side of the fence. After one-fourth mile from FS-16, take the left fork another one-fourth mile as the road contours across the east side of Squaw Butte. Where the road turns sharply southeast at a gully, leave the road and ascend in the gully on an animal track for 100' then continue on the animal track as it ascends diagonally left (south) to the slope south of the gully. Continue up the slope in open timber, passing a rocky outcrop of andesite. Reach the ridge and turn north up the ridge to the summit ledge of basalt. These rocks are part of the Strawberry Volcanic series.

BULLRUN ROCK, 7873', 12 miles RT, 2300' gain (USGS Rastus Mountain, Bullrun Rock, SMMRW, WWURD). Park as above for Squaw Butte. Hike the road west for one-fourth mile as for Squaw Butte. At the first road junction, take the right fork (FS-802) and ascend across the north slope of Squaw Butte to a road junction at a fence line one mile from FS-16. Continue west on FS-802 and northwest on FS-462 to a saddle between the north and south drainages, 6100'. From this saddle, roads go north, east, south, and west. Leave the road and ascend northwest on the ridge for 3.5 miles to the summit of Bullrun Rock.

MONUMENT ROCK, 7736', 10 miles RT, 2200' gain (USGS Rastus Mountain, Bullrun Rock, WWURD, SMMRW). Park and hike as above toward Bullrun Rock. One mile before reaching Bullrun Rock, turn southwest to Monument Rock. The impressive cairn was built by a sheepherder in the early 1900's.

UNITY, 3990', population 87, MP-213 (USGS Unity). Facilities and activities: food, stores, lodging, gas. The Unity Forest Service Station has maps and information all year. **Unity Motel and RV Park**, 97884, tel. 446-3431. Facilities and activities: tents, trailers, showers, open all year. Fee.

LONG CREEK CAMPGROUND, 4430' (USGS Rastus Mountain). From Unity, drive one mile east on US-26 and seven miles south on road FS-1680, then three miles east to the campground on Long Creek Reservoir. Facilities and activities: tents and small recreational vehicles, no trailers, fishing, swimming, boating, hiking on the Eldorado Ditch, one-fourth mile east of reservoir. No fee.

SOUTH FORK CAMPGROUND, 4380' (USGS Rail Gulch). Drive west from Unity three miles then follow the road along the south fork of the Burnt River to the campground, eight miles from Unity. The first 4.5 miles of this road (CR-600 and FS-6005) are paved and the rest is narrow and gravel. Facilities and activities: tents, recreational vehicles to 25', water from spring, fishing. No fee.

STEVENS CREEK CAMPGROUND, 4440' (USGS Rail Gulch). Go one mile past South Fork Campground (see above). Facilities and activities: tents, no trailers, vehicles to 25', water from stream, fishing. No fee.

ELK CREEK CAMPGROUND, 4500' (USGS Rail Gulch). Drive 0.5 mile past Stevens Creek Campground, then turn left (west) to the campground on the Burnt River, 10 miles from Unity. Facilities and activities: tents, vehicles to 25', water from stream, fishing. No fee.

MAMMOTH SPRINGS CAMPGROUND, 4520' (USGS Rail Gulch). Drive west of Stevens Creek Campground (see above) to the campground, 10 miles from Unity. Facilities and activities: water from spring, tents, vehicles to 25'. No fee.

ELDORADO DITCH, 4500', 30 miles RT (USGS Rail Gulch, Unity,

Rastus Mountain). **Mt. Bicycle Route.** From any of the South Fork Burnt River campgrounds, ride east 0.3 mile past South Fork campground. Turn south on the Barney Creek road (FS-6010) for two miles to a crossing of the Eldorado Ditch. Turn east on FS-1695 and follow the route of the Eldorado Ditch for 15 miles to the West Camp Creek road (FS-1680). Turn north and descend to US-26 and Unity. Return on CR-600 and FS-6005 to the starting point. This route can also be done as a loop from Unity.

TABLE ROCK LOOKOUT, 7815', 18 miles RT, 3500' gain (USGS Bullrun Rock, SMMRW). **Mt. Bicycle Route.** From any of the campgrounds along the South Fork of the Burnt River, ride east until 0.3 mile east of the South Fork Campground. Turn south on the Barney Creek Road (FS-6010). At the first intersection two miles south after leaving the South Fork of the Burnt River, turn right on road FS-030 for one mile and ascend at first west and then south on roads FS-035 and FS-045 to the Table Rock trailhead. Hike south two miles on trail FS-1960 to a lookout that is staffed during the summer months.

BULLRUN ROCK, 7873', 10 miles RT, 2400' gain (USGS Bullrun Rock, SMMRW). From any of the South Fork Burnt River campgrounds drive northeast 0.3 mile past the Southfork Campground to the Barney Creek road, FS-6010. After two miles on the Barney Creek Road (FS-6010), turn left (east) on a segment of the Eldorado Ditch road (FS-1695) for six miles to the Bullrun Creek trailhead (Trail FS-1961). This trailhead can also be reached from Unity by driving west one mile on CR-600, then south on CR-601 for five miles. Hike trail FS-1961 south and southeast, passing a junction with trail FS-1965 after three miles and joining trail FS-1973 from the right at six miles. Continue south to the ridge crest near Bullrun Rock on trail FS-365. Monument Rock is 0.5 mile south of the southernmost point of trail FS-365.

BULLRUN ROCK, 7873', 10 miles RT, 2400' gain (USGS Bullrun Rock, SMMRW). Drive as above to the Barney Creek road (FS-6010). Continue south on road FS-6010 for seven miles to the Amelia Creek trailhead (trail FS-1973). Hike south on the trail, keeping left at a junction after three miles and right at a junction with trail FS-1961 to the summit ridge at Bullrun Rock.

TABLE ROCK LOOKOUT, 7815', 5 miles RT, 2000' gain (USGS Bullrun Rock, SMMRW). Drive as above for Bullrun Rock to the Barney Creek road (FS-6010). After two miles on road FS-6010, turn right (west) on FS-030, a segment of the Eldorado Ditch road. After one mile, turn south on FS-035 and FS-045 to the trailhead, seven miles from FS-6005, the South Fork Burnt River road.

ELDORADO DITCH, high point 4600', 5 miles RT, 600' gain (USGS Bullrun Rock, WWURD). From Elk Creek campground, hike two miles south on FS-6005. Where the road turns to the west to cross the Burnt River after passing through a road cut in colorful rocks of the Strawberry Volcanics, ascend south away from the road on a logging track that intersects the Eldorado Ditch after one-fourth mile and then overlies the ditch to the west. A section of the ditch not obliterated by logging roads continues north above the Burnt River on the east side of the river. A break in the ditch just east of the intersection of the logging track and the ditch might possibly have been made intentionally during the controversy between the farmers and the miners over the use of the water. To the west, the ditch is mostly overlain by logging tracks.

TABLE ROCK LOOKOUT, 7815', 32 miles RT, 3300' gain (USGS Rail Gulch, Bullrun Rock, Little Baldy Mountain, SMMRW). **Mt. Bicycle Route.** From Elk Creek Campground (see p. 36), ride south on road FS-6005 for two miles, continuing west to ascend to and follow the line of the Eldorado Ditch for one mile. Continue west and southwest on road FS-6005, ascending to a junction near the ridge crest with road FS-2652, 6715'. Turn southeast on road FS-2652 for two miles to a junction with road FS-1370. Ascend on FS-1370 to the lookout, passing Elk Flat campground after one-fourth mile on road FS-1370.

DEARDORFF MOUNTAIN-BALDY MOUNTAIN LOOP, 7162', 7610', 20 miles RT, 3100 feet gain (USGS Rail Gulch, Deardorff Mountain, SMMRW). **Mt. Bicycle Route.** From Elk Creek campground (see p. 36), ride south one mile on road FS-6005. Turn west on road FS-6015 and ascend to the crest of the ridge, 6745', and a junction with road FS-2652. Turn northwest on road FS-2652 to the saddle between Deardorff Mountain and Baldy Mountain, 6875'. Leave bicycle and hike both ways to the two summits. Serpentine, on which vegetation grows poorly, is exposed in this area. On the return, descend southeast one-fourth mile on road FS-2652 from the Baldy-Deardorff saddle, then turn northeast on road FS-2655 to descend to meet road FS-2640 at Last Chance Creek. Turn southeast on road FS-2640 to return to Elk Creek campground.

ELDORADO DITCH, high point 5000', 20 miles RT, 600' gain (USGS Rail Gulch, Bullrun Rock, SMMRW). **Mt. Bicycle Route.** From Elk Creek campground (see p. 36), ride south on road FS-6005 for two miles ascending on the slope east of the South Fork of the Burnt River. Continue west on road FS-6005 as the road crosses Bear Creek and climbs to overlie the route of the Eldorado Ditch across the canyon of the South Fork of the Burnt River. After crossing the South Fork of the Burnt River, leave road FS-6005 at 5000', and continue to contour north and northwest on the almost level route of the Eldorado Ditch at a gradient of 4.8 feet to the mile to the beginning of the ditch at Last Chance Creek. The ditch collected water from Spring Creek and Elk Creek as it passed.

SR-245

UNITY LAKE STATE PARK, 3773' (USGS Unity, Unity Reservoir). From US-26 at MP-111, drive two miles east on SR-245, then turn northeast to the campground on Unity Lake Reservoir. Facilities and activities: electrical hookups for recreational vehicles up to site maximum of 60', tent area, water, showers, boat launch, fishing, swimming, dock. See p. 60 for a bicycle loop trip. Fee.

BURNT RIVER CANYON. From MP-3 to MP-6, SR-245 passes through a narrow, picturesque canyon carved by the Burnt River in Columbia Basalt lava flows.

HEREFORD, 3658', (USGS Hereford, Beaver Dam Creek). At MP-10 on SR-245, 10 miles from US-26, a former town here on the Burnt River supplied the cattle ranches in the region. Facilities and activities: food, store.

BRUNO RANCH, 3500' (USGS Wendt Butte). At MP-21 on SR-245, 25 miles from Baker City or 21 miles from US-26, turn east on CR-1123 for 0.2 mile to the entrance. Facilities and activities: bed and breakfast, tents, trailers, picnicking, bicycling, open all year. Fee. Address: PO Box 51A, Bridgeport 97819, tel. 446-3468.

BRIDGEPORT, 3380' (USGS Bridgeport, Wendt Butte). At MP-21 on SR-245, 21 miles from US-26, and 25 miles from Baker City on SR-7 and SR-245, drive east on CR-1123 for five miles. Turn south across the Burnt River to a former supply center for mining in the region. No services.

GHOST TOWN LOOP, high point 5500', 40 miles RT, 2500' gain (USGS Wendt Butte, Bridgeport, Mormon Basin, BLM Brogan). **Mt. Bicycle Route.** Park at the Bridgeport turnoff from CR-1123 (see above). Ride west one-half mile then turn south, ascending Road Canyon. Where the road bends south again after turning east three miles from the bridge over the Burnt River, cross the route of the Eldorado Ditch. Pass Lacey Brothers Spring at four miles and reach the site of Eldorado, an old mining site five miles from the Burnt River bridge. The Eldorado Ditch brought water here from the headwaters of the Burnt River, more than 100 miles away. From Eldorado, continue south then east two miles to the site of Malheur City, where the only remains are gravestones. From the site of Malheur City, ride east six miles to the site of Amelia, passing Amelia Butte on the right (south) at four miles. From Amelia, turn northwest for four miles into Mormon Basin, a mining camp established by miners from Salt Lake City and a mineral producer before 1900. Many of the mines and prospects are situated on Pedro Mountain, 6453', to the northeast from Mormon Basin, and California Mountain, 5679', to the southeast.

Creeks arising in a one square mile in Mormon Basin flow in three different directions. Basin Creek flows south into Willow Creek and the Malheur River, ending in the Snake River. The south fork of Dixie Creek drops east into the Burnt River at Dixie, and Clarks Creek goes northwest into the Burnt River near the site of Bridgeport.

From Mormon Basin, turn northwest through Glengarry Gulch to ride eight miles down Clarks Creek, passing the site of Clarksville, another supply center and mining community site. From the site of Clarksville, ride west through the site of Chinatown, an early settlement of Chinese miners, into the Bridgeport Valley on the Burnt River. Cross the river and turn left (southwest) to Bridgeport and the starting point.

US-26

WETMORE CAMPGROUND, 4335' (USGS Pogue Point). This campground on US-26 at MP-203, 10 miles north of Unity, has the following facilities and activities: tents, trailers to 25', handicapped accessible trail, water, hiking. No fee.

YELLOW PINE CAMPGROUND, 4400' (USGS Pogue Point). On US-26 at MP-202, 11 miles north of Unity. Facilities and activities: tents, trailers to 25', handicapped accessible trail, water. No fee.

OREGON CAMPGROUND, 4800' (USGS Pogue Point). On US-26 at MP-200. Facilities and activities: tents, trailers to 25', water. No fee.

BLUE MOUNTAIN SUMMIT, 5109', MP-199 (USGS Pogue Point). This ridge separates the John Day River drainage on the north from the Burnt River drainage on the south.

STEEP POINT, 6685', 20 miles RT, 2500' gain (USGS Austin, Deardorff Mountain, Rail Gulch). **Mt. Bicycle Route.** Park near the junction of US-26 with road FS-2645, MP-196. Ride south on road FS-2645, ascending along Squaw Creek for ten miles to the ridge. Ride or hike north one mile to the summit.

ELKHORN RIDGE LOOP, high point 6720', 25 miles RT, 3000' gain (USGS Austin, Deardorff Mountain). **Mt. Bicycle Route.** At MP-192 on US-26, park near the junction with road FS-2640. Ride southeast on this road, ascending the Dry Fork of Clear Creek. At Elkhorn Spring, 5700', 11 miles from US-26, turn south on the ridge, bending west after 1.5 miles to continue up the ridge to the Elkhorn Microwave Site, 6720'. Return north 0.5 miles to a road junction, 6571'. Turn left and descend west and southwest. Go right (northwest) after one-half mile, passing Looney Spring with a primitive campground, then continue down Clear Creek on road FS-2635 to return to US-26. Turn right (east) one mile to the starting point.

AUSTIN JUNCTION, 4500' (USGS Austin, Bates). Facilities and activities: food, store, lodging, gas. Seasonal.

DIXIE CAMPGROUND, 5200' (USGS Bates). Near MP-184, turn north of US-26 to the campground. Facilities and activities: tents, trailers to 25', water, hiking. No fee.

DIXIE SUMMIT SKI AREA, 5200' (USGS Bates). Near MP-184 on US-26, the area has the following facilities and activities: cross country skiing, snowmobiling, snopark.

DIXIE BUTTE LOOKOUT, 7592', 12 miles RT, 2500' gain (USGS Bates). **Mt. Bicycle Route.** From Dixie Summit, ride north on road FS-2610 to the lookout. From this viewpoint, Strawberry Mountain is almost directly south (194°), and Bullrun Rock in the Monument Rock Wilderness is southeast (136°). Rock Creek Butte northeast of Sumpter in the Elkhorn Range is northeast (58°).

FIRESIDE LODGE, 5000' (USGS Bates). At MP-183 on US-26 just west of Dixie Summit. Facilities and activities: cabins, campground with hookups, tent area, showers, country western dancing monthly, restaurant, open all year. Address: Prairie City OR 97869, tel. 820-4677.

PRAIRIE CITY, 3540', population 1145 (USGS Prairie City). Facilities and activities: food, stores, lodging, gas. The Prairie City Forest Service Station has maps and information. The depot of the Sumpter Valley Railway, built in 1910, is still in use as a museum, but the railroad tracks are gone.

DeWitt Museum. From US-26 in Prairie City, drive south on Main Street for one-half mile to a park with the museum, which uses the old Sumpter Valley Railroad depot. Open May 15 to October 15, 10am to 3pm, Thursday through Saturday.

Depot Campground. Drive as above to the Prairie City Park. Facilities and activities: pull throughs and full hookups for recreational vehicles of any size, grass tent area, showers, disposal. Fee. tel. 820-3605.

Events and Activities: Fourth of July celebration with parade, bicycle race from Seneca, fireworks. **Strawberry Mountain Llamas** has day treks on weekends. Telephone: 820-3746.

PRAIRIE CITY FOREST LOOP, high point 6000', 70 miles RT, 3900' gain (USGS Prairie City, Roberts Creek, Logan Valley East, Crane Prairie, Little Baldy Mountain, Isham Creek). **Bicycle Route.** This route is entirely pavement. Ride southeast from Prairie City on CR-62 in the valley of the John Day River. At MP-8, continue right (south) on CR-14 at the junction with road FS-13, entering the Malheur National Forest after four miles and reaching a junction with road FS-16 at 25 miles from Prairie City. Turn southeast on FS-16, crossing the first high point of the loop,

5900 ', then rounding north to a junction with road FS-13 at 42 miles from Prairie City . Ride north on FS-13, ascending above the North Fork of the Malheur River and crossing a pass, 6000', to the Deardorff Creek drainage before returning to the outgoing route, CR-62. Turn right (northwest) to return to Prairie City. The mileage for the trip can be reduced by 16 miles and the elevation gain reduced by 500' by starting the loop from any of the campgrounds along CR-14 or FS-16.

BALDY MOUNTAIN–DEARDORFF MOUNTAIN LOOP, high point 7610', 30 miles RT, 4000' gain (USGS Isham Creek, Deardorff Mountain). **Mt. Bicycle Route.** Drive eight miles southeast of Prairie City on CR-62. Park at the junction with road FS-13. Ride FS-13 four miles east to a junction, then turn north (left) on road FS-1344. Go right (east) after three miles at a junction. Continue east on this road (FS-1344), taking the left fork at all road junctions, staying on the ridge to Baldy Mountain, 12 miles from CR-62 and 7610'. From the summit of Bald Mountain, ride east one mile to Deardorff Mountain, 7162'. Continue northeast from the summit of Deardorff Mountain along the ridge, turning left (west) at a road junction after passing the Elkhorn Microwave Site. Keep left at road junctions, descending to the bottom of the canyon of Reynolds Creek, then descend along Reynolds Creek on road FS-489. After joining road FS-2635, turn left (south) to road CR-62 and the starting point, one mile southeast on CR-62.

BLUE MOUNTAIN HOT SPRINGS, 4269' (USGS Roberts Creek). From Prairie City, drive south eight miles on CR-62 and three miles on CR-14. Facilities and activities: tents, trailers, swimming, showers, seasonal. tel. 820-3744. Fee.

LOOKOUT MOUNTAIN, 8033', 14 miles RT, 3000' gain (USGS Roberts Creek, Little Baldy Mountain). Drive 13 miles southeast and south of Prairie City on CR-62 and CR-14 and park at the trailhead, one mile south of the Malheur National Forest boundary. Hike east and south on the Sunshine Flat trail (FS-369) to the summit.

TROUT FARM CAMPGROUND, 4923' (USGS Roberts Creek). From Prairie City, drive eight miles southeast on CR-62 and seven miles south on CR-14. Facilities and activities: tents, trailers to 25', water. No fee.

CRESCENT CAMPGROUND, 5170' (USGS Roberts Creek). This minimum campground is two miles south of Trout Farm campground (see above) and 16 miles from Prairie City. Facilities and activities: tents, trailers to 25', fishing. No fee.

STARVATION ROCK, 7120', 5 miles RT, 1500' gain (USGS Logan

Valley East, Roberts Creek, Little Baldy Mountain). Drive as above three miles past Crescent campground. Park and hike northeast on a road 0.5 miles to the trailhead. Hike trail FS-374 to the summit.

LOOKOUT MOUNTAIN, 8033', 12 miles RT, 2500' (USGS Logan Valley East, Roberts Creek, Little Baldy Mountain). Hike as above to Starvation Rock, continuing on the trail east to a road. Turn north on the road to the summit.

SHEEP MOUNTAIN, 7728', 12 miles RT, 2000' gain (USGS Logan Valley East, Roberts Creek, Little Baldy Mountain). Hike as above to Starvation Rock, continuing on the trail east to the road. Turn right (south) on the road to the summit.

LITTLE CRANE CAMPGROUND, 5560' (USGS Crane Prairie). From Prairie City, drive paved roads CR-62 and CR-14 southeast and south for 22 miles to a junction with road FS-16, then drive east and northeast on paved road FS-16 to the campground, 30 miles from Prairie City. This minimum campground on Little Crane Creek has the following facilities and activities: space for tents and small recreational vehicles, fishing, water from stream. No fee.

NORTH FORK MALHEUR CAMPGROUND, 4720' (USGS Crane Prairie). From Prairie City, drive as above past Little Crane campground and continue for five miles on road FS-16. Turn right on gravelled road FS-1675 for three miles to the campground on the North Fork Malheur River, 38 miles from Prairie City. Facilities and activities: tents, trailers to 25', fishing, water from river. No fee.

ELK CREEK CAMPGROUND, 5040' (USGS Crane Prairie). Drive as above one mile past the North Fork Malheur River campground turnoff to this minimum campground. Facilities and activities: water from creek, space for tents and small recreational vehicles, fishing. No fee.

LOOKOUT MOUNTAIN, 8033', 12 miles RT, 3000' gain (USGS Little Baldy Mountain). Drive as above two miles past Elk Creek campground to the junction of roads FS-16 and FS-13, then one mile north on FS-13 to the trailhead, 5150'. The trailhead can also be reached by driving eight miles southeast of Prairie City on CR-62 and 15 miles southeast on road FS-13. Hike west on the Sheep Creek trail (FS-371) to the summit.

LOOKOUT MOUNTAIN, 8033', 14 miles RT, 3000' gain (USGS Little Baldy Mountain). Drive eight miles southeast of Prairie City on CR-62 and 11.5 miles southeast on road FS-13 to the trailhead. Hike west and southwest on the Horseshoe Trail (FS-363) to the summit.

LITTLE BALDY MOUNTAIN, 7701', 9 miles RT, 2700' gain (USGS Little Baldy Mountain). Drive as above for Lookout Mountain at the Horseshoe trailhead. Hike west on the Horseshoe Trail (FS-363). Where the trail turns southwest, leave the trail and hike north cross country on the ridge to the summit.

TABLE ROCK, 7815', 20 miles RT, 2400' gain (USGS Bullrun Rock, Little Baldy Mountain, SMMRW). **Mt. Bicycle Route.** Drive eight miles southeast of Prairie City on CR-62 and 12 miles southeast on FS-13 to the junction with road FS-1370, 5500'. Park and ride east on road FS-1370 to 6400'. Turn northwest to a junction with road FS-2652, then east to the summit of Table Rock, a lookout that is staffed during the summer months. From the summit, Mt. Ireland is exactly north and Rock Creek Butte, in the Elkhorn Range northeast of Sumpter, is east of north (18°). Both summits are 35 miles distant.

McNAUGHTON SPRING CAMPGROUND, 4840' (USGS Strawberry Mountain, SMMRW). Drive south from Prairie City on CR-60 for ten miles to this minimum campground. The road turns to gravel after three miles and narrows at the Forest boundary. Facilities and activities: space for tents and small recreational vehicles, no trailers, water from spring. No fee.

SLIDE CREEK CAMPGROUND, 5000' (USGS Strawberry Mountain, SMMRW). Drive one mile past McNaughton Spring campground to this minimum campground. Facilities and activities: space for tents and small recreational vehicles, no trailers, water from creek, hiking, fishing. No fee.

STRAWBERRY MOUNTAIN, 9036', 10 miles RT, 3500' gain (USGS Strawberry Mountain, SMMRW). Drive one mile past Slide Creek campground (see above) to the trailhead on Strawberry Creek. Park and hike the trail west, ascending at first along Onion Creek, then ascend south on the north ridge of Strawberry Mountain to the summit.

GEOLOGY OF STRAWBERRY RANGE. The Strawberry and Aldritch Mountains over a length of about 50 miles have been raised one to two miles by folding and faulting, mostly along the John Day fault, which runs along the north side of the range. The eastern end of these mountains are layered lava flows, called the Strawberry Volcanics, that occurred during some of the time that the Columbia Basalts were emitted. Much of the lava is andesite, a light-colored rock containing more quartz than basalt, which is the predominant lava of the Columbia and Picture Gorge flows. The Strawberry Volcanics came from vents south and east of Strawberry Mountain. The remains of one of the main vents, nearly a mile in diameter, are represented by the cliffs above Little Strawberry Lake. In the western part of the range, beginning at Indian Creek Butte and extending to Aldritch Mountain, peridotite, serpentine and gabbro are exposed. These rocks were derived at great depth from the mantle that underlies the continental and oceanic plates and were intruded and solidified before this region became part of the continent.

STRAWBERRY CAMPGROUND, 5737' (USGS Strawberry Mountain, SMMRW). Drive south to the end of road CR-60, 12 miles from Prairie City. Facilities and activities: tents and small recreational vehicles, no trailers, fishing, hiking, water. No fee.

STRAWBERRY LAKE, 6263', 2.5 miles RT, 600' gain (USGS Strawberry Mountain, SMMRW). Park in the hiker parking area at the end of road CR-60 south of Prairie City. Hike south to the lake, passing the Slide Lake trail junction on the left after one mile. Many camp sites are available at the lake.

STRAWBERRY FALLS, 6700', 5 miles RT, 1100' gain (USGS Strawberry Mountain, SMMRW). Hike as above to Strawberry Lake. Continue around the east side of the lake to the falls.

STRAWBERRY MOUNTAIN, 9036', 13 miles RT, 3500' gain (USGS Strawberry Mountain, SMMRW). Hike as above from the trailhead at the south end of the road on Strawberry Creek. After passing the falls, the trail turns northwest and north to the summit.

SLIDE MOUNTAIN, 8521', 12 miles RT, 3000' gain (USGS Strawberry Mountain, SMMRW). From the Strawberry Lake trailhead (see above), hike south one mile, then turn east on the Slide Lake trail (FS-372) for another mile to a trail junction (FS-372B). Take the left (upper) fork and ascend east on switchbacks. After one mile, go left on trail FS-385. Where the trail (FS-385) reaches a saddle and junction, 7800' and four miles from the Strawberry Lake trail, leave the trail and hike north cross country over the shoulder of Graham Mountain to the summit.

GRAHAM MOUNTAIN, 8570', 12 miles RT, 3000' gain (USGS Strawberry Mountain, SMMRW). Hike as above to the saddle south of Slide Mountain, 7800'. Leave the trail and hike east cross country up the ridge to the summit.

STANDARD MINE–COPPEROPOLIS MINE, high point 5000', 12 miles RT, 1200' gain (USGS Dixie Meadow). **Mt. Bicycle Route.** From Prairie City, drive north three miles on CR-58 to the end of the pavement, 3800'. Park and ride north on Dixie Creek for two miles. Turn northeast and ride up Standard creek for two miles to the site of the Standard Mine, at one time the largest producer of cobalt ore in the state. Continue up Standard Creek to the end of the road at the Copperopolis Mine where tourmaline crystals have been found in the mine tailings.

ARCH ROCK, 4594', 30 miles RT, 2000' gain (USGS Susanville, Cougar Rock). **Mt. Bicycle Route.** From MP-171 on US-26, four miles west of Prairie City, drive north on CR-18 for 10 miles to Four Corners, the end of the paved road and a four-way intersection, 5279'. Park and ride north on road FS-36, passing Eagle Rock at two miles, 4800', then descending along Camp Creek. Where Cougar Creek joins from the east at a road junction, ten miles from the starting point and 3953', turn right (south) 0.5 mile to a trailhead. Leave bicycle and hike one-fourth mile east to Arch Rock.

COUGAR ROCK, 6169', 15 miles RT, 2000' gain (USGS Cougar Rock, MFPCR). **Mt. Bicycle Route.** From the north end of paved CR-18 at Four Corners (see above under Arch Rock), park and ride north two miles to Eagle Rock. Turn right (east) three miles on road FS-3640, then left (north) one-half mile. Leave bicycle and hike northwest to the summit.

INDIAN CREEK BASIN, 7000', 13 miles RT, 2900' gain (USGS Strawberry Mountain). From MP-170 on US-26, drive eight miles south on CR-55, CR-71, and FS-7101 to the trailhead near the boundary of the Malheur National Forest. Hike south on the Indian Creek trail (FS-364) into the basin and a junction with trail FS-201. From Indian Creek basin, Strawberry Mountain is four miles and Indian Creek Butte is two miles.

SHEEP ROCK, 6400', 6 miles RT, 1800' gain (USGS Strawberry Mountain). Drive as above to the trailhead for Indian Creek basin. Hike south on the Indian Creek trail (FS-364) for 2.5 miles, to 6100'. In a opening in the forest, ascend west to the saddle south of the summit. Follow the ridge to the open summit with views of the John Day river valley.

BALDY MOUNTAIN, 7358', 8 miles RT, 2000' gain (USGS Pine Creek Mountain). At MP-168, six miles west of Prairie City, drive six miles south from US-26 on CR-54 and FS-5401 to the end of the pavement, at the Malheur Forest Boundary, 5500'. Hike south on the road for 0.5 mile. Where the road bends west, leave the road and ascend south and southeast up a ridge cross country, passing two roads and the Chambers Mine at 6500'.

PRAIRIE DIGGINGS, 3600' (USGS Castle Creek). At MP-165, 10 miles west of Prairie City and three miles east of John Day, drive southeast on CR-52 for one mile. Turn east 1.5 miles to an abandoned placer mining area. Nearly every gully and slope in this region where water flowed or could be brought by ditch was mined at some time in the past.

JOHN DAY. See p. 126.

MT. VERNON. See p. 125.

GEOLOGIC SITE, 2700' (USGS Shop Gulch). At MP-144, nine miles west of Mt. Vernon, turn south from US-26 and stop at a road cut, 0.1 mile from US-26. The John Day fault is marked by a low gap in the road cut. North of the fault, beds of the Mascall Formation, which overlies the Picture Gorge Basalts, slope gently to the south. As a result of north-south compression, south of the fault these same beds of the Mascall Formation slope steeply to the north. Fossil leaves, seed pods, and snail shells can be found in the beds south of the fault. Two-tenths of a mile farther south, vertical layers of the Picture Gorge Basalts are exposed along Fields Creek Road. To the north across the John Day River gently sloping layers of the Picture Gorge Basalts have been displaced upward along the Belshaw fault at their southern edge. Between the exposures of the Picture Gorge Basalts to the north and the John Day River, the Mascall Formation is exposed in the White Hills, a locality for collecting fossil leaves.

BILLY FIELDS CAMPGROUND, 4000' (USGS Big Weasel Springs). At MP-144 on US-26, drive south six miles on road FS-21 to this minimum campground. Facilities: space for tents and recreational vehicles, water from stream. No fee.

FIELDS PEAK, 7362', 8 miles RT, 3000' gain (USGS Big Weasel Springs). From US-26 at MP-144, drive south eight miles on road FS-21 and two miles south of Billy Fields campground, to a junction with road FS-115. Park and hike east on roads FS-115 and FS-2160 to the beginning of trail FS-212. Follow trail FS-212 to the summit.

McCLELLEN MOUNTAIN, 7043', 18 miles RT, 2600' gain (USGS McClellen Mountain, Big Weasel Spring). **Mt. Bicycle Route.** At MP-144 on US-26, drive south 13 miles on road FS-21 to a junction with road FS-2170. Turn left (east) staying on FS-21 for two miles to a junction with road FS-011 at the site of Lemon Cabin. Park and ride north on road FS-011 for two miles to Tex Creek and a junction with road FS-102. Continue north on FS-102 for 0.5 mile, then follow Tex Creek on road FS-132 to the junction of Miner Creek and Tex Creek, seven miles from road FS-21. Leave bicycle and hike along Tex Creek for one mile then ascend northeast one mile to the summit, passing west of Packsaddle Gap.

OREGON MINE CAMPGROUND, 4315' (USGS Big Weasel Springs). Drive as above for Billy Fields campground on road FS-21. Continue south to the end of the pavement, 13 miles from US-26. Turn right (northwest) on road FS-2170 one-half mile to this minimum campground on a branch of Murderers Creek. Facilities: space for tents and small recreational vehicles, water from creek. No fee.

ALDRITCH MOUNTAIN LOOKOUT, 6991', 30 miles RT, 3000' gain (USGS Big Weasel Springs, Aldritch Mountain). **Mt. Bicycle Route.** From Oregon Mine campground, ride west down Murderers Creek on road FS-2170, taking a right fork (northwest) at two miles to stay on road FS-2170, and another right fork (north) on road FS-070 at four miles from the campground. At a junction seven miles from the campground, turn northwest on road FS-2150 to ascend Aldritch Ridge to the lookout, passing Big Weasel Springs at eight miles, Little Weasel Springs at ten miles, Cedar Grove Botanical Area where tree seed is grown, and Frankie and Johnny Summits. The summit of Aldritch Mountain provides a spectacular view to the north over the John Day river valley. Serpentine rock is exposed in many places on Aldritch Ridge.

HORSE MOUNTAIN, 5386', 6 miles RT, 1200' gain (USGS Big Weasel Springs, Flagtail Mountain). From Oregon Mine campground, hike south on the road up Horse Creek to the ridge. Follow the ridge south to the high point.

OREGON MINE, 5100', 4 miles RT, 900' gain (USGS Big Weasel Springs). From Oregon Mine campground, hike north on the ridge west of Oregon Mine Creek to reach the mine. Much of the rock exposed here is serpentine.

HORSE MOUNTAIN LOOP, high point 5000', 15 miles RT, 750' gain (USGS Big Weasel Springs, Flagtail Mountain). **Mt. Bicycle Route.** From Oregon Mine campground (see above), ride west on road FS-2170 to a junction with road FS-2490. Turn left on FS-2490 and go west and southwest over a ridge to another branch of Murderers Creek to meet road FS-2480. Follow road FS-2480 four miles as it ascends Murderers Creek, turning right on road FS-2180 up Beaverdam Creek. After two miles, this road turns north to a junction with road FS-21. On reaching FS-21, turn left (west) to return to Oregon Mine campground.

BLUE RIDGE LOOP, high point 5280', 26 miles RT, 1500' gain (USGS Big Weasel Springs, Aldritch Mountain South, Graylock Butte, Flagtail Mountain). **Mt. Bicycle Route.** From Oregon Mine campground, ride west on road FS-2170 for two miles to a junction. Continue west on road FS-2490 for one mile then on road FS-203 for two miles to rejoin road FS-2490, bending south and again southwest. Turn south on road FS-389 as it ascends over Blue Ridge, 4900', crossing road FS-228 at the crest of the ridge. On reaching road FS-24, turn right (east) and continue on FS-24 along Deer Creek and the North Fork of Deer Creek through an old mining district. After eight miles on FS-24, turn north to follow roads FS-641, FS-377, and FS-2180, descending along Dans Creek to road FS-21. On reaching road FS-21, turn left (west) to the starting point. This route can be extended eight miles with little increase in elevation gain by staying on road FS-641 for five miles to road FS-401 and descending along Lemon Creek to FS-21 and the starting point.

GEOLOGIC SITE, 2400', MP-132 (USGS Dayville). The 70' thick reddish rimrock at the top of the slope directly north across the John Day River is a welded tuff, from a volcanic ash flow five million years old and known as the Rattlesnake Formation. Immediately below the Rattlesnake

Formation is the older Mascall Formation, a sedimentary deposit known for its fossils. The Mascall Formation overlies the Columbia Basalts of the Picture Gorge lava flows, best seen in Picture Gorge to the west along the John Day River. The Picture Gorge basalt layers overlie the John Day formation, exposed to the west in John Day Fossil Beds National Monument. The valley here has been eroded from the Mascall Formation.

DAYVILLE, 2360', population 144, MP-131 (USGS Dayville). Facilities and activities: food, stores, lodging, gas. **Events:** Fourth of July celebration with dance, horse races, parade, picnic, roping contest, tel. 987-2375. **Fish House Inn and RV Park**, PO Box 143, 97825, tel. 987-2124, tents, trailers, no hookups. Fee. **South Fork Minimart & RV Park**, PO Box 42, 97825, tel. 987-2106, tents, trailers, electrical and water hookups. Fee.

RUDIO MOUNTAIN, 5760', 30 miles RT, 3500' gain (USGS Dayville, Sheep Ridge). **Mt. Bicycle Route.** From Dayville, ride west on US-26 for 0.5 mile then north on Franks Creek Road (CR-1), going right (east) at a road junction after 12 miles. In the saddle between the summits, keep right (south) to the highest summit of Rudio Mountain. Return to the saddle and ride north to the lookout (5676').

MURDERERS CREEK LOOP, high point 5200', 55 miles RT, 3600' gain (USGS Dayville, Aldrich Gulch, Aldritch Mountain South, Aldritch Mountain North, Big Weasel Spring). **Mt. Bicycle Route.** From Dayville, ride south, ascending along the South Fork of the John Day River on road CR-42 for 15 miles to the junction with Murderers Creek, 2939'. Turn left and follow Murderers Creek east, passing Murderers Creek Ranch. At six miles from the South Fork of the John Day River, turn northeast on road FS-2160 ascending away from Murderers Creek along Thorn Creek to enter the Malheur National Forest in one mile. Rejoin Murderers Creek one mile before passing Oregon Mine campground. One mile after passing Oregon Mine campground, turn left (north) on paved FS-21 to ascend over Aldritch Mountain Ridge (5200') to reach US-26. Turn left (west) to Dayville.

SOUTH FORK OF THE JOHN DAY RIVER, high point 4300', 90 miles RT, 2300' gain (USGS Dayville, Aldrich Gulch, Suplee Butte, Izee, Lewis Creek, Graylock Butte). **Mt. Bicycle Route.** From Dayville, ride south on gravel, ascending along the South Fork of the John Day River. Join paved road CR-67 after 30 miles and reach Izee at 38 miles. Continue up the South Fork of the John Day River to the end of the pavement, 45 miles from Dayville.

MASCALL RANCH, 2300' (USGS Picture Gorge East). At MP-125, four miles west of Dayville, this area is the type locality for the Mascall Formation, a fossil-bearing sedimentary rock deposited 15 to 12 million years ago.

PICTURE GORGE, 2200' (USGS Picture Gorge East and Picture Gorge West). Stop at MP-125, a viewpoint near the east end of the Gorge and the beginning of the John Day Fossil Beds National Monument. From MP-125 on US-26 to MP-123 on SR-19, the road follows the John Day River through this spectacular canyon, cut by the river in the Picture Gorge Basalts, which are contemporary with the Columbia Basalt lava flows farther east. More than 15 lava flows have been counted. These flows occurred from 20-12 million years ago. The river carved the narrow canyon in the last half million years and the five benches at the east entrance to the gorge mark stages in the down cutting. The mesa to the southwest from Picture Gorge consists of the Rattlesnake Formation on top of the Mascall Formation, both more recent than the Picture Gorge Basalts. The basalt layers were tilted during the uplift of the Aldritch Mountains to the south.

JUNCTION SR-19, 2231', MP-124 (USGS Picture Gorge East, Picture Gorge West). At this junction, leave US-26 to drive north on SR-19.

SHEEP ROCK OVERLOOK, 3360', MP-122 (USGS Picture Gorge West, Picture Gorge East). Two miles south of the Cant Ranch and one mile north of US-26, a viewpoint and exhibit provides a view north to a remnant cap of Picture Gorge Basalt resting on an exposure of nearly 2000' of the John Day Formation. The layers to the south of a fault that runs diagonally through the face below Sheep Rock are offset 70'-100' upward. This fault can be clearly seen in the picture of Sheep Rock shown on the John Day Fossil Beds brochure (GPO 1993–342-398/80004 Reprint 1993). A Thomas Condon Memorial is also located here.

JOHN DAY FOSSIL BEDS NATIONAL MONUMENT, 2200', (USGS Miller Flat, Mount Misery, Picture Gorge East and Picture Gorge West). The lands of the National Monument begin at MP-125 on US-26 and end north of MP-118 on SR-19. The Headquarters building at the Cant Ranch, at MP-121, two miles north of US-26 on SR-19, has displays of some of the fossils found in the area as well as informative talks and videos. The total area of the National Monument is 14,000 acres.

GOOSE ROCK, 2000', MP-120 (USGS Picture Gorge West). The pebble conglomerate making up this rock was deposited in a near shore environment before 60 million years ago as this area was becoming part of the continent. The Goose Rock conglomerate ends abruptly on the north at the Middle Mountain faults, where the Picture Gorge Basalt has been displaced downward more than 2000'. These faults run east-west, one of them following the base of Middle Mountain.

BLUE BASIN FOSSIL BEDS, 2100', MP-118 (USGS Picture Gorge West). This area, part of the John Day Fossil Beds National Monument, has a 0.5 mile trail into the fossil beds with displays of models of fossils that have been found in the area, and a three mile loop trail to an overlook.

Guided tours begin in May (10am, check at Cant Ranch Headquarters).

CATHEDRAL ROCK, 2000', MP-116 (USGS Mount Misery). A large block of the John Day Formation collapsed from the slope to the west to partially block the John Day River.

FOREE FOSSIL BEDS, 2000', MP-114 (USGS Mount Misery). A picnic area with restrooms and water has short trails into the fossil beds. Overlying the fossil beds of the John Day formation are thick layers of the Picture Gorge member of the Columbia Basalts.

ASHER'S RV PARK, 2000', MP-114 (USGS Mt. Misery). Facilities and activities: tents, trailers, partial hookups, seasonal. Fee. Address: HC 82, Box 113, Kimberly, 97848. Telephone: 934-2712.

BASALT DIKES, 1900' (USGS Mount Misery). At MP-109, the vertically standing rocks to the southeast and 0.5 mile up hill are part of a dike system that was one of the fissures from which part of the Picture Gorge lavas originated. At MP-107, a parking area on the west side of the highway provides pedestrian access to the John Day River. The cliffs rising above the river on the west side are part of this dike system. The polygonal ends of the columns in the basalt, which developed during cooling, are exposed in the cliff just above the river. The columns lie horizontally in contrast to the vertical columns normally seen in horizontal basalt lava flows, for example, in Picture Gorge. The dike system can also be seen going off to the northwest as a row of pinnacles.

KIMBERLY, 1828', MP-105 (USGS Kimberly). Facilities and activities: store, gas (open daily).

SR-402. From Kimberly, turn east on pavement.

THOMAS ORCHARDS, 1850' (USGS Kimberly). Drive 0.5 mile east of Kimberly on SR-402. U-pick peaches, apricots, cherries, apples, and pears. Telephone 934-2870.

LONE PINE PARK, 1900' (USGS Kimberly). Drive one mile east of Kimberley on SR-402 to this minimum campground on the John Day River. Facilities and activities: fishing, hiking, tents, trailers, no hookups. No fee.

BIG BEND PARK, 1950' (USGS Bologna Basin). Drive three miles east on SR-402 from Kimberley to this minimum campground on the John Day River. Facilities and activities: fishing, hiking, tents, trailers, no hookups. No fee.

MONUMENT, 2007', population 162 (USGS Monument). Drive 13 miles east on SR-402 from Kimberley. Several buildings remain from the earliest settlement. Facilities and activities: food, store, gas. **Elkhorn Tavern**

and RV Park: tents, trailers, showers, laundromat. Fee. Address: Monument 97864, tel. 934-2244. **Events:** Mid-July, Grasshopper Festival with roping contests, barrel racing, wild cow milking. Contact Archie Osburn, General Delivery, 97864.

MONUMENT MOUNTAIN LOOKOUT, 3875', 12 miles RT, 2000' gain (USGS Monument). **Mt. Bicycle Route.** From the town of Monument, ride north on CR-670 for four miles. Turn east to the summit, which has a lookout tower, a microwave relay station, and an impressive view of the John Day River country.

NORTH FORK JOHN DAY RIVER, high point 2200', 30 miles RT, 200' gain (USGS Monument, Johnny Cake Mountain, Slickear Mountain). **Mt. Bicycle Route.** From Monument, ride north along the North Fork of the John Day river to the junction with the Middle Fork of the John Day River.

SUNKEN MOUNTAIN, 4117' (USGS Hamilton). Two miles west of Hamilton on SR-402 and 21 miles from SR-19, the tumbled and hummocky terrain south of SR-402 is the remains of a landslide in the John Day Formation. Bare walls of light-colored volcanic ash beds indicate active parts of the landslide. Slopes covered with grass or trees have been inactive long enough for the vegetation to grow. As stream erosion carries material away from the lowest part of the slide, the valley wall becomes oversteepened and a new slide occurs. The volcanic ash of the John Day Formation weathers to clay which becomes slippery when wet. Once a rupture has occured, the slide material can continue to move on a slope of low angle. The western scarp of Hamilton Mountain to the south exposes this same formation.

HAMILTON MOUNTAIN LOOP, high point 5000', 36 or 42 miles RT, 3600' gain (USGS Monument, Courthouse Rock, Hamilton, Fox, Street Mountain). **Mt. Bicycle Route.** From Monument, ride or drive three miles south on road SR-402 toward Hamilton. At a road junction, ride south on CR-6, passing Barber Pole Butte on the right (west) after four miles and Courthouse Rock on the left (east) at seven miles. Reach the site of Courtrock School at eight miles and the site of Courtrock at 12 miles. Turn east and ascend over the Hamilton Mountain Range, 4700', to reach road CR-9 at 22 miles from SR-402. Turn north over the Long Creek Mountain Range, high point 5000', to rejoin SR-402, passing through a portion of the Malheur National Forest. Turn left (west) on SR-402 to return to the starting point.

SUNKEN MOUNTAIN LOOP, high point 4000', 25 miles RT, 2000' gain (USGS Monument, Courthouse Rock, Hamilton, Street Mountain). **Mt. Bicycle Route.** From Monument, ride south and southeast ten miles on SR-402. Near the community of Hamilton, turn south on road CR-7 and ascend south over the shoulder of Sunken Mountain to reach road CR-6. Turn north to return to SR-402. Continue north to Monument.

GEOLOGIC SITE, 4300' (USGS Fox, Hamilton). Stop at MP-25 on SR-402. Long Creek Mountain to the southeast consists of 1500' of Picture Gorge Basalt flows. Round Basin in the foreground (southeast) eroded in the soft ash of the John Day Formation beneath the Picture Gorge Basalts, which can be seen in road cuts where the highway crosses Basin Creek. The east-west Hamilton fault is marked by the gulch to the left below the parking area. The fault extends east along the northeast edge of Round Basin and passes at the northern foot of Long Mountain. Movement on the Hamilton fault has dropped the Picture Gorge basalts about 1000'. North of the fault, Basin Creek has cut only a narrow V-shaped valley in the basalts compared with the wide Round Basin that the creek eroded in the John Day formation.

SR-7

Baker City to Austin Junction

Begin at Post Office Square in Baker City, MP-51. Drive south on State Route 7.

GRIFFIN GULCH (USGS Baker, Bowen Valley, Blue Canyon, Wingville). South of MP-49, SR-7 crosses Griffin Gulch, named for Henry Griffin of Portland, Oregon, who made the first discovery of gold in Baker County on October 23, 1861. He, with three companions, was searching for the lost Blue Bucket mine, supposed to have been discovered by an Oregon Trail emigrant party (see Oregon Historical Quarterly 20:219, June 1919).

AUBURN, 3600' (USGS Blue Canyon, WWBRD). Find a junction south of MP-44. The town of Auburn, five miles west of here in Blue Canyon and having at one time as many as 5,000 people, sprang into existence after the nearby discovery of gold. The town was the seat of Baker County until 1868. Now nothing is left but acres and acres of piled boulders left from placer mining, hard-to-find graveyards, and the remains of a reservoir and a ditch that was dug to bring water from Elk and Wilson Creeks and from creeks farther north. Now the Baker City water supply system uses parts of route of this ditch.

To find the Auburn site, drive west on the old Auburn road (CR-722 & FS-7220), passing the Wildlife Feeding Station on the left (south) of the road at 3.5 miles. After passing the Feeding Station, continue for 1.5 miles to where a minor dirt track turns off to the right (north). Park and walk this track 0.5 mile to the bottom of Blue Canyon and the site of Auburn. The cemeteries are on a knoll 0.5 mile west of the road that continues northwest up the ridge between Blue Canyon Creek and Freezeout Gulch. The area shows much evidence of old mining activity. For example, a faint ditch line begins 0.5 mile to the northwest up Blue Canyon from the junction with Freezeout Gulch. This ditch line contours around the ridge into Freezeout Gulch. Road FS-7225, which leaves FS-7220 one mile northwest of the dirt road to Auburn and near the National Forest boundary, passes the old Auburn Reservoir in the southwest corner of Section 4, T10S, R39E.

ELKHORN WILDLIFE AREA, 4100' (USGS Blue Canyon). A feeding station to provide winter sustenance for large animals through the winter is located 3.5 miles west of SR-7 on a road that begins south of MP-44. The reserved area is south of the road to Auburn.

SALISBURY, 3647'. South of MP-42, at the junction with SR-245, this intersection was the beginning of the Dooley Mountain Toll Road to

Bridgeport and later a station on the Sumpter Valley Railroad. Now, SR-245 follows near or on the route of the old toll road for the first six miles. The route of the toll road then goes over the east shoulder of Dooley Mountain to end at Bridgeport.

BALD MOUNTAIN, 6683', 8 miles RT, 2500' gain (USGS Brannan Gulch, Dooley Mt.). From Salisbury junction on SR-7, drive three miles south on SR-245 to the junction with the Stices Gulch road on the right. Park and hike south on the road in the floor of Stices Gulch for two miles. Turn west on road FS-1130, following the stream bed for one mile. Where the road turns south away from the stream bed, ascend south of west cross country to the summit.

DOOLEY MOUNTAIN SUMMIT, 5392' (USGS Dooley Mt.). Drive eight miles south from Salisbury on SR-245. This summit has partial views northwest to the Blue Mountains and south into the Burnt River valley and the hills beyond.

COLUMBIA BASALTS. From MP-44 to MP-38 on SR-7, lava flows of the Columbia Basalts crown the valley rims along the road.

MASON DAM AND PICNIC AREA. West of MP-35, turn left (south) to the base of the dam and a picnic area with fishing access to the Powder River. No camping.

BALD MOUNTAIN LOOP, 6683', 30 miles RT, 2800' gain (USGS Phillips Lake, Blue Canyon, Beaverdam Creek, Brannan Gulch). **Mt. Bicycle Route.** Begin at Union Creek campground or at parking near Mason Dam. Ride east on SR-7, turning south at the east end of Phillips Lake to cross Mason Dam. Ride south on road FS-1145 for seven miles then go left (east) on Skyline Road (FS-11) to the summit. From the summit of Bald Mountain, continue east to road SR-245. Turn left and descend north to SR-7. Turn left to return to the starting point.

PHILLIPS LAKE SOUTH SHORE TRAIL, 4080', 12 miles RT, minimum gain (USGS Phillips Lake). Park at the south end of Mason Dam, leaving SR-7 near MP-34. Hike west near the south shore of Phillips Lake, passing three hike-in or boat-in campgrounds with minimum facilities and two drive-in campgrounds, to the west end of the lake in the midst of dredge tailings. Water birds, deer, and elk sometimes feed in this area. This trail is part of a cross-country ski trail system.

PHILLIPS LAKE BOAT LAUNCH. West of MP-34, turn south to the boat launch ramp near the north end of Mason Dam.

PHILLIPS LAKE NORTHSHORE TRAIL, 4100', 8 miles RT, minimum gain (USGS Phillips Lake). Drive as above to the boat launch parking at the north end of Mason Dam. Hike west along the north shore of Phillips

Lake to Social Security Point, passing through Union Creek Campground. Begin this trail also from Union Creek Campground.

UNION CREEK CAMPGROUND, 4100', (USGS Phillips Lake). Near MP-32, turn south into the campground on Phillips Lake, a reservoir on the Powder River. Facilities and activities: Pull throughs and full hookups for recreational vehicles of any size, water, boat launch, showers, hiking, bicycling, swimming, boating. Fee. Address: HCR 87, Box 929A, Baker City OR, 97814. tel. 894-2210.

INDIAN ROCK POINT, 4824', 3 miles RT, 600' gain (USGS Phillips Lake). Find the beginning of the trail across SR-7 from the entrance to Union Creek Campground. The trail offers views of the extent of the dredging in Sumpter Valley.

AUBURN GHOST TOWN LOOP, high point 5000', 30 miles RT, 1500' gain (USGS Phillips Lake, Blue Canyon, Bowen Valley, WWBRD). **Mt. Bicycle Route.** From Union Creek Campground, ride east on SR-7 for one-fourth mile then go north from SR-7 on road FS-2225 up Union Creek for two miles. Turn right (northeast) on road FS-7220, passing after two miles a branch road on the right that descends in California Gulch, another mining district. Stay on road FS-7220 to descend east on the gentle slope of the south rim of Blue Canyon. Pass a junction with road FS-7225 at five miles from SR-7. At six miles from SR-7, road FS-7220 leaves the Wallowa-Whitman National Forest. East of the forest boundary, a short road goes to a Blue Canyon overlook. Continue southeast on road FS-7220, now CR-722, for one-fourth mile to the junction with a dirt road that descends north into Blue Canyon and the site of Auburn at the junction of Blue Canyon and Freezeout Gulch. Turn and ride on this dirt road north and northwest one-half mile beyond the junction of the two canyons to the site of the cemeteries. These are on a minor summmit south of the road. Follow the dirt road north to join road FS-7225 near an old reservoir that was fed by the Auburn ditch. Stay on road FS-7225, descending northeast and east near Elk Creek. Road FS-7225 becomes CR-714 on leaving the National Forest and CR-714 can be followed east to intersect with road SR-7. On reaching SR-7, turn south to Salisbury junction and west to return to the starting point at Union Creek Campground.

SKYLINE ROAD LOOP, high point 5800', 30 miles RT, 2000' gain (USGS Phillips Lake, Beaverdam Creek, Sumpter, WWBRD). **Mt. Bicycle Route.** From Union Creek Campground, ride west on SR-7 to MP-30, then south on the South Shore road, passing Southwest Shore and Miller Lane Campgrounds. At three miles from SR-7, turn south up Dean Creek. Continue south up the Dean Creek road to the intersection with the Skyline Road, FS-11, nine miles from SR-7. Turn west and northwest on Skyline Road on or near the crest of the ridge to a junction with SR-7 near Huckleberry Mountain. Turn right to go east and north on SR-7 into Sumpter Valley to return to Phillips Lake and the starting point.

MARBLE PASS LOOP, high point 7542', 25 miles RT, 3500' gain (USGS Phillips Lake, Elkhorn Peak, WWBRD). **Mt. Bicycle Route.** From Union Creek Campground on Phillips Lake, ride east on SR-7 for one-fourth mile, then turn up Union Creek on road FS-2225, going left at the first intersection into road FS-7220, two miles from SR-7. At three miles from SR-7, turn right (northwest) on SR-7240, contouring north and northwest across several stream gullies for seven miles to a junction with road FS-6510. Turn right (north) on FS-6510 and ascend north and northeast for four miles to the beginning of the Chemical Lime Company limestone quarry, now inactive. Stay on the road as it ascends past and through the heaps of crushed limestone left from the quarry operation. After passing the quarry, continue east to reach Marble Pass. Leave bicycle at the pass and hike south one mile to the summit of Marble Point (WWBRD). Return on road FS-6510 to road FS-7240. Turn right (south) for 3.5 miles to reach SR-7, then go left (east) four miles on SR-7 to Union Creek Campground.

MOWICH PICNIC AREA, 4100' (USGS Phillips Lake). West of MP-32, turn south. This area has access to Phillips Lake.

DREDGE TAILINGS, MP-31 to Sumpter (USGS Phillips Lake, Sumpter). The remains of decades of dredging for gold fill the valley bottom for ten miles.

SOUTHWEST SHORE CAMPGROUND, 4100' (USGS Phillips Lake). West of MP-30, turn south, then east on FS-2220 to the campground on the south side of Phillips Lake, two miles from SR-7. Facilities and activities: tents, trailers, hiking, bicycling. No fee.

MILLER LANE CAMPGROUND, 4100' (USGS Phillips Lake). Drive as above three miles from SR-7 to the campground. Facilities and activities: tents, trailers, hiking, boating, bicycling, fishing. No fee.

BLACK MOUNTAIN, 6646', 10 miles RT, 2600' gain (USGS Phillips Lake). From either of the south shore campgrounds of Phillips Lake, hike east on the southshore road to the Dean Creek Road. Turn south for 1.5 miles, then go left (southeast) on the road up Little Dean Creek, keeping left at junctions to maintain a southeast direction. After 2.5 miles at a saddle, 5750', leave the road and ascend east in open timber on a subsidiary ridge to the summit.

DEER CREEK CAMPGROUND, 4400' (USGS Phillips Lake). West of MP-29, turn right (north), then immediately left on a road that becomes FS-6550. At 3.4 miles, turn right on FS-6530 to the campground, four miles from SR-7.

TWIN LAKES, 7665', 7701', 7 miles RT, 2300' gain (USGS Phillips Lake, Elkhorn Peak). Drive as above toward Deer Creek Campground. At 3.4 miles, where the road crosses Deer Creek, continue north up Lake Creek. Park at the road end, seven miles from SR–7. The last 0.5 mile of this road is narrow with no turnouts. Hike the trail three miles to the first lake. The second lake is another 0.5 mile. Spectacular cliffs of altered sea floor rocks form the valley wall on the west.

ELKHORN PEAK, 8931', 9 miles RT, 3500' gain (USGS Phillips Lake, Elkhorn Peak). Drive and hike as above to Twin Lakes. Continue on the trail east past the first lake to the junction with the Elkhorn Crest Trail, 7900'. Turn south on the trail for a few feet, then leave the trail, ascending southeast up the north ridge of Elkhorn Peak, first on the east side of the ridge, then on the crest of the ridge or just below the crest on the west side. The rocks here are altered sediments accumulated on the sea floor, and known as the Elkhorn Peak argillite. Dikes of andesite penetrate the ridge south of the summit and the slope leading down to Twin Lakes.

ROCK CREEK BUTTE, 9106', 11 miles, 3700' gain (USGS Phillips Lake, Elkhorn Peak). Hike as above for Elkhorn Peak to the junction of the Twin Lakes trail with the Elkhorn Crest Trail. Turn north on the Elkhorn Crest Trail. After one-half mile, the trail crosses a saddle to the east side of the crest and traverses through colorful cliffs of altered sea floor sediments. After the trail crosses back to the west side of the ridge, go 500' on the trail then turn right (north) off the trail up a 50' wide alpine meadow. Continue north to the summit on the gentle west side of the ridge.

ELKHORN PEAK, 8931', 10 miles, 3400' gain (USGS Phillips Lake, Elkhorn Peak). **Quarry Route.** West of MP-29, turn right into a road that becomes FS-7240, passing immediately the road left to Deer Creek Campground. After driving 3.4 miles from SR–7, go left on road FS-6510, turning right (north) at a junction 4.2 miles from SR–7, where a road goes left to Deer Creek Campground. Park at the beginning of the limestone quarry, six miles from SR–7 and 5600'. From this point on the road becomes steeper, gullied, and may be washed out in places. Hike up the road beside and through the quarry around piles of crushed limestone for one mile. Near the top of the quarry, from the junction with a road west into the quarry where the main road turns sharply northeast, continue northeast on the main road for one-fourth mile to the junction with another spur road to the west above the quarry. Turn west on this road for 100', then ascend north to the broad crest of "Quarry" Ridge. Follow this ridge east in open timber and sagebrush to meet the Elkhorn Crest Trail at 7900'. Turn north on the Elkhorn Crest Trail for one mile until the trail turns west to contour around the west side of Elkhorn Peak. At this point, leave the trail and ascend north to the summit, keeping west of the summit ridge on the open, gentle slope. Several false summits make short descents necessary. At several places, the altered sea floor rocks of the summit ridge are penetrated by dikes of volcanic rock.

"QUARRY" POINT, 8255', 7 miles rt, 2700' gain (USGS Phillips Lake, Elkhorn Peak). Hughes Lane in Baker City points almost directly at this summit, the distinct small point south of Elkhorn Peak on the western skyline. Hike as above on the quarry route toward Elkhorn Peak, turning north for one-fourth mile after joining the Elkhorn Crest Trail to the first 'window' view to the Powder River Valley. Turn southeast from the trail and ascend to the summit, first on the east side of the crest, then on or west of the crest.

MARBLE PASS, 7542', 8 miles RT, 2000' gain (USGS Elkhorn Peak, Marble Point). Park at the limestone quarry on road FS-6510 (see above under Elkhorn Peak, Quarry Route, p. 58). Hike up the road to the pass. Outcrops of limestone are exposed in the road cut at the pass and in the minor summit to the north.

MARBLE POINT, 7931', 10 miles RT, 2400' gain (USGS Elkhorn Peak, Marble Point, WWBRD). From Marble Pass (see above), hike south up an obvious trail to the broad, gentle plateau with a choice of summits. No marble is exposed on Marble Point. This is the summit as named on WWBRD and USGS Marble Point.

McEWEN. West of MP-29 on SR-7 a store and gas station mark the location of what was once an important stage stop and later a station on the Sumpter Valley Railway. The village is named for Thomas McEwen, who operated the stage and livery stable here. Before the dredge, the valley grew hay.

SUMPTER VALLEY RAILROAD. West of MP-28, turn south to the facilities of the partially restored Sumpter Valley Railroad. All of the rolling stock, including a show-piece Heisler gear-drive locomotive, is original equipment of the Sumpter Valley Railroad, recovered from places as far away as Alaska. The railroad was completed to nearby McEwen in July of 1891 and by 1910 ran to Prairie City, 80 miles from Baker City. The railroad operated until 1947, carrying logs, wood products, and other freight. The restored train carries passengers weekends and holidays from Memorial weekend to the end of September and for special trips. Address: PO Box 389, Baker City 97814, tel. 894-2268.

SUMPTER JUNCTION. West of MP-26 is the junction with the road to Sumpter, three miles to the northwest (see p. 94).

HUCKLEBERRY MOUNTAIN–BIG HUCKLEBERRY BUTTE, 5786', 5918', 4 miles RT, 1000' gain (USGS Sumpter, WWBRD). Park at Larch Summit, MP-22. Hike southeast on or near the ridge crest, and part of the way through an old forest fire, with views of the Elkhorn Range to the north.

BALD MOUNTAIN, 6683', 40 miles RT, 3000' gain (USGS Sumpter, Phillips Lake, Beaverdam Creek, Brannan Gulch). **Mt. Bicycle Route.** West of MP-20, park and ride east on Skyline Road (FS-11) to the summit, passing Sheep Rock, Spud Spring, and Camp Crunch Spring.

WHITNEY, 4164' (USGS Whitney). East of MP-15, several decaying buildings on the North Fork of the Burnt River mark the site of a once important logging center for the Sumpter Valley Railroad. The route of the railroad can still be seen crossing the valley. The sawmill burned in 1918. Agate limb casts have been found to the northeast.

NORTH FORK BURNT RIVER LOOP, high point 4164', 45 miles RT, 800' gain (USGS Whitney, Unity Reservoir, Pogue Point, WWURD). **Mt. Bicycle Route.** The almost level road (CR-529, CR-535) to the southeast from Whitney along the river joins SR-245 in 20 miles. Turn left (west) on SR-245 through the narrow Burnt River canyon and around the south side of Unity Reservoir (water, restrooms), then ride north on CR-575 to rejoin the road along the North Fork of the Burnt River at the King Ranch and return to the starting point.

CAMP CREEK, high point 5496', 20 miles, 1300' gain (USGS Whitney, WWURD). **Mt. Bicycle Route.** The road (CR-507 and FS-19) to the northwest up Camp Creek from Whitney travels past old placer mines. From the high point at the crest of the ridge, return south on roads FS-1960 and CR-503 to SR-7. Turn east to the starting point.

NORTH FORK BURNT RIVER, 5000', 20 miles RT, 1000' gain (USGS Greenhorn, WWURD). **Mt. Bicycle Route.** Near MP-11 and five miles west of Whitney on SR-7, park at the road junction and ride west and northwest up the river on road CR-503, FS-1042 for six miles. Turn north to a saddle and four-way road junction, 5000', where Olive Creek descends north. Turn east three miles on road FS-1046 into the Geiser Creek basin. Descend near Geiser Creek past the sites of the Geiser, Bonanza, and Golden Boy mines to return to CR-503, SR-7, and the starting point.

TIPTON, 5076', MP-8 (USGS Whitney). Located at the junction of SR-7 with the Howard Meadow Road, nothing remains of a logging center that supplied the Sumpter Valley Railroad.

GREENHORN, 6300' (USGS Greenhorn). At the Tipton junction, MP-8, drive west on FS-1035 to this once important mining center. Only a few old cabins remain, some in the process of being restored for use. The historic jail has been moved to be part of the Canyon City museum. Tempskya fern fossils have been found west of here in mine dumps and placer diggings.

VINEGAR HILL, 8131', 8 miles RT, 2000' gain (USGS Greenhorn, Vinegar Hill, WWURD). From Greenhorn, hike the ridge west to the summit, passing through an old mining district.

AUSTIN, 4115' (USGS Austin). Near MP-2, drive north one mile. Once a logging community, with a postoffice established in 1888, this area now raises cattle. No services.

BATES, 4074' (USGS Bates, Austin). West of SR-7 at MP-1, at one time Bates was a large lumber mill and a terminus of the Sumpter Valley Railroad. In 1994, only a concrete wall remained from the sawmill.

DEERHORN CAMPGROUND, 4000' (USGS Bates). From SR-7 at MP-1, drive five miles north on CR-20 on a paved road down the Middle Fork of the John Day River. Facilities and activities: tents, trailers to 25', hiking, fishing, bicycling. No fee.

MIDDLE FORK CAMPGROUND, 3840' (USGS Vinegar Hill). Drive as above past the Deerhorn Campground for seven miles from SR-7. Facilities and activities: tents, trailers to 25', hiking, fishing, bicycling. No fee.

VINEGAR HILL, 8131', 25 miles RT, 4100' gain (USGS Bates, Vinegar Hill, WWURD). **Mt. Bicycle Route.** From Deerhorn Campground, ride three miles southeast up the Middle Fork of the John Day River on CR-20 to the junction with FS-2010, three miles from SR-7. Ride north up Vincent Creek on road FS-2010 for five miles. Turn northwest at a junction, continuing on FS-2010 to circle around the south ridge of Vinegar Hill to reach the northwest ridge at a road junction. Turn southeast up the ridge to the summit.

INDIAN ROCK LOOKOUT, 7353', 40 miles RT, 4000' gain (USGS Vinegar Hill, Boulder Butte, Desolation Butte, WWURD). **Mt. Bicycle Route.** From the Middle Fork Campground, ride two miles northwest down the Middle Fork of the John Day River. Turn right at the outlet of Granite Boulder Creek on road FS-4550 for one mile to a junction. Turn left (northwest), staying on FS-4550 to contour across the drainages of Beaver Creek, Dry Creek, Wray Creek, Badger Creek, Big Boulder Creek, and Myrtle Creek. After 12 miles in a generally northwest direction and one mile past Myrtle Creek, turn right (northwest) at a "Y" and go two miles on road FS-539 to join road FS-45. Turn north three miles to the Indian Rock road junction. Ascend east two miles on road FS-539 to the summit.

DAVIS CREEK LOOP, high point 4900', 25 miles RT, 1500' gain (USGS Vinegar Hill, Bates, Dixie Meadows). **Mt. Bicycle Route.** From the Middle Fork Campground, ride northwest along the Middle Fork of the John Day River for three miles. At the first junction after Granite Boulder Creek, turn left (south) on road FS-4550, keeping left after one-fourth mile on road FS-791 to reach the trailhead one mile from CR-20. Ride the trail (FS-244), ascending gradually south and east across the drainages of Little Butte Creek and Deerhorn Creek to cross a saddle, 4900'. Descend south to Davis Creek, then go east along Davis Creek into a road (FS-2614) that reaches US-26 near Austin Junction. Turn left (northeast) on US-26 and north on SR-7 for one mile. Ride northwest on CR-20 to return to the starting point on the Middle Fork of the John Day River.

SUNSHINE FOREST SERVICE STATION, 3642' (USGS Boulder Butte). Drive 15 miles northwest on CR-20 down the Middle Fork of the John Day River from SR-7 at MP-1 near Bates. Facilities and activities: maps and information during the summer.

GALENA–SUSANVILLE, high point 4200', 30 miles RT, 1000' gain (USGS Bates, Vinegar Hill, Boulder Butte, Susanville). **Mt. Bicycle Route.** From the Middle Fork Campground (see above), ride northwest on CR-20 down the Middle Fork of the John Day River, passing much evidence of the mining that took place along the river in the past. At ten miles from the Middle Fork Campground, turn right (northeast) on road FS-45 for one mile. Turn left (north) on roads FS-947 and FS-914 for two miles into the area that was the Susanville mining district. Several roads give access to old mines. From Susanville, descend southwest along Elk Creek to the location of Galena on the Middle Fork of the John Day River, another old mining center. To return to the starting point, ride southeast up the Middle Fork of the John Day River.

AUSTIN JUNCTION, 4234' (USGS Austin). MP-0. Junction of SR-7 with US-26. Facilities and activities: food, store, gas, lodging. Seasonal.

SR-86

Baker City to Oxbow

From Baker City, drive north on I-84 for two miles to Exit 201. Turn east on SR-86.

OREGON TRAIL, 3300' (USGS Baker). One mile from I-84 on SR-86, turn north on Linley Lane, passing east of the Baker City Municipal Airport. At four miles from SR-86 near the intersection with SR-203, Linley Lane crosses the route of the Oregon Trail. No marking. Look southeast to the Oregon Trail Interpretive Center on Flagstaff Hill to the see the route followed by the Oregon Trail emigrants.

SR-203

POWDER RIVER, 2700' (USGS Keating). From the intersection of Linely Lane with SR-203 (see Oregon Trail above) or from MP-297 on I-84, drive east on SR-203 to a crossing of the Powder River in Lower Powder Valley, a cattle and hay-growing region irrigated by water from Thief Valley Reservoir ten miles upstream.

TABLE MOUNTAIN, 3755', 6 miles RT, 700' gain (USGS Sawtooth Ridge). At MP-26 on SR-203, three miles north of the bridge over the Powder River, turn east on Blue Mountain Road and stop at a viewpoint after 100 yards. The flat tableland to the east ending in sharp bluffs are lava flows from Sawtooth Crater (see below).

PONDOSA, 3229' (USGS Medical Springs). Drive as above on SR-203 across the Powder River to Pondosa at MP-21, the site of a Collins Pine Lumber Company sawmill from about 1930 to 1950. Facilities and activities: food, store, sawdust, deck available for events. tel. 853-2351.

MEDICAL SPRINGS, 3388' (USGS Medical Springs). Drive as above past Pondosa to MP-20 on SR-203. This community once had a sanatorium based on the local hot mineral springs with full medical staff. The swimming pool still exists but it is not open to the public.

SAWTOOTH CRATER, high point 5282', 20 miles RT, 2500' gain (USGS Flagstaff Butte, Sawtooth Ridge). **Mt. Bicycle Route.** From Medical Springs, ride southeast on road FS-70, reaching the Sawtooth Ridge area after eight miles. At 10 miles from Medical Springs, turn north to circle through the caldera of Sawtooth Crater for one mile. Where the road turns west, leave bicycle and hike northwest to the high point. Continue riding west to reach the outgoing route, FS-70, after passing Sardine Spring.

Return to Medical Springs on FS-70. Sawtooth Ridge is the remains of a volcano that was active during the time the Columbia Basalts were emitted but it produced andesite lava rather than basalt.

TAMARACK CAMPGROUND, 4440' (USGS Bennett Peak). From Medical Springs, drive 1.6 miles southeast on Collins Road (FS-70), then northeast 13 miles on Big Creek Road (FS-67) to Eagle Creek. Cross Eagle Creek and drive southeast one-fourth mile to the campground on Eagle Creek, 15 miles from SR-203 at Medical Springs. Facilities and activities: tents, trailers to 25', water, fishing, hiking.

BENNET PEAK, 7099', 17 miles RT, 2500' gain (USGS Bennet Peak, WWECW). **Mt. Bicycle Route.** From Tamarack campground (see above), ride northeast on road FS-7750, beginning across the road from the campground. At the first intersection, turn south, continuing on FS-7750. Keep left at the next intersection and go right at the third. After two miles, leave FS-7750 to the right (north) on road FS-100 for two miles. At 5800', turn right (east) on FS-130 and ascend in three miles to the summit.

TWO COLOR LAKE, 7100', 22 miles RT, 2700' gain (USGS Krag Peak, Bennet Peak, WWECW). **Mt. Bicycle Route.** Ride as above for Bennet Peak. Continue northeast on the ridge to reach the lake.

SANGER LOOP, high point 5000', 20 miles RT, 1600' gain (USGS Bennet Peak, Balm Creek Reservoir, Flagstaff Butte, Sparta Butte, WWECW). **Mt. Bicycle Route.** From Tamarack campground (see above), ride west on road FS-67 for two miles to a junction, then south on road FS-390 four miles to the Collins Road, FS-70. The last two miles of FS-390 passes through the area of the mining community of Sanger. Sanger Gulch and the Sanger Mine are to the east. From the Sanger road junction, continue southeast on road FS-70, descending along Goose Creek for two miles and rounding east two miles to another road junction (FS-7020). Turn north on road FS-7020, descending steeply to Eagle Creek. Cross the river and ride northwest up the river to Tamarack Campground and the starting point.

TWO COLOR CAMPGROUND, 4813' (USGS Bennett Peak). Drive two miles north of Tamarack campground (see above) to Two Color campground on Eagle Creek. Facilities and activities: tents, trailers to 25', water, fishing, hiking.

FLAGSTAFF BUTTE LOOKOUT, 6521', 20 miles RT, 2200' gain (USGS Bennett Peak, Flagstaff Butte, WWECW). **Mt. Bicycle Route.** From Tamarack campground or Two Color campground, ride west on road FS-77 then north up West Eagle Creek. In West Eagle Meadow, cross the creek on a bridge and ascend south and west up Trout Creek to the next road junction on the crest of a ridge. At this junction, turn north to the lookout on the ridge between Trout Creek and the headwaters of Catherine Creek. Return southeast from the lookout to road FS-77 and continue southeast, then descend along Glendenning Creek, passing the old Basin Mine. Just past the site of the mine, turn south to the Big Creek Road, FS-67. Turn left on FS-67 (southeast) and continue east and north at road junctions to reach Eagle Creek and Tamarack or Two Color campgrounds.

TWO COLOR FOREST SERVICE STATION, 4813' (USGS Bennet Peak). The Forest Service Station, two miles northeast of Two Color campground on Eagle Creek, has maps and information during the summer months. The building is available for rental use during the winter months. Contact Pine Ranger District, General Delivery, Halfway OR 97834, telephone: 742-7511.

BOULDER PARK TRAILHEAD, 4991' (USGS Bennet Peak). The trailhead is two miles beyond Two Color campground (see above) and 21 miles from Medical Springs.

POINT 8881, 8881', 10 miles RT, 4000' gain (USGS Bennet Peak, WWECW). Hike west and northwest from the Boulder Park trailhead on the trail to West Eagle Meadow, ascending along Boulder Creek. At the high point, 7400', where the trail levels and begins to contour west, leave the trail and hike cross country up the ridge, at first north, then northeast for 1.5 miles to the summit of this granite peak.

NEEDLE POINT, 9027', 15 miles RT, 4200' gain (USGS Krag Peak, Eagle Cap, WWECW). From Boulder Park trailhead (see above), hike northeast up Eagle Creek toward Eagle Lake. At six miles, the trail turns west up Cached Creek to a trail junction. Turn right (northeast) on this trail, the Eagle Lake trail, for one mile. Leave the trail and hike west cross country to the summit.

EAGLE LAKE, 7500', 15 miles RT, 2600' gain (USGS Krag Peak, Eagle Cap, WWECW). From Boulder Park trailhead (see above), hike northeast on the trail up Eagle Creek, taking the right fork at six miles to continue northeast to the lake, one of the sources of Eagle Creek.

LOOKINGGLASS LAKE, 7302', 15 miles RT, 2400' gain (USGS Bennet Peak, Krag Peak, WWECW). From Boulder Park trailhead (see above), hike northeast up Eagle Creek for 4.5 miles. Turn south and ascend three miles to the lake, lying in a basin under Hummingbird Mountain.

HUMMINGBIRD MOUNTAIN, 7984', 17 miles RT, 3100' gain (USGS Bennet Peak, Krag Peak, WWECW). Hike as above to Lookingglass Lake. From the lake, hike northwest cross country to the summit.

BEAR LAKE, 7160', 14 miles RT, 2200' gain (USGS Bennet Peak, Krag Peak, WWECW). From the Boulder Park trailhead, hike northeast on Eagle Creek, taking the Lookingglass Trail west at 4.5 miles. At one mile from Eagle Creek, turn left (north) to Bear Lake.

TOMBSTONE LAKE, 7421', 14 miles RT, 2000' gain (USGS Bennet Peak, Steamboat Lake, WWECW). From Tamarack Campground (see above, p. 64), drive west and north seven miles on road FS-77 to the trailhead in West Eagle Meadow, 5480' and 19 miles from Medical Springs on roads FS-70, FS-67 and FS-77. From SR-203 at MP-13, 13 miles from Union, drive 14 miles on road FS-77. Hike north, taking the left fork at three miles.

DIAMOND LAKE, 7041', 16 miles RT, 2400' gain (USGS Bennet Peak, Steamboat Lake, WWECW). Hike as above one mile past Tombstone Lake to Diamond Lake, lying in a basin south of China Cap.

ECHO LAKE, 7222', 10 miles RT, 1800' gain (USGS Bennet Peak, WWECW). From the trailhead in West Eagle Meadow (see above under Tombstone Lake), hike north on the trail toward Tombstone Lake. At three miles on the trail, turn right (east) at a trail fork to ascend steeply to the lake.

TRAVERSE LAKE, 7718', 12 miles RT, 2300' gain (USGS Bennet Peak, WWECW). Hike as above one mile past Echo Lake to Traverse Lake.

POINT 8653, 8653', 12 miles RT, 3200' gain (USGS Bennet Peak, Steamboat Lake, WWECW). Hike as above to Echo Lake. On reaching Echo Lake, turn north and hike cross country to the summit.

CRATER LAKE, 7434', 14 miles RT, 3100' gain (USGS Krag Peak, WWECW). From Tamarack campground (see above, p. 64), drive southeast on Eagle Creek road (FS-77), for six miles. Turn east five miles on the road along East Eagle Creek (FS-7745), passing at two miles the site where the moving picture "Paint Your Wagon" was filmed in 1969. The road ends at a washed out bridge, 4360'. Ford East Eagle Creek and hike northeast on the road along the creek for two miles, then ascend east on the Little Kettle Creek Trail to the lake in a basin surrounded by Krag Peak, Truax Mountain, and Granite Mountain. The lake, which previously drained into the Imnaha River, now feeds water through a tunnel west into Kettle Creek and Eagle Creek. The equipment for controlling the flow of water into the tunnel was restored in 1963.

KRAG PEAK 9048', 18 miles RT, 4700' gain (USGS Krag Peak, WWECW). Hike as above to Crater Lake. From the campground on the north shore of the lake, ascend the slope north cross country to the east ridge. Continue up the east ridge to the summit pyramid. Ascend in broken rocks to the summit and a comprehensive view of the Eagle and Cornucopia Mountains. Eagle Cap, 9595', is seven miles almost directly north (354°)

and Cornucopia Mountain, 8650', is four miles southeast (138°). Imposing Red Mountain, 9500', is 2.5 miles directly east.

TRUAX MOUNTAIN, 8040', 18 miles RT, 3700' gain (USGS Krag Peak, WWECW). Hike as above to Crater Lake. From the west end of the lake, hike southwest cross country to the summit.

SR-86

OREGON TRAIL, 3363' (USGS Baker). At 2.5 miles from I-84 on SR-86, as SR-86 bends northeast to ascend into the foothills, turn north on gravelled Sunnyslope Road. This road intersects the Oregon Trail route two miles from SR-86, at a cross road (no marking). At this point, the general direction of the Oregon Trail is northwest (324°) toward an area where the Powder River meanders in the flat valley land.

OREGON TRAIL HISTORICAL MONUMENT, 3700' (USGS Virtue Flat). At MP-6 on SR-86, a stone pillar beside the highway commemorates the Oregon Trail.

OREGON TRAIL, 3645' (USGS Virtue Flat). At MP-7, where the Ruckles Creek Road turns south down Ruckles Creek, SR-86 crosses the route of the Oregon Trail. Drive southeast on Ruckles Creek Road 2.5 miles to a road junction. One mile south of this intersection, where the road bends southeast, it overlies the Oregon Trail route for one mile.

NATIONAL HISTORIC OREGON TRAIL INTERPRETIVE CENTER, 3945' (USGS Virtue Flat). At MP-7 on SR-86, turn left (north) to the Interpretive Center on the top of Flagstaff Hill. The Interpretive Center has displays, exhibits, artifacts, audio-visual programs, films, and programs. The center overlooks a well-preserved segment of the Oregon Trail. Four miles of trails, some barrier-free and with informative displays, give access to much of the area and to the actual ruts of the Oregon Trail. The surrounding sagebrush steppe looks much as it did when the Oregon Trail immigrants travelled here 150 years ago. The Interpretive Center is operated by the Bureau of Land Management, Post Office Box 987, Baker City OR 97814. The Center is open 9am to 6pm, May 1 to September 30 and 9am to 4pm October 1 to April 30. Admission free. Parking is available for vehicles up to a combined length of 49'. No overnight parking.

A reproduction of a pioneer encampment displays the tools and equipment used by the immigrants.

A miners camp has many artifacts from the early mining days in Baker County.

Throughout the year, special programs use the indoor theater. An outdoor ampitheater in planning will have the Baker Valley and the Blue Mountains as a background. A schedule of activities is available from the Bureau of Land Management in Baker City (see address above).

Flagstaff Mine, a former gold lode mine, is adjacent to the Interpretive Center. The filled-in shaft opening is still visible.

KEATING, 2720' (USGS Keating). At MP-10 on SR-86, turn northeast six miles to the community of Keating in Lower Powder Valley, a hay growing region. No services.

CLOVER CREEK FORMATION. The type locality of this geological formation, consisting of volcanic and other material accumulated on the ocean floor and as islands before the accumulation area was added to the continent, extends along Clover Creek. From Keating, drive east three miles to Clover Creek. The oldest part of this formation, exposed at the Harsin Ranch, is made up of volcanic flows, pyroclastic material, and altered sediments. A more recent part of the formation is exposed along Tucker Creek. Drive northeast from Keating three miles.

LOWER POWDER VALLEY, 2700' (USGS Keating). After passing the Keating road junction, SR-86 descends into a wide valley where hay and cattle are the chief agricultural products.

LAKE SEDIMENTS, 2600' (USGS Keating). At MP-15, sediments deposited in a lake lie on top of Columbia Basalts.

GLASGOW BUTTE LOOP, 4922', 20 miles RT, 2300' gain (USGS Glasgow Butte, BLM Baker City). **Mt. Bicycle Route.** At MP-20 on SR-86, one-half mile west of a bridge over the Powder River, park at an intersection and ride south on Five Mile Road, going right (south) at a "Y" one mile from SR-86. At six miles from SR-86, go left (east) toward Glasgow Creek. Continue east six miles to a high point south of Glasgow Butte. Leave bicycle and ascend 0.5 miles north to the summit and an overall view of the Lower Powder Valley, little changed in a century. A dike of Columbia Basalt is exposed at the summit. The rocks to the south and west are serpentine, peridotite is exposed to the east, and gabbro is exposed to the north. Return to bicycle, continue east one mile then turn north down Five Mile Creek, taking the left branch at road junctions to stay on the plateau above the Powder River. Return to the outgoing route one mile from SR-86. Go right (north) to the starting point.

COLUMBIA BASALTS, 2600' (USGS Glasgow Butte). Near MP-23, at the Sparta road junction, basalt lava flows poured into a lake and cooled beneath the sediments of the lake. Find pillows and mixes of sediments with volcanic glass.

VOLCANIC TUFF, 3200' (USGS Glasgow Butte). At two miles on the Sparta road, beyond a farmhouse, the road passes exposures of a volcanic tuff.

WALLOWA TERRANE, 3400' (USGS Sparta Butte). From MP-23

drive four miles northeast on Sparta Road (CR-852). Turn north on roads CR-891 and FS-70 for six miles. Turn east on road FS-7015 to descend Empire Gulch Road to Eagle Creek. The Martin Bridge limestone of the Wallowa Terrane is exposed in road cuts near Eagle Creek. Fossilized fragments of an ichthyosaur were found 100 yards north of the junction of Paddy Creek with Eagle Creek.

SPARTA, 4092' (USGS Sparta). At MP-23 on SR-86, drive north on CR-852 eight miles to the site of Sparta, briefly a mining center around the beginning of the present century. The following mines were active at one time: Rosebud, Gypsy Union, Gem, and Del Monte. None of these mines have been active in recent years. No services.

SPARTA BUTTE, 4944', 5 miles RT, 1000' gain (USGS Sparta). From Sparta, hike north on the Old Ranger Station road (FS-70) for one mile then turn west cross country one mile to the summit. The site of the Union Mine is on the northwest flank of Sparta Butte. Sparta Butte is the cone of a volcanic vent that emitted part of the Columbia Basalts.

OCEANIC CRUST TERRANE, 2500' (USGS Sparta). A diorite of age 220 million years is exposed at MP-26. Geologists think this rock could be the root of an island arc that became part of the North American continent. This exposure of diorite extends six miles along the Powder River and two miles north. North of the diorite, the Clover Creek greenstone is exposed (see above), centering around Cup Spring and Dempsey Creek south of Eagle Creek. Dikes of the Clover Creek greenstone are exposed in the diorite trending north from the Powder River beginning one mile east of Pittsburg Gulch.

LANDSLIDE, 2300', MP-30 (USGS Sparta). In September of 1984, a landslide here from the slopes north of the river closed SR-86 for three months. The road was rebuilt over the hill south of the former route.

OCEANIC CRUST TERRANE, 2300' (USGS Sparta). At MP-34, gabbro, a rock formed from the earth's mantle, is exposed. This rock was mixed into the oceanic crust and was carried along to become a part of the continent. This exposure of gabbro extends along the south side of the Powder River east as far as Canyon Creek.

RICHLAND, 2203' population 161, area population 927 (USGS Richland). This community at MP-41 on SR-86 has the following facilities and activities: food, stores, lodging, gas.

Camping and RV Parks: Hewitt County Park, 2090' (USGS Richland). From SR-86 at MP-43, one mile east of Richland center, drive southeast two miles to the park, situated on Brownlee Reservoir. Facilities and activities: tent area, recreational vehicles of any length, fishing, power boats, boat ramp, dock, showers, gas, marine supplies. The water temperature in August is 75°. Open all year. tel. 893-6147. **John Holcomb Park**, 2090' (USGS Richland). Located on Brownlee Reservoir near Hewitt Park, this park now has parking, boat launch ramp, and dock. Camping sites are planned. **Eagle Valley RV Park**, 2200' (USGS Richland). This park is on SR-86 in Richland. Facilities and activities: pull throughs and full hookups for recreational vehicles of any size, showers, laundry. tel. 893-6161.

Cornucopia Wilderness Pack Station offers back country pack trips in the Wallowa Mountains, Route 1, Box 50, Richland, 97870, winter tel. 893-6400, summer tel. 742-5400. The pack station is at Cornucopia.

COLUMBIA BASALT DIKES, 2500' (USGS Sturgill Creek, Connor Creek).
Dikes of Columbia Basalts are exposed from mile 15 to mile 20 on the road leading south to Huntington from Richland. This dike system extends into the mountains north and west of Cornucopia.

EAGLE FORKS CAMPGROUND, 2960' (USGS Sparta Butte).
From Richland, drive 11 miles north up Eagle Creek on road FS-7735. Facilities and activities: tents, trailers to 25', water, fishing, hiking.

EAGLE CREEK LOOP, high point 4825', 30 miles RT, 2000' gain
(USGS Sparta Butte, Balm Creek Reservoir, WWECW). **Mt. Bicycle Route.** From the Eagle Fork campground, ride north on road FS-7735, ascending Little Eagle Creek. After three miles, turn left (northwest) at a road fork, 3900', and continue on road FS-7735 along Snow Fork Creek for 1.5 miles to 4500'. Contour south one mile, then descend into the canyon of Eagle Creek. Ride north along Eagle Creek one mile to the bridge. Cross and turn south downstream for two miles, then ascend west on the Empire Grade to a road junction, three miles from Eagle Creek. Turn south and southeast for three miles on FS-70 to a junction with the Old Ranger Station Road, FS-70-05, in Forshey Meadow. Turn east, taking east or northeast forks at road junctions to descend to Eagle Creek north of Puzzle Creek. Puzzle Creek is the unnamed creek shown on the Wallowa-Whitman Forest Map (1990 edition) between Dempsey Creek on the north and Shanghai Creek on the south. On reaching Eagle Creek, turn southeast to the starting point.

RICHLAND-PINE VALLEY SUMMIT, 3700', MP-48 (USGS Richland, Posy Valley).
Between the Eagle Valley at Richland and the Pine Valley at Pine, SR-86 ascends over a grassy ridge which provides grazing for cattle and sheep. At the crest, the Cornucopia Mountains stand out to the north.

PINE, 2580' (USGS Posy Valley).
This community east of SR-86 at MP-53 has the following facilities and activities: food, store, gas.

PINE FOREST SERVICE STATION.
From MP-53 on SR-86, drive

one mile east to this station which provides maps and information year around on weekdays.

HALFWAY, 2590', population 311, area population 1,177 (USGS Posy Valley, Halfway). From MP-53 on SR-86 in Pine, drive two miles northwest on CR-413. This community has the following facilities and activities: food, stores, lodging, gas. **Pine Valley Community Museum**, on CR-413 in the center of the commmunity, has a collection of regional artifacts. Open weekends in summer, 10am to 4pm. Address: PO Box 673, Halfway 97834, 742-2983. **Clear Creek Gardens and Game** has tours of a buffalo ranch, Wednesday and Sunday, 10am and 3pm, June to Labor Day and by reservation at other times. Address: PO Box 559, Halfway, 97834, 742-6558. **Wallowa Llamas.** Back country tours in the Wallowa Mountains, Route 1, Box 84, Halfway 97834, 742-2961, 742-4930. **Canyon Outfitters.** Fishing, hunting, and river trips, PO Box 893, Halfway 97834, tel. 742-4110.

HALFWAY PICNIC GROUND, 3100' (USGS Jimtown, Richland). Drive west from Halfway three miles to the picnic ground. The Posy Valley irrigation canal runs at the edge of the picnic ground.

JIM TOWN, 2903' (USGS Jimtown). Drive four miles northwest on CR-413 from SR-86 at MP-53. No services.

CARSON, 3360' (USGS Jimtown). Drive paved road CR-413 for seven miles northwest of SR-86 at Pine. No services.

McBRIDE CAMPGROUND, 4750' (USGS Jimtown). Drive five miles west of Carson on the Carson Grade (road FS-7710). The campground is on Summit Creek and Brooks Irrigation Canal and has the following facilities and activities: tents, trailers, hiking, fishing, bicycling, water.

SUMMIT POINT TRAILHEAD, 6800' (USGS Jim Town). From McBride Campground (see above), drive north five miles on road FS-7715 to the trailhead. From this trailhead, Crater Lake is seven miles one-way and 800' gain.

CORNUCOPIA PEAK, 8650', 8 miles RT, 2000' gain (USGS Jim Town, Cornucopia, WWECW). From Summit Point trailhead (see above), hike north on trail FS-1885 for 2.6 miles to the junction with trail FS-1868. Leave the trail at the junction and hike northeast to the crest of the ridge. Follow the ridge northeast to the summit.

SUMMIT POINT LOOKOUT, 7006', 10 miles RT, 2300' gain (USGS Jimtown). **Mt. Bicycle Route.** From McBride campground (see above), ride north on road FS-7715 to a lookout that is staffed during the summer months.

PLACER MINE, 3800' (USGS Jimtown). Three miles north of Carson and 10 miles from SR-86 at Pine on CR-413, the road passes an operating placer gold mine. The mine uses modern techniques of sediment control and land restoration and doesn't contaminate Pine Creek.

CORNUCOPIA, 4700' (USGS Cornucopia). From Carson (see above), drive five miles north on a gravel road (CR-413) to the site of an old mining community, an important gold and silver producing area until 1942 and, for many years, the most productive mine in eastern Oregon. To explore this site where several buildings remain, turn right just before the bridge over Pine Creek and drive 0.25 mile to a large parking area. Walk south to cross the bridge over Pine Creek. The Cornucopia Pack Station is 0.25 mile beyond the parking area.

CORNUCOPIA PEAK, 8650', 10 miles RT, 4000' gain (USGS Cornucopia, WWECW). Park as above for Cornucopia. Cross the bridge and hike south on the road on the west side of Pine Creek 0.25 mile to cross to the south side of Jim Fiske Creek. Turn west and ascend at first on a four-wheel track then on a trail up Jim Fiske Creek. At 7400', where the trail turns southwest on a contour, leave trail and ascend northeast cross country to the southeast ridge of Cornucopia Peak. Ascend northwest on the ridge to the granitic summit.

PINE CREEK TRAILHEAD, 4827' (USGS Cornucopia). From SR-86 at MP-53 near the community of Pine, drive CR-413 for 12 miles northwest and north, passing through the communities of Halfway, Jim Town, and Carson. The road becomes gravel after passing Carson. One hundred yards before reaching a bridge that crosses over Pine Creek into the site of Cornucopia, turn right on a dirt road that ascends over mine tailings for 0.5 mile to the trailhead. Parking here is limited. One-fourth mile after the turnoff, the road to the trailhead passes a large parking area that is suitable for trailers and large vehicles. From the trailhead, trails go up the West Fork of Pine Creek and the East Fork of Pine Creek. The Simmons Creek Trail leaves the East Fork trail one mile north of the trailhead.

RED MOUNTAIN, 9555', 14 miles RT, 5000' gain (USGS Cornucopia, WWECW). From the Pine Creek trailhead (see above), hike west up the trail along the West Fork of Pine Creek (Pine Lakes Trail, FS-1880) to the junction of the Middle Fork of Pine Creek with the West Fork, three miles from the road and the western end of the almost level valley. Continue on the trail for 0.5 mile as it ascends away from the valley. Leave the trail where the trail turns west toward Pine Lakes, 5800', and hike northwest up the slope above the Middle Fork, avoiding brush, going directly toward Red Mountain to reach a valley. Cross east of Red Mountain Reservoir and continue up the open grassy slopes to the northwest. Ascend a talus ramp to the north ridge of Red Mountain. Turn south to the summit.

PINE LAKES–CRATER LAKE–IMNAHA RIVER LOOP, high

point 8400', 30 miles RT, 5500' gain (USGS Krag Peak, Cornucopia, WWECW). From the Pine Creek trailhead (see above), hike northwest up the valley of the West Fork of Pine Creek on trail FS-1880, passing the Cornucopia Wilderness Pack Station on the left, white mine tailings on the right, and crossing the East Fork of Pine Creek after 0.2 miles. After three miles, reach the upper end of the valley (camping) and begin to ascend on the switchback trail into the upper meadows of the West Fork of Pine Creek. After leaving the almost level valley, the trail begins to pass exposures of the granitic Cornucopia batholith, which is generously laced with dikes of dark-colored Columbia Basalts. In several places the trail crosses or passes near these dikes. After five miles, at 6700', ford the creek below the waterfall that descends from the Pine Lakes outlet (camping). Reach Pine Lakes, 7600', in seven miles (camping).

From the upper Pine Lake, trail FS-1880 ascends north on switchbacks, then contours west before turning south to climb past a small lake to a saddle, 8400'. Descend west from the pass to reach a junction with trail FS-1885 at three miles from Pine Lakes. Turn north on trail FS-1885, contouring across the west face of Granite Mountain for two miles to the junction with the Cliff Creek Trail. Go left 0.5 mile on trail FS-1945 to Crater Lake, 7600' and six miles from Pine Lakes. For day trips from Crater Lake, see p. 66 and below.

To continue the loop, return east from Crater Lake to trail FS-1885 and descend north above Cliff Creek, crossing several streams dropping from the meadows below the ridge north of Krag Peak. On nearing the Imnaha River at 6100', take the left fork to reach a ford on the Imnaha River. A well-preserved cabin stands in the woods north of the ford. Camping near the river in a large meadow is one-fourth mile west upstream from the ford.

Leaving the campground on the Imnaha River, descend east along the South Fork of the Imnaha River, passing the lower Cliff Creek trail junction after one mile and reaching the Blue Creek Trail junction at 1.5 miles, marked by a campsite between the trail and the river and a talus slope descending from the north that almost reaches the trail. Ford the river and ascend on trail FS-1865 for 2.8 miles to a trail junction where FS-1865 turns east. Take the right (southwest) fork on trail FS-1896 and climb steeply for 1.2 miles to the Blue Creek–Norway Creek saddle (camping). If the ditch that crosses this saddle is not flowing, hike northwest on the trail along or near the ditch to find streams and a spring within 0.5 mile.

From the Blue Creek–Norway Creek saddle, descend south above Norway Creek, reaching a four-wheel track after two miles in the saddle between Norway Creek and Simmons Creek. Continue southeast down this steep road to reach and cross the East Fork of Pine Creek. Turn southwest to reach the starting point at Cornucopia. (For day trips from this loop, see the following eight trips).

POINT 8800, 8800', 4 miles RT, 1200' gain (USGS Krag Peak, WWECW). From the upper Pine Lake, hike north and west on trail FS-1880 until the trail turns south. Leave the trail and ascend northwest into the basin closed on the north and west by granite ridges. Ascend west on a scree ramp to the ridge crest. Turn north to the summit, which consists of an exposure of the Cornucopia batholith.

GRANITE MOUNTAIN, 9040', 6 miles RT, 1500' gain (USGS Cornucopia, Krag Peak, WWECW). This is the summit that is named Granite Mountain on the maps. The rock is not granite but altered sea-floor sediments that have weathered to a dark red. From the upper Pine Lake, hike north on trail FS-1880 for one-fourth mile, 100' west of the last switchback, until directly below a 20' wide dark-colored basalt dike in the light-colored granitic rocks above. Find a faint way trail that ascends briefly toward the cliffs above, turning at first northeast to climb above a talus slope then north to reach a flowery meadow (no reliable water) in one-half mile after leaving trail FS-1880. Cross the meadow north to ascend a grass ramp to the south ridge of Granite Mountain. Continue up the ridge, turning northwest at 8700' to reach the summit.

SHEEP MEADOW, high point 7769' to 8800', 6 miles RT, 300'-2200' gain (USGS Krag Peak, WWECW). From the camping site on the north shore of Crater Lake, go north in the meadow across the trail for 100'. This is the first meadow west of the Cliff Creek (northeast) end of the lake. Before reaching the rocks, turn northeast to continue up in an open glade to a bench where a faint way trail is visible. The way trail is an old sheep driveway. Contour north for 0.5 mile, staying below the rocks and talus slopes of Krag Peak, and following, where visible, this old sheep driveway to reach a flower covered meadow with pond and stream, 7769'. Find an old sheepherder camp complete with stove in the woods north of the pond. Continue north on the bench for one mile to a view into a basin that shelves toward the Imnaha River and is enclosed by a curving, serrated ridge. From near this viewpoint, Point 8680', with a view to Eagle Cap and the other summits of the Wallowa Mountains, can be reached by ascending west up a sandy, alpine slope to reach the ridge crest just north of a vertical, dark-colored Columbia Basalt dike. Turn north to the summit viewpoint. Point 8837', the next summit south of Point 8680', is talus to the summit.

DEER MEADOW, high point 7900', 3 miles RT, 400' gain (USGS Krag Peak). From Crater Lake, hike east on trail FS-1845 to the junction with trail FS-1885. Turn south on FS-1885 for 300'. Turn east on a faint way trail that soon becomes more visible to ascend into a meadow with stream and crescent-shaped pond (camping).

HAWKINS PASS, 8350', 12 miles RT, 2500'-3500' gain (USGS Eagle Cap, Cornucopia, Krag Peak, WWECW). From the camp on the Imnaha River above the upper Cliff Creek trail junction, hike west on trail FS-1816 in woods and meadows into the glacial cirque that encloses the source of the South Fork of the Imnaha River. The nearly vertical walls of this cirque are white marble and other brilliantly colored rocks. At the pass, find a mineral prospect with exposures of garnet crystals. The summit east of the pass, Point 8640', is easily reached and gives a view of a corner of Wallowa Lake. The summit to the west, Point 9040', can also be reached without difficulty.

MARBLE MOUNTAIN, high point 8644', 8 miles RT, 3500' gain (USGS Cornucopia, WWECW). From camp at the junction of the Blue Creek trail and the South Fork Imnaha River trail, hike east down the South Fork of the Imnaha River for two miles. Turn north and ascend to Boner Flat on trail FS-1801. The trail junction occurs in a meadow and may be obscure but once above the meadow the trail reappears. In Boner Flat, a meadow area at 7300' with no reliable water, leave the trail and ascend the ridge west cross country to the first summit, 8644', and a view into the tumbled region at the head of the North and Middle Forks of the Imnaha River.

POINT 8862, 8862', 4 miles RT, 1300' gain (USGS Cornucopia). This summit bears 320° from the Blue Creek–Norway Creek saddle. From camp at the Blue Creek–Norway Creek saddle, hike northwest on trail FS-1887 along the ditch to the end of the ditch below the source of Blue Creek. Leave the trail and ascend west along the creek, passing several springs that form the source, to a clear view of the steeper slope to the west. Note a diagonal line in the middle of the slope that ascends north to just below the saddle to the left of the northernmost summit. Head for the lower left end of this line to find an old, overgrown trail. Follow this trail northwest until it disappears on a rock outcrop. Continue northwest diagonally upward to the saddle. Turn north and ascend on sandy scree on the west side of the summit block to the summit ridge 20' north of the summit.

SUGARLOAF MOUNTAIN, 8000', 8 miles RT, 1800' gain (USGS Cornucopia, WWECW). From camp at the Blue Creek–Norway Creek saddle, hike south on trail FS-1887, the Sugarloaf Trail. Where the trail descends in the valley of the East Fork of Pine Creek to cross trail FS-1865, trail FS-1887 disappears in meadows. After crossing obvious trail FS-1865, ascend northeast in meadow to find trail FS-1887, which crosses to the north side of the ridge at the next saddle east. Where the trail crosses the west shoulder of Sugarloaf Mountain, leave the trail and hike northeast to the highest point, with views of the rolling hills toward and across the Snake River and the Seven Devils Mountains in Idaho.

FISH LAKE CAMPGROUND, 6662' (USGS Deadman Point). From Halfway, drive north on gravelled Fish Lake Road, FS-66, 29 miles to the campground on Fish Lake. Facilities and activities: fishing, tents, trailers to 25', water, boat launch, no power boats, snowpark.

SUGARLOAF MOUNTAIN, 8000', 10 miles RT, 1500' gain (USGS Deadman Point). From Fish Lake campground, hike west from the north end of the lake. Continue west and north on trail FS-1869, passing east of the Sugarloaf Reservoir. One-fourth of a mile past the reservoir, at a trail junction, turn west on the ridge trail (FS-1887) to the trail high point. Where the trail begins to descend, turn north cross country to the summit.

DEADMAN POINT, 7760', 10 miles RT, 1200' gain (USGS Deadman Point). Hike as above toward Sugarloaf Mountain. At the trail junction one-fourth mile north of Sugarloaf Reservoir, continue north on the Deadman Canyon trail (FS-1869) to the pass. At the pass, turn northeast and hike cross country to the summit.

RUSSELL MOUNTAIN LOOKOUT, 7508', 10 miles RT, 1000' gain (USGS Deadman Point). **Mt. Bicycle Route.** From Fishlake campground (see above), ride north and east for two miles on road FS-66 to a junction. Turn north on road FS-450 to reach the lookout.

TWIN LAKES CAMPGROUND, 6500' (USGS Deadman Point). Drive on road FS-66 past Fish Lake to the campground on Twin Lakes, 35 miles from Halfway. Facilities and activities: tents, trailers, fishing, water, no power boats.

JUNCTION WALLOWA MOUNTAINS LOOP, 2279' (USGS McLain Gulch). At MP-63, SR-86 meets FS-39, the Wallowa Mountains Loop Road (see p. 107).

NORTH PINE REST AREA, 2861' (USGS McLain Gulch). From MP-63 on SR-86, drive north five miles on FS-39 to this picnic ground.

McLAIN POINT, 5109', 6 miles RT, 3500' gain (USGS McLain Gulch, Oxbow, HCNRA). From the North Pine Rest Area (see above), hike a branch road from the rest area, at first northeast to a ford across North Pine Creek, then southeast to the end of the road. Ascend cross country to ridge. Turn north one mile on the ridge to the summit.

OXBOW-COPPERFIELD, 1725' (USGS McLain Gulch). At MP-70 on SR-86, this community has the following facilities and activities: food, stores, lodging, gas, post office.

Oxbow Power Plant. Tours of the generating station of the Idaho Power Company that generates a maximum of 190 megawatts and one million kilowatt hours of electricity per year are available at noon, Mountain Time.

Camping and RV Parks: Hell's Canyon Sportsmen Park. Located on Pine

Creek, at MP-69 on SR-86. Facilities and activities: pull throughs and full hookups for recreational vehicles of any size, fishing, hiking, store, gas, showers, laundry, open all year. Fee. PO Box 243, Oxbow 97840. tel. 785-3393 or 800-453-3393. **Copperfield Park.** This Idaho Power Company campground, on the shore of the Snake River below Oxbow Dam, has the following facilities and activities: pull throughs and full hookups for recreational vehicles of any size, fishing, hiking, showers, water, swimming, grass tent area. Fee. tel. 785-3323, reservations 800-422-3143.

Oxbow Dam. From Copperfield Park, hike two miles southeast on the road south of the campground, keeping left at the first road junction after crossing the bridge over Pine Creek to pass the powerplant and ascend over the layered basalts of the Oxbow to the dam and powerplant intake.

Boat and Float Trips: AAA Shuttle Service, PO Box 265, Oxbow, 97840, tel. 785-3305 or 800-551-7409. **Hell's Canyon Adventures**, PO Box 159, Oxbow, 97840, tel. 785-3352 or 800-422-3568.

BROWNLEE DAM, 2100' (USGS Brownlee Dam). From Oxbow on SR-86, drive 13 miles south to this 395' high dam on the Snake River with a generating capacity of 585 megawatts. Visiting hour: noon, Mountain Time.

McGRAW CABIN, 2800', 12 miles RT, 1300' gain (USGS Homestead). From Oxbow, drive north on the west side of the Snake river for nine miles to a parking area at Ballard Creek. Park and hike north along the river four miles to the boundary of the Hell's Canyon National Recreation Area. Continue one-half mile northeast along the Snake River, then ascend the trail up McGraw Creek for three miles to the site of the cabin.

COPPER CREEK LOOP, 5480', 41 miles RT, 3500' gain (USGS Homestead). **Mt. Bicycle Route.** From Copperfield Park or Sportsman's Park, ride seven miles north of SR-86 at Oxbow on the west side of the Snake River (road CR-1039). Continue northwest up the road that follows near the power line to the high point at the crest of the ridge. Descend to FS-39. Turn left and continue down road FS-39 to join SR-86. Turn left to return to Oxbow and the starting point.

SHEEP MOUNTAIN, 4935', 12 miles RT, 3500' gain (USGS Oxbow, McLain Gulch). From Copperfield Park, hike south on CR-71 for 0.3 mile past the Pine Creek bridge to a power line. Leave the paved road and ascend west on a dirt road under the power line to the ridge, passing in the first 0.2 mile a storage tank and electrical sub-station. Continue southwest up the ridge, first on roads, then on a faint trail. Near the first summit, bypass a ledge of Columbia Basalts by ascending diagonally left (southeast). From the first summit, 4141', continue southwest one mile on the ridge to the true summit. The rocks of the ridge are part of the Columbia Basalts.

HELLS CANYON DAM, 1350' (USGS White Monument). From Oxbow, cross the Snake River and drive 27 miles north on the Idaho side of the river. Cross the 330' high dam to the Oregon side of the river. The generating capacity of the dam is 391 megawatts. Visiting hour: noon, Mountain Time.

HELL'S CANYON INTERPRETIVE CENTER (USGS White Monument, Squirrel Prairie). Facilities and activities: maps, geologic and other information, boat launch. A trail goes west for 0.5 miles up Short Creek to an Indian site. Another trail goes north down the Snake River for one mile to the site of an old homestead.

FS-73

Elkhorn Scenic Byway:
North Powder to Sumpter

Begin road log miles at exit 285 from Interstate 84, the North Powder Exit. Drive southwest on road signed: Anthony Lakes, 20 miles.

PILCHER CREEK RESERVOIR, 3850' (USGS Tucker Flat). Where the Anthony Lake road turns south, four miles from I-84, continue west four miles on road signed Pilcher Creek Reservoir, then go two miles north on a gravel road. Facilities and activities: tents, trailers to 25', boat launch, fishing, no hookups.

ELKHORN WILDLIFE AREA, 3700' (USGS Tucker Flat). Drive as above from I-84 for Pilcher Creek Reservoir. Where the road to the reservoir branches north eight miles from I-84, continue west one mile to a station where elk are fed during the winter.

ELKHORN DRIVE SCENIC BYWAY. At mile five from I-84, turn west on the Elkhorn Scenic Byway. Haines, on US-30, is eight miles south from this intersection and Baker City is 20 miles.

NORTH POWDER RIVER ROAD, high point 6000', 14 miles RT, 1700' gain (USGS Rock Creek, Anthony Lake, WWBRD). **Mt. Bicycle Route.** After driving three miles west on the Elkhorn Scenic Byway from the junction of the road from North Powder and the Elkhorn Scenic Byway, turn south on the Muddy Creek road, CR-1144, for 3.6 miles to the unmarked Bulger Flat road. Turn right (west) for two miles and park at a road junction, 4316'. Ride west, keeping left at the first "Y" after 0.1 mile and right at the next "Y". At a third "Y", take either road, the roads rejoin. Reach a bridge over the North Powder River after one mile. After crossing the river, follow the road west, south and southwest up the valley of the river, avoiding frequent logging spurs right and left. Pass a sign board three miles from the North Powder River bridge at the boundary of the Wallowa-Whitman National Forest: Red Mountain Lake, four miles; Summit Lake, five miles, North Powder River trail, five miles. Cross Twin Mountain Creek at five miles from the North Powder River bridge and continue ascending southwest to the Red Mountain Lake trailhead, seven miles from the starting point and 6000'.

TWIN MOUNTAIN, 8897', 16 miles RT, 4600' gain (USGS Rock Creek, Anthony Lake, WWBRD). **Mt. Bicycle Route.** Ride as above on the

North Powder River road to Twin Mountain Creek, 5800' and five miles from the North Powder River bridge. Leave bicycle and hike northwest on the east side of the creek into Twin Mountain Meadow. Continue north to the saddle between the North Powder River and Dutch Flat Creek, 7600'. Turn east and northeast on the ridge to the summit. According to the USGS map, the west summit is one foot higher than the east summit.

RED MOUNTAIN LAKE, 7123', 17 miles RT, 2900' gain (USGS Rock Creek, Anthony Lake, WWBRD). **Mt. Bicycle Route.** Ride the North Powder River Road for six miles from the North Powder River bridge (see above). Leave bicycle and hike southeast 1.3 miles to the lake, lying in a glacial cirque north of Red Mountain.

SUMMIT LAKE, 7247', 20 miles RT, 3000' gain (USGS Rock Creek, Anthony Lake, WWBRD). **Mt. Bicycle Route.** Ride as above one mile past the Red Mountain Lake trailhead, to 6200'. Leave bicycle and hike south two miles to the lake.

MEADOW LAKE, 7172', 19 miles RT, 2900' gain (USGS Rock Creek, Anthony Lake). **Mt. Bicycle Route.** Ride as above on the North Powder River Road (see above) two miles past the Red Mountain Lake trailhead. Turn north 0.5 mile to the lake.

LOST LAKE, 7363', 21 miles RT, 3100' gain (USGS Rock Creek, Anthony Lake). **Mt. Bicycle Route.** Ride as above two miles past the Red Mountain Lake trailhead to the Lost Lake trail junction. Turn north two miles to the lake.

COLUMBIA HILL, 8117', 25 miles RT, 3900' gain (USGS Rock Creek, Anthony Lake, Bourne, WWBRD). **Mt. Bicycle Route.** Ride the North Powder River Road (see above). Continue southwest past the Red Mountain Lake trailhead, ascending the road on the slope on the north side of the river. Reach the Elkhorn Crest Trail in three miles from the Red Mountain Lake trailhead. At the junction with the Elkhorn Crest Trail, turn right (west) to Cracker Saddle, 7600', where the slope drops steeply north to the North Fork John Day River. Leave bicycle and hike south up the ridge to the summit of Columbia Hill.

NORTH POWDER RIVER, 3700', mile 9 (USGS Rock Creek). In summer, the river at this bridge is much reduced by removal of water for irrigation.

DUTCH FLAT CREEK TRAILHEAD, 4800' (USGS Rock Creek). At mile 13 on FS-73, drive west one mile on road FS-7307.

DUTCH FLAT CREEK, 4800' to 7900', 21 miles RT, 3100' gain (USGS Rock Creek, Anthony Lakes). Hike south then west from the Dutch Flat Creek trailhead. At one mile, Dutch Flat Creek is actively cutting a deeper channel in a terminal glacial moraine. One mile further, a moraine persisted long enough to impound a lake that stored sediments to make the present meadow. A short branch trail to the left (south) goes to a campsite on the meandering creek. Also here, trees and large boulders standing on earth islands give evidence of past floods from waters temporarily impounded by avalanches farther up the valley. In the next several miles, the trail goes over and around granite outcrops rounded and flattened by glacial action. Reach Dutch Flat Lake, 7326', at 10 miles, and Dutch Flat Saddle, 7900', on the Elkhorn Crest National Recreation Trail at 10.5 miles.

ANTHONY CREEK CAMPGROUND, 4400' (USGS Anthony Butte).
At mile 14.5 on FS-73, drive seven miles north and east on FS-7312, a narrow gravel road. This campground is also accessible from Pilcher Creek Reservoir by driving west on roads FS-4330 and FS-7312 for six miles. Facilities and activities: tents, small recreational vehicles, water from stream, hiking. No fee.

HIGH MOUNTAIN, 6629', 6 miles RT, 2300' gain (USGS Anthony Butte).
From Anthony Creek campground (see above), hike southwest up ridge, passing east of the first summit, 5708'.

VAN PATTEN LAKE, 7396', 4 miles RT, 1,000' gain (USGS Anthony Lakes).
At mile 18, park in the Little Alps snowpark, 6400'. Hike up the road, which begins first to the east for 0.5 mile then turns back to the west, becoming a trail after one mile.

VAN PATTEN BUTTES, 8729', 8648', 8 miles RT, 2600' gain (USGS Anthony Lakes).
Hike as above to Van Patten Lake. At outlet dam, note notch to the southwest in the skyline ridge. This notch is the key to the easy ascent of Van Patten Buttes. Continue on trail around the west side of the lake until the shoreline turns south. Ascend southwest, entering a narrow valley, keeping to the right (west) side of the valley along the steep slopes descending from Van Patten Buttes. Avoid avalanche debris and brush when necessary by ascending west wall of the valley twenty to fifty feet where glacier carved benches provide easy, brush free travel. Continue ascending southwest, detouring 100 yards west as valley narrows briefly to pass a cascade. Return to the original line through a narrow defile, passing an old campsite. The valley then widens into a sloping meadow ending in a talus field. Pass this talus field on the left, then ascend southwest to the notch seen from the dam. Turn right (west) and hike up bouldery ramp on the south side of the ridge crest, avoiding the steep rocks of the ridge crest. Ramp ends at the summit plateau. The 8648' summit is immediately south (left) and the 8729' summit is west across the sandy, almost level, sparsely timbered plateau. This sandy area is an example of decomposed granite (see p. 84, Stop 4).

ELKHORN CREST TRAILHEAD, 7200', mile 20 on FS-73 (USGS

Anthony Lakes). Facilities available: restrooms, no water. Trail junctions on the Elkhorn Crest Trail: Black Lake Trail, 0.5 miles; Dutch Flat Saddle, 3 miles; Cunningham Saddle, 5 miles; Lost Lake, 7 miles; Peavy Trail, 10 miles; Pole Ridge Trail, 16 miles; Twin Lakes Trail, 19 miles; Marble Pass and road FS-6510, 23 miles.

BLACK LAKE, 7344', 2 miles RT, 300' gain (USGS Anthony Lakes). From the Elkhorn Crest Trailhead on road FS-73, hike the Elkhorn Crest Trail south 0.5 miles, then turn right one-half mile to the lake. A trail from Anthony Lake joins from the right (west) shortly before the turnoff to Black Lake.

ANGELL PEAK, 8646', 6 miles RT, 1800' gain (USGS Anthony Lakes). From the Elkhorn Crest Trailhead on road FS-73, hike two miles south on the Elkhorn Crest Trail. At the top of the third 50' to 80' switchback west of the pond visible below in Antone Creek basin, find a granite wall next to the trail that is marked by almost level intersecting narrow white bands. Leave the trail just above this wall, 8100', and turn northwest (325°) away from the trail and ascend in open woods until directly east of a black pyramidal point above on the ridge crest. Turn west and ascend toward the base of this rocky promontory. On reaching the red-stained base of this rock, turn southwest and ascend ramp to the ridge crest. Ascend the gentle slope in the scattered rocks of the crest briefly, then an open heather and grass slope just west of the crest. When this open slope is closed by trees and steep rocks, contour southwest through tumbled rocks from the lower west edge of the open area onto another open heather and grass slope. This 10 to 20 yard wide ramp ascends on the west side of Angell Peak north ridge to within a few feet of the summit. Note prospect with fragments of greenish quartz at the south edge of the summit plateau.

DUTCH FLAT SADDLE, 7900', 6 miles RT, 1000' gain (USGS Anthony Lakes). From Elkhorn Crest Trailhead (see above), hike the Crest Trail south for three miles. A trail from the north joins at Dutch Flat Saddle.

DUTCH FLAT LAKE, 7326', 7 miles RT, 1600' gain (USGS Anthony Lakes). Hike as above to Dutch Flat Saddle then descend east on trail to the lake.

DUTCH FLAT PEAK, 8525', 7 miles RT, 1600' gain (USGS Anthony Lakes). Hike as above to Dutch Flat Saddle. Continue south on the Elkhorn Crest Trail for 100', then ascend south through open woods to the summit, keeping 50' to 100' below the ridge crest on the west side. The summit gives a view north to the peaks overlooking Anthony Lake, down Dutch Flat Creek, and of the peaks to the east and south: Twin Mt., Red Mt. and Mt. Ruth.

ANTHONY LAKES FOREST SERVICE STATION. At mile 20,
turn south toward Anthony Lake. Information and maps are available here during the summer months.

ANTHONY LAKES CAMPGROUND, 7100' (USGS Anthony
Lakes). From the Anthony Lakes Forest Service Station turn east then south into the campground. Facilities and activities: piped water, tents, trailers, boating, no power boats. Fee.

HOFFER LAKES, 7472', 2 miles RT, 400' gain (USGS Anthony
Lakes). Drive the road west and south around Anthony Lake to the parking area. Walk the trail east around the south side of the lake to the Hoffer Lake trail just east of Parker Creek. From the Anthony Lake Campground, walk south around the east side of the lake to the beginning of the trail.

The Forest Service has prepared a self-guided Nature exhibit for the trail to Hoffer Lakes:

1. **Granite Boulder.** This large boulder weighs more than 60 tons. It was once part of the higher mountains in the background until glacial action broke it loose and carried it here.

   This rock is granodiorite, commonly called *granite*, and is the most common rock in this area. it is composed of several different minerals. The dark, shiny, flakey material is mica; the bulk of the lighter-colored material is a combination of feldspar and quartz.

   The four-inch band running diagonally across the boulder is a *dike*. These dikes result when cracks below the earth's surface are filled with molten rock of a different kind than the parent material. Dikes often remain on ridges when the more erosive adjacent rocks wear down. The dikes shown here are small, but in many places they are large, often several feet or more thick.

   The small, dark, rectangular body above the dike on the pointed end of the boulder is an *inclusion*. An inclusion results when some molten rock material cools faster than the bulk of the parent lava mass.

2. **Gunsight Mountain.** The peak to the east, 8,366 feet high, is the fourth highest peak in the Anthony Lakes area (highest is Angell Peak, 8,688'). The name is derived from the notch at its summit which is symbolic of the rear sight on a rifle. Notice the trees growing on this rocky mountain. How can trees grow on these solid granite surfaces? Stop 5 should give you some clues.

3. **A Lake of the Past.** This small meadow was once a miniature mountain lake formed when water filled the depression created by the glacier. As erosion occurred and water plants lived, died, and decayed through the ages, silt was deposited until finally the lake was filled to form the meadow before you.

4. **Water Against Rock.** The coarse nature of the minerals forming granite allows water to penetrate the outer surfaces of these boulders. As the water freezes and expands, small pieces of rock are chipped away. Small cracks develop in the boulder. This expanding power of freezing water gradually breaks up the rock. Through the years this boulder will eventually be reduced to soil and fine sand. Note the granitic sand around the rocks. It seems impossible for anything to grow on a rock, yet there is one plant that can. See it at the next stop!

5. **Plant Pioneers.** The light-green crusty plant appearing on some rocks is a *lichen* (pronounced "like-en"). An elementary type of plant life, this is the first plant to become established upon the bare rock surface. These plants also aid in breaking down the rock by producing an acid which eats into the rock. This begins the millions-of-years process of reducing rock to soil. Eventually the action of water and plants, plus other erosional processes, will wear down the solid granite mass of Gunsight Mountain.

Deposits left by glacial ice are called *glacial drift*. This boulder and others like it visible from the trail are examples. Notice the splitting that has occurred on the back of the boulder from frost action.

Do you recognize the dark irregular deposits in these rocks similar to the rock at Stop 1? They are further examples of inclusions.

6. **The Followers.** After lichens make a foothold on rocks, mosses and other small plants follow. These followers continue to add to the soil deposits started by the lichens. Eventually sufficient soil deposits are built up support higher plant life.

7. **The "Power" of Trees.** The soil deposits started by the primitive lichen and added to by the mosses eventually are used by trees. As the tree grows, its roots penetrate small cracks in the rock. These cracks are expanded until splitting occurs as can be seen here. In this way, vegetation slowly follows up the path of a retreating glacier.

8. **Hoffer Lakes.** Hoffer Lakes was once a single lake created when the natural dam (a terminal moraine) behind you (north) was deposited by a glacier. Soil accumulations have since divided the lake and reduced its area as shown by the amount of meadow present.

Glaciers are formed when large amounts of snow accumulate and remain year around. As additional snow builds up on these perennial snowfields, the lower layers of the snowpack change to ice. This ice layer then becomes plastic-like and begins to move downhill. The glacier continues to move as long as large amounts of snow fall each year. When a climate change occurs and less snow falls, the glacier retreats to eventually disappear.

The birthplace of an alpine glacier is called a *cirque*, an amphitheater-shaped feature with an extremely steep headwall. The steep headwall is formed when melting water from the growing glacier penetrates the rock beneath. This water then freezes and expands, breaking up the surface rock which is then picked up by the moving ice.

Notice the cirque extending along the ridge between the two peaks to the south.

9. **Hanging Valley.** The valley to the east, an unusual geologic feature, is a *hanging valley* or canyon. As a glacier moves downhill it must move along a relatively straight path. The main canyon is cut down more quickly by greater amounts of ice than side canyons. The side canyons are then left hanging above the main canyon so that, after the ice has disappeared, the streams flow out to the edges of cliffs and form waterfalls.

10. **Action of Moving Ice.** Go to the south end of the upper lake. One of the main processes in glacial erosion is *plucking*, which includes any manner in which debris is picked up and incorporated into the moving ice mass. The pits in the wall to the south were made when water percolated into joints and cracks, then froze and expanded, causing blocks of rock to be pried loose.

Glacial erosion also includes *abrasion*. The glacier's undersurface is studded with rock fragments of many sizes. With these fragments acting as teeth, the slowly moving ice bites into the bedrock beneath, making long scratches and grooves as may be seen on many rocks near here.

Do you recognize the small rock ridges on these and surrounding rocks? They are further examples of dikes.

11. **Glacial Valley.** The valley in which Hoffer Lakes lie is a glacial valley in miniature. Notice the characteristic "U-shaped" cross section with a fairly flat valley floor and steep sidewalls. To the south is the cirque with a vertical headwall. The sidewalls may not necessarily be solid rock as they are here but are commonly composed of debris scooped from the valley floor and sidecast much the same as a furrow in plowing. The furrows that parallel the glacier's course are *lateral moraines*. As a glacier moves downhill material is scooped up and pushed in front of the moving ice. When the glacier recedes, this ridgelike accumulation of debris remains and is called a *terminal moraine*.

(The above Nature Trail Log was adapted from: **Trail of the Alpine Glacier**, *Wallowa-Whitman National Forest*).

West of the first Hoffer lake, a trail continuing to the Lakes Lookout skirts extensive flower meadows that in the past were lakes that now have filled in completely. Another branch of trail turns east to an upper lake with a steep granite face dipping sharply into the lake on its east side from the north ridge of Lees Peak.

LEES PEAK, 8626', 6 miles RT, 1600' gain (USGS Anthony Lakes). Hike as above to Hoffer Lakes (see p. 83). Turn left (east) toward the upper lake, passing the lakes on the north side and continuing southeast on a trail into a valley, ascending near the stream. After one-fourth mile from the upper Hoffer Lake, and after passing the second ridge dropping north from Lees Peak, turn right (southwest) and ascend a gentle slope, first in open timber, then on more open meadow toward the summit that forms the southwest wall of Angell Basin. The slope steepens before reaching the gentle summit plateau with its many protruding granite blocks. A block fifteen feet high at the south end of the plateau forms the highest summit but the ascent of this block should be left to climbers.

GUNSIGHT MOUNTAIN, 8342', 7 miles RT, 1500' (USGS Anthony Lakes). Hike as above to Hoffer Lakes. Continue southeast following the stream into Angell Basin, passing the route to Lees Peak one-fourth mile from the upper Hoffer Lake. In the meadow where the stream turns south and just before reaching the steep slopes of the north ridge of Angell Peak, turn northwest (left) and ascend diagonally in open woods toward the saddle south of the summit. Continue to the summit on the gentler west side 50' to 100' below the crest of the south ridge.

BLACK LAKE, 7344', 2 miles RT, 300' gain (USGS Anthony Lakes). From Anthony Lake campground, hike south to find the trail near the end of the east side road. After passing Lilypad Lake, join the Elkhorn Crest Trail briefly before turning right (south) to the lake.

ANTHONY LAKE SHORELINE TRAIL, 7131', 1 mile RT, no gain (USGS Anthony Lakes). From any of the campgrounds or picnic areas near the lake, walk the gravelled path around the lake. Some of the fireplaces were built in the 1930's by the Civilian Conservation Corps.

MUD LAKE CAMPGROUND, 7091' (USGS Anthony Lakes). At mile 20 on FS-73, turn right (north) to the campground near Mud Lake, a lake with marshy shoreline and lily pads in summer. Facilities and activities: tents, trailers to 25', hiking, fishing, water. Fee.

ANTHONY LAKES SKI AREA, 7200', mile 20 (USGS Anthony Lakes). Facilities and activities: chair lift, groomed cross country ski trails, food, snopark, restrooms. Seasonal.

LAKES LOOKOUT, 8522', 5 miles RT, 1600' gain (USGS Anthony Lakes). Park in the Anthony Lakes Snowpark, east of the buildings of the ski lift operation. Hike south up the ski lift service road to the ridge. At the first road junction, turn left and ascend the ridge south on a road or trail half mile to a parking area. The trail to the summit continues up the west side of the ridge. The summit provides a panoramic view of the

Anthony Lakes peaks and many others. Ironside Mt. is 48 miles south and Mt. Ireland is 8.5 miles southwest. Distinctive Mt. Emily, with its abrupt east face, is 35 miles slightly east of north and west of La Grande.

GRANDE RONDE LAKE SNOPARK, 7222' (USGS Anthony Lakes). Near mile 20, turn right (north) into a parking area. Facilities: toilet, no water.

GRANDE RONDE LAKE CAMPGROUND 7146' (USGS Anthony Lakes). At mile 21 on FS-73, turn right (north) one-fourth mile. Facilities and activities: fishing, hiking, water, non-power boating, picnicking. Fee. This lake is the beginning of the Grande Ronde river, which flows north through La Grande to the Snake River.

ELKHORN SUMMIT, 7392', mile 21 on FS-73 (USGS Anthony Lakes). The undulating forest to the north is the Grande Ronde river watershed.

CRAWFISH BASIN, 7200', 4 miles RT, 600' gain (USGS Anthony Lakes, Crawfish Basin). At mile 23 on FS-73, drive right (east) on FS-210 and again right on FS-187 to a signboard marking the trailhead, 2 miles from FS-73. Hike south above Crawfish Basin with views of the extensive meadow, a former lake now filled by sediment. Note islands of rocks or trees dotting the meadow. Use various way trails to descend and explore the meadow.

DUTCH FLAT SADDLE, 7900', 4 miles RT, 400' gain. Begin as above on the Crawfish Basin Trail and continue to the junction with the Elkhorn Crest Trail.

LAKES LOOKOUT, 8522', 2 miles RT, 800' gain (USGS Anthony Lakes). Drive as above to the Crawfish Basin Trailhead. Hike up the trail on the west side of the ridge to the summit.

FOREST FIRE! mile 24. A lightning-set forest fire burned more than 6,000 acres here in 1986. A pine beetle infestation had killed many trees, leaving them more vulnerable to fire.

CRAWFISH LAKE, 6893', 3 miles RT, 700' gain (USGS Crawfish Lake). At mile 24 on FS-73, turn right (south) and park at the beginning of road FS-218. Hike the road southeast, then cross the creek and ascend near the outlet stream to the lake. Crawfish Meadow can be reached by hiking east from the north end of the lake. A trail to Cunningham Saddle on the Elkhorn Crest Trail follows the south side of the meadow.

CRAWFISH LAKE, 6893', 3 miles RT, 800' gain (USGS Crawfish Lake). At mile 29, where FS-73 makes a sharp U-bend, park at the trailhead east of FS-73 and hike up the trail to the lake.

PEAVY CABIN, 5900' (USGS Anthony Lakes, Crawfish Lake). At mile 31 on FS-73, drive three miles east on a bumpy road (no high centers). The cabin was built by the Civilian Conservation Corps and used by Professor Peavy of the Department of Forestry, Oregon State University.

MOUNT RUTH, 8600', 12 miles RT, 3000' gain (USGS Anthony Lakes, Crawfish Lake). From Peavy Cabin (see above), hike south on the old road near the North Fork of the John Day River (Peavy Trail). After two miles, the trail leaves the river and climbs east, reaching the Elkhorn Crest trail four miles from the Peavy Cabin. Turn left (north) on the Elkhorn Crest Trail for two miles. After contouring across the cliffs and talus descending from Mt. Ruth, at the point where the trail crosses the west ridge of Mt. Ruth, 7800', turn southeast up an open, sandy, grass slope through occasional trees to the north ridge of Mt. Ruth. Ascend south on crest of ridge, or just below the crest on west side, to the summit.

SUMMIT LAKE, 7247', 12 miles RT, 2600' gain (USGS Anthony Lakes, Crawfish Lake, Bourne). From Peavy Cabin (see above), hike as above on the Peavy Trail to its junction with the Elkhorn Crest Trail. Turn right one-fourth mile to Cracker Creek saddle, then east on an almost level trail to Summit Lake.

LOST LAKE, 7363', 11 miles RT, 2600' gain (USGS Anthony Lakes, Crawfish Lake). From Peavy Cabin (see above), hike three miles east on the Cunningham Cove trail to Cunningham Saddle and the Elkhorn Crest Trail. Turn right (south) on the Elkhorn Crest Trail two miles to the Lost Lake trail junction. Descend east to Lost Lake.

MOUNT RUTH, 8600', 13 miles RT, 3000' gain (USGS Anthony Lakes, Crawfish Lakes). From Peavy Cabin (see above), hike east on the Cunningham Cove trail to Cunningham saddle and the Elkhorn Crest Trail. Turn right (south) on the Elkhorn Crest Trail, passing the Lost Lake trail junction after two miles. One mile past the Lost Lake trail junction, as the trail crosses the west ridge of Mount Ruth, turn southeast from the Elkhorn Crest Trail and ascend southeast (see Mount Ruth above).

BALDY LAKE, 7788', 12 miles RT, 2600' gain (USGS Crawfish Lake, Mt. Ireland). At 31 miles on FS-73, turn left (south) and park at the trailhead. Follow the trail south, crossing Baldy Creek several times and, about halfway to the lake, the old power line clearcut that ran from Fremont Powerhouse to Bourne. From the lake, a trail continues east over Crown Point Ridge into the Cable Cove mining area.

JUNCTION FS-52, 5200', mile 35 (USGS Trout Meadow). This paved road goes west 41 miles to Ukiah.

CRANE FLATS, 5500', mile 36 to mile 39 on FS-73 (USGS Trout Meadow, Granite). At some seasons, deer and elk feed in the meadows early and late in the day.

CRANE CREEK TRAIL, 4500', 8 miles RT, 1,000' gain (USGS Trout Meadow). At mile 37, park at the trailhead and hike west, descending along Crane Creek to the North Fork John Day River.

LA BELLEVUE MINE LOOP (USGS Trout Meadows, Crawfish Lake). **Mt. Bicycle Route.** A network of roads beginning near mile 37 on road FS-73 and two miles south of the junction of FS-73 with FS-52 leads to the Continental Mine, the La Bellevue mine, other mines, and the site of Cabell City, two miles east of FS-73 on Onion Creek at 5800'. Cabell City was a supply center for miners before 1900.

ROAD FS-7340, high point 6800', 16 miles RT, 1000' gain (USGS Granite, Mt. Ireland). **Mt. Bicycle Route.** This road at mile 38.5 on FS-73 goes to the Buffalo Mine, the Cox tunnels, the Blue Ribbon Mine, and beyond.

BALDY LAKE, 7788', 7 miles RT, 2000' gain (USGS Mt. Ireland, Crawfish Lake). At mile 39, drive six miles east on FS-7345 to the trailhead near the clearcut for the power line from the Fremont Power House to Bourne.

COUGAR-INDEPENDENCE MINE, 5000' (USGS Granite). At mile 41, pass the remains of mines that produced gold and silver until about 1940.

CHINESE WALLS, mile 42 (USGS Granite). The walls of boulders paralleling the stream bed were stacked by Chinese to get deeper into the stream bed. They reworked placer claims after earlier miners. Now, archeologists are reworking the diggings looking for artifacts left by the miners. A pamphlet describing the archeological findings is available from the Baker County Tourist Information Office.

GRANITE, 4683', mile 44, population 8 (USGS Granite). "Albert G. Tabor first struck gold just below the present town of Granite on the Fourth day of July 1862. Tabor named his claim the Independence since the strike was made on Independence day, and the town that sprang up around the strike was also called Independence. However, the name was changed to Granite in 1876 when the people applied for a post office and found there was already an Independence, Oregon. Granite was a center of mining activity for over 80 years. Today activity has ceased with nothing remaining but the town and a wealth of history." Quoted from Wallowa-Whitman National Forest. Several buildings in various states of decay still remain scattered throughout the townsite and the cemetery has many gravestones from the earliest days. Facilities: store, gas, food, lodging. **The Granite Store** has parking and electrical hookups for recreational vehicles. Address: Granite Route Box 20, Sumpter 97877.

SILVER BUTTE, 6191', 16 miles RT, 3000' gain (USGS Granite, Olive Lake, Silver Butte). Across road FS-73 from the turnoff to Granite, drive west on FS-10 for 1.5 miles, then turn right on FS-1035 along Granite Creek for 3.5 miles. A final 0.3 miles left (west) on FS-1035-010 ends at the confined parking area by the trailhead (no trailers), 4300'. The trail begins high on the north slope above Granite Creek to avoid private land along the creek, then descends to cross the creek on a bridge. Five hundred feet after crossing Lake Creek (the large creek entering Granite Creek from the south), the metal box just below the trail covers a spring. Look for the freely flowing outlet. After passing through a generous campsite near the North Fork John Day River, cross the bridge over the river, 3936', turn right (north) then immediately west and ascend through sparse woods to an open plateau where several thick stands of young trees have regrown after a fire. On reaching a road, turn right (south) one-fourth mile to the rocky summit with views to the east, south, and north. Desolation Butte Lookout, 7028' and seven miles away, is at 236° and Mount Ireland Lookout is 12 miles away at 110°.

FREMONT POWER HOUSE, 4939' (USGS Granite, Olive Lake). Leave road FS-73 as above for Silver Butte but remain on road FS-10 for five miles, passing dredge and placer tailings along Granite Creek and Clear Creek, to the power house, built in 1908 to supply electricity to the mines in the area as far as Bourne. It was in operation until October 1967, supplying not only the local area, but also the regional electrical supply net. A similar power station west of Haines, Oregon, built a few years earlier with equipment dating from 1901 and 1902, still generates up to a megawatt of electricity using water from Rock Creek Lake.

OLIVE LAKE CAMPGROUND, 6000' (USGS Olive Lake). Leave road FS-73 at the Granite turnoff and drive west 12 miles on road FS-10. Facilities and activities: tents, trailers to 25', water, hiking, fishing, boating, bicycling.

BEN HARRISON PEAK, 7830', 12 miles, 2000' gain (USGS Olive Lake, Desolation Butte, Vinegar Hill). From Olive Lake Campground, hike south on the east side of the lake on roads and trails, passing a meadow that was the reservoir supplying the Fremont Power House. At Saddle Camp on the summit of a ridge of the Greenhorn Mountains, turn left (southeast) to a pass at Dupratt Spring. Ascend east to the open summit of the peak.

BOUNDARY FOREST SERVICE STATION, 4727', mile 47 (USGS Mt. Ireland). This cabin, with its pleasant indoor workmanship, was built by the Civilian Conservation Corps in the 1930's and is used by Forest Service work and fire crews.

MOUNT IRELAND, 8321', 7 miles RT, 2400' gain, mile 48.5 (USGS Mt. Ireland). Eleven miles west of Sumpter or four miles east of Granite, turn north on road FS-7370. Pass a spur road to the right at 0.6 miles, a spur road to the left at 0.8 miles, then turn left (north) at 2.4 miles. Three hundred feet past the turnoff pass a sign 7370. At 3.0 miles from the paved road, drive right at a sign: Mt. Ireland Lookout Trail one mile. Park 3.2 miles from the paved road, then hike west on a blocked logging track with a sign: Mt. Ireland Lookout Trail 0.5 mile. Reach old-growth forest in one-half mile, passing a sign at one-fourth mile: Mt. Ireland Lookout three miles. One mile after leaving the parking area, the trail passes a small clearcut and a road. After another mile, the trail turns up the open south ridge and passes the junction with the trail to Downie Lake. Three hundred feet before this trail junction, at the edge of the forest, a faint trail goes southwest to Big Dipper Spring. From the lookout, Mt. Rainier is 216 miles at 310°, Mt. Adams is 180 miles at 300°, and Mt. Hood is 167 miles at 282°. The lookout is staffed from July into October.

DOWNIE LAKE, 6600', 7 miles RT, 2000' gain (USGS Mt. Ireland). Hike as above toward Mt. Ireland to the junction with the Downie Lake Trail at 7300' on the south ridge of Mt. Ireland and two miles from the parking area. Turn right (east) and descend to Downie Lake.

GOLD SPRING AND CENTER, 5300', mile 52 (USGS Mt. Ireland). This site was a supply center for the mines and a stop for the stage coach from the Columbia River to Sumpter. The buildings are gone, but the spring remains, feeding an ever-flowing fountain beside the highway.

BLUE SPRING SUMMIT AND SNOPARK, 5864', mile 53 (USGS Mt. Ireland). Named for Blue Spring below the road to the west, now only a trickle from a trampled swamp.

ELKHORN VIEWPOINT, mile 54. Park at a wide shoulder for the view of the Elkhorn Range. Rock Creek Butte is 10 miles at 64° and Elkhorn Peak is 11 miles at 72°.

McCULLY FORK CAMPGROUND, 4553', mile 58 (USGS Bourne). This campground is three miles west of Sumpter. A ditch west of the campground supplied water for placer mining in the valley to the east.

GRAYS PEAK, 6802', 8 miles RT, 2500' gain (USGS Mt. Ireland, Bourne). A challenge for orienteers: Find the summit! Begin at McCully Forks Campground, three miles west of Sumpter. Walk north on the west side of the creek to the end of the road. Ascend west in the clearing under the power line to a road, crossing an old mining ditch just above the campground. Turn right (north) on this road one-fourth mile to the gully at the north edge of a clear cut. Ascend this gully on a bulldozer track 500' (200' gain) to another road. Turn right (northwest) on the road and contour one-half mile. Just before the road reaches a saddle, turn right (northeast) on a road blocked by two earthen vehicle barriers. Continue on this road 600' as it veers to the east, then turn left (north) into a road with 3' to 6' trees (1993) growing in the track. Go one-half mile on this road, ascending slightly, to a four-way junction with a well-travelled gravel road (5400'). From this junction, go southwest on the only road that goes uphill. After one-fourth mile, turn north (right), and continue uphill on the more travelled road, taking the left fork where a gate closes the right fork. After passing the gate, go right uphill (north) at the first fork then left (west) toward the summit at the second fork. After the road ends, ascend northwest cross country to the summit ridge, then turn south along the ridge, stepping over and around windfallen trees. The summit is a tangle of fallen trees and large granite blocks. The rocky ridge 200' south of the summit gives an open view to the south and east.

ROCK CREEK BUTTE, 9106', 10 miles RT, 2400' gain (USGS Elkhorn Peak, Bourne). From Sumpter, drive north up the Cracker Creek road toward Bourne for 2.4 miles from the paved Sumpter-Granite road. Turn right away from Cracker Creek road on the Pole Creek Ridge road (FS-5536) and drive five miles to the the trailhead at 6800'. Hike the trail (FS-1624) north to a junction with the Elkhorn Crest Trail. Turn right (east) to the south ridge of Rock Creek Butte. Leave the trail and ascend north cross country to the summit.

WIND CREEK PEAK, 7642', 7 miles RT, 3000' gain, (USGS Bourne). From the paved road to Granite just west of Sumpter, drive the road north toward Bourne. Park where the road crosses Wind Creek, 3.1 miles from the turnoff from the Granite-Sumpter road. Walk the road northwest along Wind Creek, continuing west on the road after the road turns sharply away from the creek. The ridge visible to the northwest at the beginning of the hike is the Elkhorn Crest and the rocky summit of Wind Creek Peak is seen briefly from the road along the creek 1.5 miles from the Cracker Creek road. One-fourth mile after the road bends left (west) away from the creek, turn right (north) off the road up an open timbered valley, passing a mine entrance. Continue ascending north in open woods and occasionally on broken rocks to the summit, passing another mining prospect. The easy-appearing west ridge is steeper in places and more complex.

CABLE COVE, 6800', 12 miles RT (USGS Bourne). Drive five miles north on the Cracker Creek road toward Bourne from the Granite-Sumpter road turnoff just west of Sumpter. Park and hike west on the road up Silver Creek (FS-5540). This road sometimes has heavy truck traffic and driving is not advisable. Cable Cove was a center for mining around 1900 but only mine dumps and a few artifacts remain.

CROWN POINT, 8006', 16 miles RT, 3000' gain (USGS Bourne). **Mt. Bicycle Route.** Park and ride up the road along Silver Creek to the clearing at 6500'. After reaching Cable Cove (see above), leave bicycle and hike west on road that ascends below the mine dumps on the south-facing ridge to Crown Point Ridge. Turn south to the summit, which overlooks Baldy Lake and Mt. Ireland.

BOURNE, 5300' (USGS Bourne). From the highway just west of Sumpter, turn north and drive six miles along Cracker Creek, passing an old dredge hull in a pond of Cracker Creek at one mile. Bourne never had a devastating fire, but most of the buildings have disappeared, partly the result of scavenging and partly from a flood in 1937. Bourne was the end of the power line from the Fremont Power House and the transformers that terminated the power line are still standing near where they were placed, nearly 90 years ago. To see them, walk north until the road divides, then west across Cracker Creek. Turn north 100' on the west side of the creek to find the transformers. The clear cut for the power line is still visible going off to the west. Bourne has no facilities for travellers.

"The Golconda, Columbia, North Pole, E and E and other hard rock mines are an inseparable part of our historical heritage. Bourne, named after Senator Jonathan Bourne, Jr. of Portland, who was intensely interested in Oregon mining is located almost in the geographical center of the Northpole-Columbia lode, which is the most extensive gold lode in northeast Oregon. The combined, continuous ore body is thought to have produced about $9,000,000 in gold. Today activity is sporadic and limited; of the future we can only guess." (*Wallowa-Whitman National Forest*).

COLUMBIA HILL, 8117', 10 miles RT, 3500' gain (USGS Bourne). From the end of the road in Bourne, where the road divides into three 4-wheel drive tracks, hike the left (west) road over Cracker Creek. Follow this road west one mile to where the road descends steeply west below the Columbia Mine dump. Immediately after passing below the mine dump, contour northwest 100' across a small creek and then ascend slightly west of north, passing several collapsed buildings and many artifacts left by the miners. After one-half mile, cross a road, and continue ascending on or near the ridge crest, finding an obvious track going slightly west of north. Stay on this track, either on the crest of the ridge or on the more open west side of the ridge to avoid windfalls and tumbled rocks. Cross an open meadow area, continuing to go slightly west of north and staying on the west side of the ridge leading toward Columbia Hill. At 7200', after passing west of a small summit of tumbled rocks, the trees thin and Columbia Hill becomes visible in the distance (340°) to the right (east) of a 7813' summit. Go directly toward Columbia Hill to the saddle between the 7813' summit on the west and a 7595' summit on the southeast (right) to find a trail that contours north across the east face of the rocky 7813' summit to the ridge immediately south of Columbia Hill. Go north to the summit, crossing an 80' wide granitic dike just south of the 7611' point on the ridge between the 7813' summit and Columbia Hill. This dike is part of the granitic mass of the Bald Mountain batholith exposed in the summits to the north that begins south of Mt. Ruth and extends north to the peaks around Anthony Lake. This granitic intrusion supplied the energy and some of the metals for the mineralization in this area.

SUMPTER, 4400', mile 61, population 119 (USGS Bourne). "The bustling, boom town of Sumpter stretched from here westward to the Powder River at the peak of the mining boom. The mining camp was named for Fort Sumter, South Carolina, by five ex-confederate soldiers who discovered gold near here in 1862. The Sumpter Valley Railroad reached Sumpter in 1896 and the town began to boom until at one time it had 3,500 people. On August 13, 1917 the dreaded fate of many mining towns occurred, fire raged through the town and destroyed eleven city blocks including nine brick buildings. The fire and dwindling returns from gold mining ended the boom." (*Wallowa-Whitman National Forest*).

Facilities in Sumpter include: stores, taverns, restaurants, lodging, picnic ground, gas, Post Office, Forest Service station. A gold dredge that ceased operation in 1954 sits in a pond at the edge of town is now a State Park. A planned restoration of the dredge will allow tours. The partially restored Sumpter Valley Railroad now ends at the edge of town near the dredge. It operates on weekends in the summer and at other times by arrangement (see p. 59).

Events: Sumpter Valley Country Fair and Flea Market is held on the weekends of Memorial Day, Fourth of July, and Labor Day. Address: PO Box 513, Sumpter, 97877, 894-2264. **Snowmobile Run** from Sumpter to Granite is held in January. **Elkhorn Crest Sled Dog** races are held in February.

Camping: China Diggins RV Park. Located at the beginning of the road to Bourne at the west edge of Sumpter. Facilities and activities: tents, trailers, hiking. tel. 894-2264. **Gold Rush RV Park.** Located at the beginning of the road to Bourne at the west edge of Sumpter. Facilities and activities: tents, trailers, electrical hookups, open all year. Telephone: 800-560-5434, 523-5433. **Sumpter Pines RV Park.** At east edge of Sumpter off the connecting road to SR-7. Facilities and Activities: hookups, hiking, near dredge and Sumpter Valley Railroad. PO Box 504, 97877, tel. 894-2328.

SR-82

La Grande to Wallowa Lake

ISLAND CITY, 2742', population 696 (USGS La Grande SE). Facilities and activities: food, stores, gas, park with picnic tables.

IMBLER, 2731', population 299 (USGS Imbler). Facilities and activities: food, store.

MOUNT HARRIS LOOKOUT, 5359', 8 miles RT, 2600' gain (USGS Imbler). From Imbler at MP-12, drive two miles east on Hull Lane, then 0.5 mile north on Grays Creek Road. Park at Striker Lane. Hike east and south on the road to the summit of this state lookout.

SUMMERVILLE, 2700', population 111 (USGS Summerville, Imbler). From SR-82 at MP-14, drive west two miles. Facilities and activities: store, gas, post office.

ELGIN, 2716', population 1,586, area population 3,259 (USGS Elgin). Facilities and activities: food, stores, lodging, gas.

Chamber of Commerce, on SR-82 at Albany and Eighth Sts., Box 391, 97827, tel. 437-1971.

Opera House and City Hall. Built in 1912 and recently restored, the Opera House has movies every weekend and other programs throughout the year, including plays produced by the Eighth Street Players, a repertory group (437-9182).

Elgin Park. Drive east on Cedar from SR-82 to the Grande Ronde river. Boat launch.

Elgin Mobile Home Park, full hookups for recreational vehicles, no tents, self-contained only, no restroom. Drive north on 15th Street from SR-204. tel. 437-1491.

Events: Elgin Stampede. Second weekend in July, 437-3853. **Riverfest,** third weekend in June, 437-1080.

Backcountry Trips: Marsh Tilden Float Trips, 437-9270. **T.R.T. Raft Rentals,** PO Box 893, 97827, 1610 Alder St., tel. 437-9270 or 800-700-RAFT, rubber raft and kayak rentals plus equipment.

SR-204. From Elgin, drive northwest on SR-204.

ANDIES PRAIRIE SNOPARK, MP-26 (USGS Andies Prairie). Find the snowpark 15 miles northwest of Elgin.

UMATILLA BREAKS VIEWPOINT, 5100' (USGS Andies Prairie). At MP-24, a pull-off provides a view over the headwaters of the Umatilla River.

WOODLAND CAMPGROUND, 5200' (USGS Andies Prairie). At MP-24, 17 miles northwest of Elgin. Facilities and activities: tents, pull throughs for trailers to 25', no water. No fee.

WOODLAND SNOPARK, 5200' (USGS Andies Prairie). The snowpark is 0.1 miles northwest of Woodland Campground.

LOOKINGGLASS TRAIL, high point 5500', 20 miles RT, 2500' gain (USGS Andies Prairie, Tollgate, Jubilee Lake, Partridge Creek). **Mt. Bicycle Route.** From Woodland campground, ride 0.3 miles northwest on SR-204 then one mile east on road FS-3725. Turn left on road FS-3701 and descend north to the trailhead, five miles from SR-204. Descend to Lookingglass Creek, 3050'. Ascend two miles northwest along the creek, leaving the creek at 4000' to continue ascending northwest. Reach SR-204 at Spout Springs, 5450'. Turn left (east) two miles to the starting point at the campground.

SPOUT SPRINGS SKI AREA, high point 5450', MP-22 (USGS Tollgate). East of Tollgate on SR-204, and 20 miles northwest of Elgin, the area has the following facilities and activities: snowpark, water, food, trailhead, dinner theater, mountain bike rentals and trails, cross country and downhill skiing with T-bar and chair lifts. Restaurant closed Monday and Tuesday in off season. No camping.

MORNING CREEK, 5200', MP-20 (USGS Tollgate). Facilities and activities: snowpark, barrier-free picnic area.

WOODWARD CAMPGROUND, 4950' (USGS Tollgate). At MP-20, drive west to the campground near Langdon Lake. Facilities and activities: tents, trailers to 25', picnicking, water, hiking. View of lake but no access. Fee.

McINTYRE LOOKOUT, 5300', 6 miles RT, 500' gain (USGS Tollgate). From Woodward campground, hike west on SR-204 for one mile. Turn north on roads to the lookout on the highest point with views over the Umatilla National Forest.

TOLLGATE, 4892', MP-20 (USGS Tollgate). Tollgate Forest Service Station has maps and information. **Tollgate Trailfinders Snowmobile Club,** warming hut, Route 1, Box 77A, Weston, 97886. For snow information, call 566-2784.

TARGET MEADOWS CAMPGROUND, 4800' (USGS Tollgate). From Tollgate, drive two miles north on FS-6401 to the campground. Facilities and activities: tents, trailers to 25', water, hiking, bicycling. Fee.

JUBILEE LAKE CAMPGROUND, 4700' (USGS Jubilee Lake). From Tollgate, drive 12 miles east and north on gravel road FS-64 to the campground on the lake. Facilities and activities: tents, trailers to 25', water, barrier-free facilities, fishing, boat launch, hiking. Fee.

LOOKOUT MOUNTAIN LOOP, 5229', 30 miles RT, 1000' gain (USGS Jubilee Lake, Fry Meadows, Wenaha Forks). **Mt. Bicycle Route.** Ride east from Jubilee Lake campground on road FS-6413. Road FS-6236 joins from the south at five miles, road FS-6232 joins from the south at eight miles, and road FS-6415 joins from the north at 10 miles. At 12 miles, turn right (south) onto road FS-62 and after one-fourth mile, turn right again to the lookout summit. Return, making left turns, on roads FS-62 and FS-6413 for two miles, then turn northwest on road FS-6415 on the ridge that separates the drainages of the Wenaha River on the north and the Grande Ronde River on the south. Continue west, passing Peerless Spring, Timothy Forest Service Station, 4674', and Timothy Springs trail-head. At the junction with road FS-64 where the road begins to descend, turn south on road FS-6403, passing Mottet campground. After passing the campground, take the first left fork to return to Jubilee Lake and the starting point.

MOTTET CAMPGROUND, 5280' (USGS Jubilee Lake). Drive to Jubilee Lake (see above). Continue on FS-64 for one mile. Turn north on FS-6411 two miles to FS-6403 and continue north on FS-6403 two miles to the campground. Facilities and activities: tents, trailers to 25', hiking. No fee.

WALLA WALLA RIVER LOOP, 5648', 20 miles RT, 3000' gain (USGS Jubilee Lake, Bone Spring). **Mt. Bicycle Route.** From Mottet camp-ground at the Walla Walla River trailhead, descend northwest to the south fork of the Walla Walla River. Turn north and ascend the trail along the river six miles to the trailhead on road FS-65. Turn right on this road for two miles to the intersection with road FS-64. Turn right (south) on the ridge that separates the drainages of the Walla Walla River on the west and the Wenaha River on the east. Pass Squaw Spring campground. Where road FS-6415 turns east, continue south to Mottet campground.

SQUAW SPRING CAMPGROUND, 5600' (USGS Bone Spring). Drive as for Mottet campground (see above). Continue east and north on FS-6403 for two miles to the junction with FS-64. Turn north four miles on FS-64 to the campground on the ridge between the Walla Walla river and the Wenaha River. Facilities and activities: tents and small recreational vehicles only, no trailers.

SR-82

MOUNT MORIAH, 5587', 20 miles RT, 2100' gain (USGS Cricket

Flat, Minam, Mount Moriah). **Mt. Bicycle Route.** At MP-27 on SR-82, five miles east of Elgin, drive south three miles to the intersection with the Minam Rim Road. Park and ride east, ascending the north fork of Clark Creek on road FS-62 to the summit of Mount Moriah, with views into the headwaters of the Minam River.

ELK POINT–ROCK SPRINGS LOOP, high point 6030', 30 miles RT, 2700' gain (USGS Cricket Flat, Mount Moriah, Minam, Gassett Bluff). **Mt. Bicycle Route.** Park and ride as above for Mount Moriah, continuing south on the Minam Rim Road (FS-62) to Elk Point, 5600', a view point into the Minam River drainage and the summits beyond and 10 miles from the starting point. Continue to the Rock Springs Viewpoint, another two miles. From the Rock Springs viewpoint, go west to Line Bluff, the high point, then turn north to return on the Minam Rim Road past Elk Point. After passing Elk Point, turn left (northwest) at the first road junction (FS-430) to descend the Middle Fork of Clark Creek, passing the Clark Creek State Forest Station. Keep right at further road junctions to return to the starting point.

MINAM SUMMIT, 3524', MP-28 (USGS Cricket Flat). This plateau is the top of a flow of Columbia Basalts. Many of the individual flows are exposed in road cuts on the descent to the Minam River (see below).

MINAM RIVER, high point 3400', 15+ miles RT, 500' gain (USGS Cricket Flat, Minam, Mount Moriah). **Mt. Bicycle Route.** At MP-31 on SR-82, one mile east of Minam Summit, park and ride seven miles south on the Minam River road to the boundary of the Eagle Cap Wilderness. Leave bicycle and hike up the river, a famous fishing stream. The river trail in the Wilderness is closed to bicycles.

COLLUSION POINT, 4820', 20 miles RT, 2500' gain (USGS Mount Moriah). **Mt. Bicycle Route.** Ride as above on the Minam River Road to the Eagle Cap Wilderness boundary. Leave bicycle and hike up the river trail for 1.5 miles. Turn east just south of Trout Creek and ascend on the Cougar Ridge Trail to the first open summit and viewpoint.

COLUMBIA BASALTS. Between MP-31 and MP-33, SR-82 descends past many layers of Columbia Basalts freshly exposed by recent highway construction. The red layers indicate the tops of flows that were oxidized by thousands to millions of years of exposure between eruptions. Lower flows tend to be more decomposed and higher flows more massive.

MINAM RIVER STATE PARK, 2500' (USGS Minam). At MP-34 SR-82, on the west side of the river, turn north down the river to the park. Facilities and activities: picnicking, fishing access, tents, trailers, site maximum 71', water. Fee.

BIG CANYON FISH FACILITY, 2500', MP-35 (USGS Minam). This

installation, at Big Canyon Road, traps returning steelhead and salmon to be taken to hatcheries for spawning. The young fish from the hatchery are acclimatized to the water here before being released. These fish will then return here when ready to spawn.

COUGAR RIDGE, 6760', 30 miles RT, 4000' gain (USGS Minam, Wallowa, Fox Point, Mount Moriah). **Mt. Bicycle Route.** At MP-35 on SR-82, one mile east of the Minam River bridge, 2950', park at the Big Canyon Fish Weir. Ride southeast on the Big Canyon Road (FS-8270) for ten miles. At a road fork, go right, staying on FS-8270, ascending steeply to the Cougar Ridge trailhead, 5800'. Leave bicycle and hike south five miles to a viewpoint on Cougar Ridge.

BALD KNOB, 6529', 35 miles RT, 3600' gain (USGS Minam, Wallowa, Fox Point). **Mt. Bicycle Route.** Ride as above for Cougar Ridge to the road junction 10 miles from SR-82. Turn left up Sage Creek on FS-8270-050 for two miles. Turn left again, staying on FS-8270-050 and ascending away from Sage Creek, to the Bear Wallow trailhead, 17 miles from SR-82 and 6000'. Leave bicycle and hike 1.5 miles to the Bald Knob viewpoint.

WALLOWA RIVER ROADSIDE REST, 2600' (USGS Minam). At MP-36 on SR-82, three miles east of the Minam River bridge, the rest area has picnicking and access to the river for fishing. No camping.

WALLOWA RIVER ROADSIDE REST, 2700' (USGS Minam). This rest area at MP-39 on SR-82, five miles east of the Minam River bridge, has fishing access and picnicking facilities. No camping.

WALLOWA, 2941', population 748 (USGS Wallowa). Facilities and activities: food, stores, lodging, gas, park at the west edge of town (no facilities). **Wallowa Valley Stay-N-Wash RV Park**, north of SR-86 at west edge of town, has full hookups for recreational vehicles of any length, showers, laundry. Telephone: 886-6944. **Events: Fourth of July** celebration, 886-2422; **City Market**, September, 886-8145.

HUCKLEBERRY MOUNTAIN, 7552', 20 miles RT, 4000' gain (USGS Fox Point, Lostine). **Mt. Bicycle Route.** From the town of Wallowa, drive south on Bear Creek Road, FS-8250, for eight miles to the junction of Bear Saddle Road, 3600'. Park and ride at first east, then southeast, ascending Little Bear Creek on road FS-8250 and maintaining a southeast direction at road junctions to stay on the most travelled road up Little Bear Creek. At six miles from Bear Creek Road, turn right (southwest) on road FS-160 to the trailhead, 5600', near Allen Canyon Ditch. Leave bicycle and hike two miles west on trail FS-1667 to the summit.

BOUNDARY CAMPGROUND, 3700' (USGS Fox Point). From the town of Wallowa, drive nine miles south on Bear Creek Road. Facilities and activities: tents only, fishing, hiking, water. No fee.

BAKER PEAK, 7083', 12 miles RT, 3500' gain (USGS Fox Point). From Boundary campground, hike two miles south up Bear Creek. Turn right (east) up Baker Canyon on a way trail to the summit that overlooks the Eagle Cap Wilderness to the south.

LOSTINE, 3363', population 231, area population 1,706, (USGS Lostine). Facilities and activities: food, stores, lodging, gas. **Events: Flea Market**, early July, 569-2415; **Sheepherder's Ball**, mid-September, 886-4365. **Backcountry Trips and Tours: Red's Horse Ranch**, Star Route Box 25, 97857, tel. 569-2222. Facilities and activities: lodging, hiking, meals, fishing, riding, pack trips. **Moffit Bros. Transportation**, Scenic tours and charters, PO Box 156, 97857, tel. 569-2284.

POLE BRIDGE RECREATION AREA, 4100' (USGS Lostine). From SR–82, drive seven miles south of Lostine on the Lostine River Road. Facilities and activities: picnicking, fishing.

WILLIAMSON CAMPGROUND, 4900' (USGS North Minam Meadows). Drive 12 miles south of Lostine on the Lostine River Road. Facilities and activities: tents, small trailers, fishing. No fee.

CHIMNEY LAKE, 7604', 10 miles RT, 2500' gain (USGS North Minam Meadows). Drive 15 miles south of Lostine on the Lostine River Road to the trailhead. Hike southwest on trail FS-1651 to a trail junction, 7200', then go north on trail FS-1659 to the lake, situated in a cirque below Lookout Mountain.

LOOKOUT MOUNTAIN, 8831', 12 miles RT, 4000' gain (USGS North Minam Meadows). Hike as above to Chimney Lake. Continue on the trail west to Hobo Lake then ascend north cross country to the summit.

FRANCES LAKE, 7705', 18 miles RT, 4200' gain (USGS North Minam Meadows, Chief Joseph Mountain). Drive 16 miles south from SR–82 at Lostine to the trailhead, 5300'. Hike east on trail FS-1663 over Marble Point Ridge to the lake, lying on the flank of Hurricane Divide.

MARBLE POINT, 9000', 16 miles RT, 3800' gain (USGS North Minam Meadows, Chief Joseph Mountain). Hike as above toward Frances Lake on trail FS-1663. At the crest of the ridge, 8600', leave the trail and hike south cross country to the summit.

FRENCH CAMPGROUND, 5300' (USGS North Minam Meadows). Drive 17 miles south of Lostine to the campground on the Lostine River. Facilities and activities: tents, trailers, water, fishing, hiking.

SHADY CAMPGROUND, 5400' (USGS North Minam Meadows). Drive 18 miles south of Lostine. Facilities and activities: tents, small trailers, fishing, hiking.

MAXWELL LAKE, 7800', 8 miles RT, 2300' gain (USGS North Minam Meadows). From the trailhead at Shady Campground, hike west on trail FS-1674 to the lake. Horses are not permitted on the trail.

FLAGSTAFF POINT, 8684', 10 miles RT, 3400' gain (USGS North Minam Meadows). Hike as above to Maxwell Lake then ascend north cross country to the summit.

TWO PAN TRAILHEAD, 5600' (USGS Eagle Cap). From Lostine, drive 20 miles south from SR-82 to the trailhead at the end of the road on the Lostine River. Facilities are limited: trailers not recommended, recreational vehicles to 25'. This is the trailhead into the Lostine River back country.

MIRROR LAKE, 7595', 14 miles RT, 2000' gain (USGS Eagle Cap). Hike southeast on trail FS-1662 from the Two Pan trailhead at the south end of the Lostine River road. The lake lies at the edge of a basin with many other lakes and directly under the north face of Eagle Cap, a spectacular setting.

EAGLE CAP, 9595', 18 miles RT, 4000' gain (USGS Eagle Cap, Steamboat Lake). From Two Pan trailhead at the south end of the Lostine River road, hike southeast on the East Lostine River trail to Mirror Lake. At the trail junction at the north end of the lake, turn right (west) toward the upper lake but before reaching the lake, turn left (south) toward Eagle Cap on the Horton Pass Trail, FS-1910. Before reaching Horton Pass, keep to the left (south) on trail FS-1805 to ascend Eagle Cap.

CATCHED TWO LAKE, 7980', 8 miles RT, 2400' gain (USGS Steamboat Lake, Eagle Cap). From the Two Pan trailhead at the south end of the Lostine River road, hike southwest on the Lostine River trail (FS-1670) for one mile. Turn right (west) and ascend on trail FS-1679 to the lake.

MINAM LAKE, 7374', 12 miles RT, 1800' gain (USGS Eagle Cap, Steamboat Lake). From the Two Pan trailhead, hike the Lostine River trail, FS-1670, to the lake in a wooded setting.

SPRING BRANCH WILDLIFE AREA, 3500' (USGS Lostine). Situated two miles east of Lostine on the Wallowa River, this wildlife area has beaverdams and many waterbirds in season. Open all year.

ENTERPRISE, 3740', population 1,905, area population 3,047 (USGS Enterprise). Enterprise, the seat of Wallowa County (population 6,911, area 3,150 square miles), has the following facilities and activities: food, stores, lodging, gas. A number of buildings are constructed of the local volcanic rock, including the Masonic Hall, dating from 1899, and the Courthouse, dating from 1909.

Chamber of Commerce, 107 W. 1st St., tel. 426-4622, has maps and information on weekdays. **Wallowa Mountains Forest Service Station and Hells Canyon National Recreation Area Headquarters** at the west edge of town off SR-82, has USGS and National Forest maps, information, and natural history displays. Open weekdays all year. Address: 88401 Highway 82, Enterprise OR 97828. tel. 426-4978.

Events: May Day Parade; Hot Air Balloon Rally, June, tel. 426-3271; **Wallowa County Fair,** August, tel. 426-4097, 426-3143; **Sheep Dog Trials,** August, tel. 426-4097; **Horse Show,** August, tel. 426-6483; **Hell's Canyon Mule Days,** 2nd weekend in September, tel. 432-6191, 426-6191.

Back Country Trips: Hurricane Creek Llama Treks, Route 1, Box 123, 97828, tel. 800-528-9609, 432-4455. Trips in Hell's Canyon and Eagle Cap Wilderness; **Cornerstone Outfitters,** PO Box 509, 97828, tel. 886-8415.

Camping: Outpost RV Park, 66258 Lewiston Hwy, 97828, tel. 426-4027. One mile north of Enterprise on SR-3. Facilities and activities: pull throughs and full hookups for recreational vehicles of any size, showers, laundry, open all year.

ENTERPRISE WILDLIFE AREA, 3560' (USGS Enterprise). This wildlife area, two miles west of Enterprise on SR-82 and 0.1 mile south on Fish Hatchery Road, has beavers, muskrats, mink, and waterbirds.

ENTERPRISE FISH HATCHERY, 3700' (USGS Enterprise). From Enterprise, drive west on SR-82 one mile to Fish Hatchery Road. Turn south and cross the railroad tracks to the hatchery, two miles from SR-82.

MARBLE QUARRY, 6000', 6 miles RT, 1500' gain (USGS Enterprise, Chief Joseph Mountain, WWECW). The quarry is located in Section 19, T2S, R44E. From Enterprise, drive two miles south to Eggleson Road. Turn west to continue on Black Marble Lane after one jog to the north. At the junction with Lime Quarry Road, park and hike 2.5 miles south. The quarry in the past produced black marble for monuments, then limestone for a kiln. A pile of lime left from operation of the kiln is one mile on Lime Quarry Road from Black Marble Lane.

RUBY PEAK, 8814', 12 miles RT, 4200' gain (USGS Enterprise, Chief Joseph Mountain, WWECW). Hike as above toward the Marble Quarry on Lime Quarry Road. Two miles from Black Marble Lane, turn right (south) on the first branch road after passing the Wallowa-Whitman National Forest boundary, at a sharp bend to the east. Ascend on the branch road, which soon becomes a steep, well-travelled trail, to reach Murray Saddle. Turn left at the saddle and follow the Silver Ditch for 0.5 mile. After passing a rocky buttress just above the ditch, cross the ditch and ascend east to the ridge south of Ruby Mountain. Turn north to the summit.

SR-3. From Enterprise, drive north.

VIGNE CAMPGROUND, 3500' (USGS Greenwood Butte).
Drive north from Enterprise on SR-3 for 12 miles then east on gravel roads FS-46 and FS-4625 for 23 miles to the campground on Chesnimnus Creek. Facilities and activities: tents, trailers, water, fishing, bicycling, hiking.

POISON POINT–FAIRCHILD POINT LOOP, high point 5400',
20 miles RT, 2000' gain (USGS Greenwood Butte, Billy Meadows, Poison Point). **Mt. Bicycle Route.** From Vigne campground (see above), ride east on road FS-4625, going left at road junctions to the ridge crest, 5144'. Turn left (west) on FS-46 to the summit of Poison Point, 5400'. Continue northwest along the ridge, keeping left at road junctions. After passing Dougherty Springs campground, 5100', turn south on road FS-4670 to pass Billy Meadows Forest Service Station, 4900'. Keep to the left at road junctions on road FS-4630, descending on the plateau between Billy Creek and Peavine Creek, to return to the Chesnimnus road 0.5 miles north of Vigne campground.

SUMMIT RIDGE–BUCKHORN SPRING LOOP, high point 5400',
20 miles RT, 2000' gain (USGS Poison Point, Deadhorse Ridge, Haas Hollow, Zumwalt). **Mt. Bicycle Route.** From Vigne campground, ride east on road FS-4625, keeping left at road junctions to the ridge crest, 5144', ten miles from the campground and one mile east of Poison Point. Turn right to go east and southeast on the ridge (road FS-46) for ten miles to a junction with road FS-780. Turn east on this road to Buckhorn Observatory. Return to road FS-46 and continue south then west to Thomason Meadows Forest Service Station, where roads branch right and left. Continue southwest on road FS-46, then, one mile southwest of Thomason Meadows Forest Service Station, where road FS-46 ascends southwest away from Chesnimnus Creek, turn west and north at the next junctions on FS-4695-930 to descend Chesnimnus Creek. At road FS-4625, turn left to continue down Chesnimnus Creek and return to Vigne campground.

COYOTE CAMPGROUND, 4800' (USGS).
Drive north from Enterprise on SR-3 for 12 miles then east on gravel road FS-46 to the campground, 27 miles from SR-3. Facilities and activities: tents, trailers, fishing, hiking, bicycling, hunting.

TABLE MOUNTAIN, high point 5244', 15 miles RT, 1000' gain
(USGS Billy Meadows, Table Mountain). **Mt. Bicycle Route.** From Coyote Campground, ride west on the Table Mountain road, FS-4650, to a view point into Joseph Creek Canyon. At 1.5 miles west of Coyote campground, turn south to Kirkland Lookout, the high point. Haystack Rock, 4523', stands on a ridge one mile southwest of road FS-4650 where it crosses Table Mountain, six miles west of Coyote Campground.

HORSE PASTURE RIDGE, high point 5045', 15 miles RT, 600' gain (USGS Billy Meadows, Table Mountain). **Mt. Bicycle Route.** From Coyote Campground, ride one mile west on FS-4650. Turn north to follow trail FS-1712 on an open ridge to an overlook into Joseph Creek Canyon.

DOUGHERTY CAMPGROUND, 5100', (USGS). Drive as above for Coyote Campground, staying on FS-46 to the campground, 32 miles from SR-3. Facilities and activities: fishing, hiking, bicycling, hunting.

TEEPEE BUTTE, 5260', 12 miles RT, 500' gain (USGS Billy Meadows, Teepee Butte). **Mt. Bicycle Route.** From Dougherty Campground, ride east on road FS-46, turning left at a junction 1.5 miles from Dougherty Campground and again left (west) on FS-595 at a junction two miles from Dougherty Campground. The summit of the butte is six miles from the campground. Trails from here descend into Basin Creek and Broady Creek.

WILDHORSE RIDGE, high point 5400', 18 miles RT, 600' gain (USGS Billy Meadows, Teepee Butte). **Mt. Bicycle Route.** From Dougherty Campground, ride east on road FS-46, turning left (north) at a junction 1.5 miles from the campground. Continue north at the next road junction, passing Wildhorse Spring six miles from the campground. Continue north on open Wildhorse Ridge to a viewpoint.

COLD SPRINGS RIDGE, high point 5482', 30 miles RT, 1000' gain (USGS Billy Meadows, Poison Point, Jim Creek Butte). **Mt. Bicycle Route.** From Dougherty Campground, ride east and south eight miles on road FS-46 to the junction with road FS-4680, the Cold Springs Road. Turn north on FS-4680 to the high point near a small pond, passing the branch road left (west) to Cold Springs six miles from FS-46. From the high point, the ridge continues almost level for five miles before dropping sharply toward Joseph Creek.

JIM CREEK BUTTE, 5152', 45 miles RT, 2400' gain (USGS Billy Meadows, Poison Point, Jim Creek Butte). **Mt. Bicycle Route.** From Dougherty Campground, ride as above on the Cold Springs Road, FS-4680. Continue past the high point on FS-4680, descending to Cold Springs Creek. After reaching the bottom of the valley, descend another 0.5 mile, 4400'. Leave bicycle and hike northeast up the ridge to the summit.

BOISE CASCADE FOREST TOUR. Drive 14 miles north of Enterprise on SR-3. Turn west at the entrance sign and begin the driving tour. Stops: (1) Riparian zone. (2) Overdense woodland. (3) Parking for walking tour. (4) Compare different forest management. (5) Bedding area for domestic sheep. (6) Modern forest management area. (7) Viewpoint. Walking tour (one mile): (1) Railroad logging. (2) Larch tree growing in railroad grade. (3) Pond. (4) Natural area. (5) Shelterwood harvest area. (6) Biscuit scabland. (7) Stump remnants of early logging. (8). Thinned area. Continue to parking area.

JOSEPH CANYON VIEWPOINT, 4700' (USGS Shamrock Creek).
North of MP-14, this viewpoint overlooks Joseph Canyon, in which many
layers of Columbia Basalts are exposed.

FLORA, 4338', area population 154 (USGS Flora). North of MP-10 on
SR-3 north of Enterprise, turn left (west) three miles to Flora. No facilities.
A church and school built of wood around the year 1900 still remain.

TROY, 1607' (USGS Troy). From Flora, drive west and northwest
to the Grande Ronde River. Continue southwest up the river to Troy, 16
miles from SR-3. Facilities and activities: **Shilo Inn RV Park**, Troy Rt. Box
85, Enterprise OR 97828, tel. 828-7741, 800-222-2244. Food, store, lodging,
gas, fishing, hiking, boating, electric hookups for recreational vehicles, tent
area, showers. Fee.

MUD CREEK CAMPGROUND, 1600', (USGS Troy). Drive six
miles southwest of Troy up the Grande Ronde River. Facilities and activities: tents, small trailers, boat ramp, fishing, hunting. No fee.

CR-697, FS-46

BUCKHORN CAMPGROUND, 5200' (USGS Deadhorse Ridge, HC-
NRA). From Enterprise, drive southeast on SR-82. Where SR-82 turns
south, go north one mile then east into Zumwalt Road (CR-697). Continue
on roads FS-46 and FS-46-780 to the campground, 43 miles from Enterprise.
Facilities and activities: viewpoint, hiking, bicycling, horse ramp.

CEMETERY RIDGE LOOP, high point 5360', 18 miles RT, 2800'
gain (USGS Deadhorse Ridge, HCNRA). **Mt. Bicycle Route.** From Buckhorn
Campground, ride down the Cherry Creek Road (FS-788) for seven miles.
At a trail junction, turn right and ascend east on trail FS-1731 to Cemetery
Ridge. Go south on the ridge past Buckhorn Viewpoint to return to the
campground.

DEADHORSE BUTTE, 5350', 15 miles RT, 600' gain (USGS Deadhorse Ridge, HCNRA). **Mt. Bicycle Route.** From Buckhorn Campground,
ride west to road FS-46, then north. After one mile, continue north, first
on road FS-760, then on a trail until the ridge drops steeply north.

SR-82

JOSEPH, 4190', population 1,073, area population 1,749 (USGS
Joseph). Facilities and activities: food, stores, lodging, gas, art galleries,
antique mall, impressive view of Chief Joseph Mountain to the south, es-
pecially in winter.

Chamber of Commerce, Maps and information. PO Box 13, 97846, 204
Main St., tel. 432-1015.

City Park, west of South Main St., on 4th. Facilities and activities: picnicking, playground, restrooms in summer.

Wallowa County Museum on Main Street in the First Bank building, constructed in 1888. Open end of May to September, 10am to 5pm every day. Ask to see the chimney flue carved from the local volcanic rock, made before bricks were available in the region.

Methodist Church, East 3rd and South Lake Sts., dating from 1909, is constructed of the colorful local volcanic rock.

Events: Melodrama, Thursday evenings in summer, tel. 432-6855, 432-1015; **Chief Joseph Days**, end of July, tel. 432-1015; **Bank Robbery Reenactment**, Wednesdays at noon, summer, tel. 432-1015; **Mt. Festival**, mid-August, tel. 432-4605; **Mt. Cruise**, early June, tel. 432-2215.

Back Country Trips: Outback Ranch Outfitters, PO Box 384, 97846, tel. 426-4037; **High Country Outfitters**, PO Box 26, 97846, tel. 432-9171; **Hell's Canyon Bicycle Tours**, 102 W. McCully, PO Box 483, 97846, tel. 432-2453; **Backcountry Outfitters**, 85353 Turner Lane, 97846, tel. 432-8080; **Eagle Cap Pack Station**, 59761 Wallowa Lake Hwy., 97846, tel. 432-4145; **Steen's Wilderness Adventures**, 64589 Steen Road, 97846, tel. 432-5315.

Mountain View RV Park, 83450 Joseph Hwy, 97846, tel. 432-2982, one mile north of Joseph on SR-82. Facilities and activities: full hookups for recreational vehicles of any size, showers.

SR-350

MOUNT HOWARD TRAIL, 8256', 8 miles RT, 2800' gain (USGS Joseph, WWECW). From Joseph, drive east on SR-350 for five miles. Turn south on CR-633 toward Ferguson Ridge for four miles. Park at the McCully Creek trailhead, FS-1812. Hike southwest for one mile to the Mt. Howard road. Hike the road at first north, then follow the road as it curves to the southwest to reach the summit.

FERGUSON RIDGE SKI AREA, 4500' (USGS Joseph, Kinney Lake). From Joseph, drive five miles east on road SR-350 then six miles south to the ski area. Facilities and activities: SnoPark, cross country skiing, tow.

LITTLE SHEEP FISH FACILITY, 2700' (USGS Clear Lake Ridge). Drive east and north from Joseph on SR-350 for 20 miles. Here on Little Sheep Creek, returning adult salmon and steelhead are trapped for transport to the fish hatchery for spawning. Young fish brought from the hatchery are acclimatized to the water before release. They will return here when they are adult and ready to spawn.

IMNAHA, 1965', area population 355 (USGS Imnaha). Drive 29 miles on SR-350 northeast of Joseph to this community that has the following facilities and activities: food, store, lodging (577-3112), gas, bicycling, fishing, hiking.

SADDLE CREEK CAMPGROUND, 6800' (USGS Hat Point). Drive
17 miles from Imnaha on the Hat Point Road. Facilities and activities: tents, small recreational vehicles, no trailers, hiking, bicycling, hunting. No fee.

HAT POINT LOOKOUT, 6982', 46 miles RT, 4000' gain (USGS
Imnaha, Sheep Creek Divide, Imnaha). **Mt. Bicycle Route.** At the town of Imnaha at the Imnaha River bridge, park and ride east and southeast on the Hat Point road to the observatory at the summit. Facilities and activities: camping, hiking.

SACAJAWEA CAMPGROUND, 6900', 50 miles RT, 5000' gain
(USGS Hat Point, Sheep Creek Divide, Imnaha, HCNRA). Find the campground one mile north of Hat Point. Facilities and activities: tents and small recreational vehicles, no trailers.

DUG BAR, 1005', 40 miles RT, 800' gain (USGS Haas Hollow, Dead
Horse Ridge, Cactus Mountain). **Mt. Bicycle Route.** From Joseph, drive SR-350 east and north to the end of the pavement at Fence Creek. Park and ride down the Imnaha River road to the end of the road at Dug Bar rapids. Facilities and activities: swimming, boat landing, minimum camping.

NEE-ME-POO NATIONAL RECREATION TRAIL, 1700' to 1000',
20 miles RT riding, 7.5 miles RT hiking, 1000' gain (USGS Haas Hollow, Dead Horse Ridge, Cactus Mountain). **Mt. Bicycle Route.** Park at the end of the paved road (see above for Dug Bar) on the Imnaha River, road SR-350. Ride 10 miles northeast down the Imnaha River to the Nee-Me-Poo trailhead. Leave bicycle and hike the trail to the end at Dug Bar. This trail commemorates the exodus from the Wallowa Valley in 1877 of a band of Indians led by Chief Joseph. This flight for freedom and sanctuary in Canada ended with the loss of many lives and capture by the army led by General O. O. Howard. The Indians were eventually confined to an Indian Reservation in Montana. A descriptive folder is available from the Hells Canyon National Recreation Area headquarters in Enterprise.

FS-39. Wallowa Mountains Loop Road. From Joseph, drive eight miles
east on SR-350 to the intersection with road FS-39. Turn south on FS-39.

SALT CREEK SUMMIT RECREATION AREA, 6150' (USGS Lick
Creek). Drive 19 miles east and south of Joseph on SR-350 and FS-39. Facilities and activities: cross country skiing, hiking, snopark, snowmobile routes, shelter, restrooms.

ANEROID MOUNTAIN, 9702', 14 miles RT, 4500' gain (USGS Lick
Creek, Aneroid Mountain). **Mt. Bicycle Route.** Drive SR-350 and FS-39 for

22 miles from Joseph and park at the junction with the Big Sheep Creek Road, 5500'. Ride four miles southwest on FS-39-100 to the end of the road, 6500'. Leave bicycle and hike west on trail FS-1819, ascending the Middle Fork of Big Sheep Creek. Take the left fork trail at 1.5 miles and the right fork trail (FS-1802) at three miles from the end of the road. One-half mile after passing Bonney Lakes at 7800', leave the trail and ascend north to the summit through Big Sheep Basin (see Aneroid Mountain, p. 113). Mountain sheep are often seen in this basin.

MOUNT NEBO, 8274', 8 miles RT, 2800' gain (USGS Lick Creek, Aneroid Mountain). Mt. Bicycle Route.
From road FS-39, 5500', ride west to the end of the road as for Aneroid Mountain, 6500' (see above). Leave bicycle and ascend west on the trail, taking left forks at 1.5, two, and three miles from the beginning of the trail to the saddle northwest of Mount Nebo. Leave trail and hike southeast up the ridge to the summit.

LICK CREEK CAMPGROUND, 5400' (USGS Lick Creek).
The campground is 25 paved miles from Joseph on SR-350 and FS-39. Facilities and activities: fishing, water, tents, trailers to 25', hiking.

LICK CREEK FOREST SERVICE STATION, 5400' (USGS Lick Creek).
This station has maps and information during the summer months.

GUMBOOT BUTTE, 5978', 20 miles RT, 600' gain (USGS Gumboot Butte, Lick Creek). Mt. Bicycle Route.
From Lick Creek campground, ride east on FS-39 for two miles to the junction with road FS-3930. Turn northeast on FS-3930, keeping right at the first road junction, road FS-3935. At eight miles from the campground, leave bicycle and hike 0.5 miles east to the summit, a volcanic vent that was active during some of the time that the Columbia Basalts were being erupted.

MORGAN BUTTE, 6085', 24 miles RT, 800' gain (USGS Gumboot Butte, Lick Creek). Mt. Bicycle Route.
From Lick Creek campground, ride east two miles on road FS-39. Turn northeast on road FS-3930, keeping to the left at the road junction after 1.5 miles. Take a right fork, 5700', eight miles from Lick Creek campground, going 0.3 mile toward Morgan Butte, to the end of the road at Mahogany Cow Camp. Leave bicycle and hike 0.5 miles to the summit viewpoint, a volcanic vent that was active during some of the time the Columbia Basalts were being erupted.

HARL BUTTE LOOKOUT, 6071', 40 miles RT, 1000' gain (USGS Harl Butte, Gumboot Butte, Lick Creek, HCNRA). Mt. Bicycle Route.
From Lick Creek Campground, ride as for Morgan Butte (see above). Continue past Morgan Butte on road FS-3930 for five miles, then, where FS-3930 bends east, continue northeast on FS-3930-280 to the summit. Harl Butte was a vent for the Columbia Basalt lava flows.

GUMBOOT BUTTE, 5978', 7 miles RT, 1100' gain (USGS Gumboot

Butte). Find the trailhead just west of the intersection of road FS-39 with the Imnaha River road, 34 miles from Joseph on SR-350 and FS-39. Hike northwest to the summit up the North Fork of Gumboot Creek.

IMNAHA FISH FACILITY, 3757' (USGS Puderbaugh Ridge). This fish trapping and release facility is 37 miles from Joseph on SR-350 and FS-39 then one mile left (north) on the Imnaha River Road, FS-3955.

BLACKHORSE CAMPGROUND, 4000' (USGS Gumboot Butte, Lick Creek). This campground on the Imnaha River is 39 miles from Joseph on SR-350 and FS-39. Facilities and activities: tents, trailers, water, fishing, hunting, hiking. Fee.

OLLOKOT CAMPGROUND, 4000' (USGS Gumboot Butte, Lick Creek). This campground on the Imnaha River is 41 miles from Joseph on FS-39. Facilities and activities: tents, trailers, water from pump, fishing, hiking. Fee.

IMNAHA RIVER ROAD, high point 3800', 60 miles RT, 1800' gain (USGS Puderbaugh Ridge, Jaynes Ridge, Sheep Creek Divide, Imnaha, HCNRA). **Mt. Bicycle Route.** From Ollokot or Blackhorse Campgrounds, or from the town of Imnaha, ride the Imnaha River Road along the scenic Imnaha River, passing historic ranches and trails, some of which have been in use for more than one hundred years.

COVERDALE CAMPGROUND, 4300' (USGS Duck Creek). This campground on the Imnaha River is 45 miles southeast of Joseph on FS-39 and FS-3960. The last five miles is a gravel road. Facilities and activities: tents, trailers, water, fishing, hiking. Fee.

HIDDEN CAMPGROUND, 4400' (USGS Duck Creek). This campground on the Imnaha River is 47 miles from Joseph on FS-39 and FS-3960. The last seven miles are gravel road. Facilities and activities: tents and small recreational vehicles, water, fishing. No trailers. Fee.

INDIAN CROSSING CAMPGROUND, 4500' (USGS Deadman Point). This campground on the Imnaha River is 50 miles southeast of Joseph on FS-39 and FS-3960. The last nine miles are on a gravel road. Facilities and activities: tents, trailers, water, fishing, hiking. Fee.

EVERGREEN CAMPGROUND, 4500' (USGS Deadman Point). This campground on the Imnaha River is 50 miles southeast of Joseph on FS-39 and FS-3960. The last nine miles are on a gravel road. Facilities and activities: tents, trailers, water, fishing, hunting, hiking. Fee.

IMNAHA RIVER TRAIL, high point 8000', 3500' gain (to Hawkins Pass), (USGS Deadman Point, Cornucopia, Krag Peak, Eagle Cap). From the trailhead at Indian Crossing, 4526' (see Indian Crossing campground above), the North Fork Imnaha River trail junction is nine miles, Boner Flat trail junction is 10 miles, Blue Creek trail junction is 11 miles, Cliff Creek trail junction is 12 miles, and Hawkins Pass, 8300', is 18 miles. Tenderfoot Pass, 8000', at the head of the North Fork of the Imnaha River on the Boner Flat trail, is 18 miles.

BUCK POINT OVERLOOK, 6141', 20 miles RT, 1000' gain (USGS Homestead, Puderbaugh Ridge). **Mt. Bicycle Route.** At 44 miles from Joseph on road FS-39, park and ride ten miles northeast on Hells Canyon Rim Road, FS-3965, to a viewpoint looking into the Hells Canyon above Hells Canyon Dam and east at the Seven Devils Mountains. Also at the viewpoint is a Bonneville Expedition Interpretive Sign.

McGRAW LOOKOUT, 5920', 20 miles RT, 1000' gain (USGS Puderbaugh Ridge). **Mt. Bicycle Route.** Park and ride as above for Buck Point Overlook. At a branch road right (east), nine miles from the starting point at FS-39, turn left 0.5 mile to the lookout tower, which gives a broad view of the Wallowa Mountains.

HELLS CANYON RIM ROAD 28 miles RT (USGS Homestead, White Monument, Puderbaugh Ridge, HCNRA). From road FS-39 at 20 miles from SR-86 or 44 miles from Joseph, drive north on paved road FS-3965. Three miles from FS-39 turn east to the Hells Canyon Overlook with interpretive signs, picnic tables, and restrooms. No water. Continue north on gravel road FS-3965 to the McGraw Lookout road, nine miles from FS-39. The lookout tower, with views of the Wallowa Mountains and the Seven Devils, is 0.5 mile east. The Buck Point Overlook (see above), is 10 miles from FS-39. Trail FS-1884 begins here. At 11.5 and 12 miles from FS-39, look carefully to find two places where the Snake River is visible from the road or from a few feet east of the road at the sharp drop into Thirty-two Point Creek. These places where the river is visible from the Hells Canyon Rim Road put the scale of Hells Canyon into understandable perspective. At 14 miles from FS-39, the driveable road ends at PO Saddle and a gate.

McGRAW CREEK CABIN, 2800', 18 miles RT, 3500' gain (USGS Homestead, White Monument, Puderbaugh Ridge, HCNRA). From road FS-39 at mile 44 from Joseph, or at mile 19 from SR-86, drive north on road FS-3965 for ten miles to Buck Point. Hike southeast on trail FS-1884 for six miles then southwest on trail FS-1879 to the cabin. Near the junction of FS-1884 and FS-1879 along Spring Creek, marine fossils of late Triassic age have been found in exposures of the Martin Bridge limestone.

LOOKOUT MOUNTAIN, 6792', 15 miles RT, 3000' gain (USGS Homestead, Puderbaugh Ridge, Jaynes Ridge, Squirrel Prairie). **Mt. Bicycle Route.** Drive north on the Hells Canyon Rim Road (see above) and park at PO Saddle, 14 miles from road FS-39. Ride north to the Wilderness Boundary. Leave bicycle and hike north to the summit of Lookout Mountain.

BEAR MOUNTAIN, 6895', 25 miles RT, 1400' gain (USGS White Monument, Squirrel Prairie, HCNRA). **Mt. Bicycle Route.** From the end of the road at PO Saddle, 14 miles from FS-39, and 58 miles from Joseph, ride as above for Lookout Mountain. Leave bicycle and hike north two miles to a trail junction in Squirrel Prairie. Turn right (northeast) on trail FS-1743 for three miles to the summit.

LAKE FORK CAMPGROUND, 3200' (USGS Duck Creek). This campground is 55 miles southeast of Joseph on paved roads SR-350 and FS-39 or eight miles north of SR-86 on FS-39. Facilities and activities: tents, trailers, water, fishing. Fee.

DUCK LAKE CAMPGROUND, 5200' (USGS Duck Lake). This campground is 50 miles southeast from Joseph on road FS-39 and an additional eight miles west on gravelled road FS-66 to Duck Lake. Facilities and activities: tents and small recreational vehicles, fishing, swimming, boating, no power boats. No fee.

SR-82

HURRICANE CREEK CAMPGROUND, 5000' (USGS Chief Joseph Mountain). From the town of Joseph, drive two miles west to Hurricane Creek, then south to the campground four miles from SR-82. Find campsites also at end of Hurricane Creek Road, two miles farther. Facilities and activities: tents, trailers to 25', fishing, hiking, water from stream. No fee.

HURRICANE CREEK TRAILHEAD, 5040' (USGS Chief Joseph Mountain). Drive two miles south of Hurricane Creek campground (see above), eight miles from Joseph.

LEGORE MINE, 8100', 8 miles RT, 3100' gain (USGS Chief Joseph Mountain). Hike south 400' on the Hurricane Creek trail, then turn west on trail FS-1753. After one-fourth mile, where the trail descends to Falls Creek, look for a branch trail to the right that goes directly up the slope then angles right (north) up the steep valley wall. The steep, loose gravel, switchback trail passes a mine entrance before reaching a collapsed log cabin.

LEGORE LAKE, 8957', 10 miles RT, 4000' gain (USGS Chief Joseph Mountain). From the end of the trail at Legore Mine (see above), ascend west cross country on a faint way trail to an open flat area with stream, 8300'. Continue ascending west in the lowest part of the valley in broken rocks to a U-notch to reach a second meadow, 8500'. Turn south and ascend open terrain to a saddle in the subsidiary ridge that connects with the main Twin Peaks–Sawtooth Peak ridge to the west. A way trail appears in the sandy scree about half way from the 8500' meadow to the saddle at 9080'. Descend south from the saddle to the lake.

SAWTOOTH PEAK, 9179', 11 miles RT, 4200' gain (USGS Chief Joseph Mountain). From the second meadow above Legore Mine, 8500', ascend north on steep sandy scree and broken rocks to the ridge just west of the summit. Turn northeast to the summit.

TWIN PEAKS, 9646', 13 miles RT, 4700' gain, (USGS Chief Joseph Mountain). From the meadow at 8500' on the way to Legore Lake (see above), hike southwest to the lowest saddle in the ridge between Sawtooth Peak and Twin Peaks. Turn south and continue up easy rocks on or near the crest of the ridge to reach the gentle west slope of the ridge. Follow on or near the crest of the ridge as it bends east to the twin spires of the highest summit.

ECHO LAKE, 8372', 16 miles RT, 3500' gain (USGS Chief Joseph Mountain). From Hurricane Creek trailhead (see above), hike south four miles on the trail up Hurricane Creek. Turn west and ascend on the trail to the lake.

CHIEF JOSEPH GRAVE. One mile south of Joseph on SR-82, an area with a dramatic view of Chief Joseph Mountain and Wallowa Lake and used by the Nez Perce and Umatilla Indians as a burial ground, has been preserved as a memorial. Frank David McCully, important in the founding of Wallowa County, and other pioneers are also buried here. Point Joseph of Chief Joseph Mountain is at 208°, and Twin Peaks, above Hurricane Creek, is at 250°.

WALLOWA LAKE BOAT LAUNCH. One mile south of Joseph on SR-82 at the north end of Wallowa Lake is a boat ramp and parking area with restrooms.

WALLOWA LAKE, 4600' (USGS Joseph). The basin filled by the lake was carved by glaciers during the glacial age, ending 15,000 years ago. Note the well-defined lateral and terminal moraines that contain the lake. The lake is 283' deep, four miles long, covers 1,508 acres, and the surface water temperature reaches 70° in August. Facilities and activities: stores, food, lodging, gas. Events: Jazz-at-the-Lake, mid-July, 962-3593. Alpenfest, late September, 432-4704.

WALLOWA LAKE STATE PARK, 4650' (USGS Joseph), 72214 Marina Lane, Joseph OR 97846, 432-4185. Drive 5.5 miles south on SR-82 from Joseph. Turn right (west) to the State Park campground. Facilities and activities: the park has pull throughs and full hookups for recreational vehicles up to 90', swimming, boat launch, hiking, sanitary disposal. Fee.

JOSEPH MEADOW, 7527', 10 miles RT, 3200' gain (USGS Joseph, WWECW). Begin in the Wallowa Lake State Park at the Outdoor Theater, 4300'. Head northwest uphill on a broad track. At a three foot diameter pine tree, bend right into a trail (330°). Follow the trail as it ascends across a steep slope above a gully to an "A" frame shed over the water supply, 4700'. Turn left and angle up the slope away from the gully to the crest of a ridge, then ascend a way trail west on the ridge to meet the main trail at 5000'.This trail comes from the Wallowa River above Wallowa Lake. Turn right on the trail and ascend to Joseph Meadow. The hill at the edge of the meadow is the high point.

MOUNT HOWARD GONDOLA, 8200' (USGS Joseph). Drive six miles south of Joseph on SR-82. The top of the gondola ride has views of the Wallowa Mountains and of the Seven Devils Range in Idaho. Operates in summer.

SCENIC MEADOWS RV PARK, 59781 Wallowa Lake Hwy., Joseph OR, 97846, tel. 432-9285. Drive six miles south of Joseph on SR-82. Facilities and activities: partial hookups, showers, dump station, tent area. Seasonal, fee.

PARK AT THE RIVER RV PARK, 59888 Wallowa Lake Hwy., Joseph OR, 97846, tel. 432-8800. Drive six miles south of Joseph on SR-82. Facilities and activities: full hookups, showers, tent area. Seasonal, fee.

SOUTH WALLOWA LAKE STATE PARK, 4646' (USGS Joseph). This state park is at the south end of SR-82, 6.5 miles from Joseph. Facilities and activities: picnicking, restrooms.

WALLOWA RIVER TRAILHEAD, 4600'. Drive 6.5 miles south of Joseph on SR-82. The trails starting here give access to Lake Basin and Aneroid Basin.

ANEROID LAKE, 7500', 12 miles RT, 3000' gain (USGS Joseph, Aneroid Mountain). From the Wallowa River Trailhead (see above), hike the trail southeast to the lake.

ANEROID MOUNTAIN, 9702', 18 miles RT, 5100' gain (USGS Joseph, Aneroid Mountain). Hike as above to Aneroid Lake. Continue on the trail southeast to the saddle between the lake and the drainage to the south. Leave the trail, turn north and hike cross country, passing east of the summit to reach the north ridge. Once on the ridge, turn south to the summit.

ANEROID LAKE–LAKE BASIN–WALLOWA RIVER LOOP, high point 8900', 37 miles RT, 6500' gain (USGS Joseph, Aneroid Mountain, Eagle Cap). From parking at the end of SR-82 near the South Wallowa Lake State Park, hike six miles southeast up the East Fork of the Wallowa River on trail FS-1804 to Aneroid Lake, 7500' (camping). Continue south from Aneroid Lake on trail FS-1804 for one mile to the junction of trails FS-1802 and FS-1814 at 8200'. Turn right (south) on trail FS-1814 to climb over Tenderfoot Pass, 8500', to a junction with trail FS-1831. Continue right (west) on trail FS-1831 to ascend over the pass between Pete's Point and Sentinel Peak, 8900', and reach trail FS-1820 near the West Fork of the Wallowa River (camping), ten miles from Aneroid Lake and 6600'.

From the junction with trail FS-1820 on the West Fork of the Wallowa River, go south two miles to the Frazier Lakes (camping). Turn west on trail FS-1806 to continue on the West Fork of the Wallowa River to pass Glacier Lake and cross Glacier Pass before reaching Moccasin Lake, five miles from Frazier Lake. To continue the loop, from Moccasin Lake, go southeast in Lake Basin to pass Douglas Lake and Lee Lake before reaching Horseshoe Lake, three miles from Moccasin Lake. From Horseshoe Lake, descend east three miles to rejoin the West Fork Wallowa River Trail, FS-1820. Turn north 3.3 miles to reach a junction (camping) with the Adam Creek-Ice Lake Trail, FS-1808. From this trail junction, the Wallowa Lake Trailhead is 2.8 miles north. The following ten hikes can be taken from this loop:

BONNEVILLE MOUNTAIN, high point 9200', 2 miles RT, 1700' gain (USGS Aneroid Mountain). From Aneroid Lake, ascend west on steep sandy scree to the highest point of Bonneville Mountain.

ANEROID MOUNTAIN, 9702', 6 miles RT, 2200' gain (USGS Aneroid Mountain). From Aneroid Lake, hike south on trail FS-1804 for one mile then go southeast on trail FS-1802 for one mile to a saddle. Leave the trail at the saddle and ascend diagonally northeast cross country past the apparent summit of Aneroid Mountain. Turn north on stable talus to reach the ridge east of the summit. Turn west to the summit.

MOUNT NEBO, 8274', 13 miles RT, 3200' gain (USGS Aneroid Mountain). From Aneroid Lake, hike one mile south on trail FS-1804 to a junction, then go southeast on trail FS-1802 for 5.5 miles, ascending over a saddle at 8400' before descending to 7200' and another trail junction. Turn south and ascend on trail FS-1819 until the trail turns to the northwest. Leave the trail and ascend south cross country to the summit.

PETE'S POINT, 9675', 2 miles RT, 1300' gain (USGS Aneroid Mountain). At a high point on trail FS-1831, one mile after leaving trail FS-1914 and 3.5 miles from Aneroid Lake, leave the trail and hike north to the summit on gentle terrain.

SENTINEL PEAK, 9401', 2 miles RT, 700' gain (USGS Aneroid Mountain). From the saddle between Pete's Point and Sentinel Peak on trail FS-1831 and six miles from Aneroid Lake, leave the trail and hike south up broken rocks to the summit.

HAWKINS PASS, 8350', 5 miles RT, 1500' gain (USGS Eagle Cap). From Frazier Lake, hike south on trail FS-1820 to the crest of Hawkins Pass. For summits accessible from Hawkins Pass, see p. 76.

EAGLE CAP, 9517', 6 miles RT, 2300' gain (USGS Eagle Cap). From camp at Moccasin Lake, hike west to Mirror Lake. Continue on the trail south toward Horton Pass. After one mile take the left fork (southeast) to the summit.

ICE LAKE, 7849', 10 miles RT, 2300' gain (USGS Eagle Cap, Joseph). From the junction of the West Fork Wallowa River Trail, FS-1820, and the Adam Creek–Ice Lake trail, FS-1808, hike west five miles to the lake (camping).

MATTERHORN, 9832', 4 miles RT, 2000' gain (USGS Eagle Cap). From Ice Lake, hike west on a way trail, passing Ice Lake on the north side, to reach the summit.

SACAJAWEA PEAK, 9838', 5 miles RT, 2200' gain (USGS Eagle Cap). From the northwest end of Ice Lake, find a way trail ascending northwest to the summit (see below).

CHIEF JOSEPH TRAIL, high point 7527', 15 miles RT, 3300' gain (USGS Chief Joseph Mountain). From the Wallowa River trailhead (see above), hike 0.5 mile south to a junction. Turn northwest, crossing the Wallowa River. Continue north, then ascend on switchbacks to the end of the trail in Joseph Meadow.

ICE LAKE, 7900', 15 miles RT, 3400' gain (USGS Joseph, Aneroid Mountain, Eagle Cap). From the Wallowa River trailhead at the end of SR-82, hike south on the West Fork of the Wallowa River for three miles. Turn west and ascend the trail to Ice Lake.

MATTERHORN, 9832', 16 miles RT, 5200' gain (USGS Joseph, Aneroid Mountain, Eagle Cap). From the Wallowa River trailhead at the south end of SR-82, hike south on the West Fork of the Wallowa River three miles to the Ice Lake trail junction. Take the right fork (west) trail and ascend west, passing Ice Lake on the north side. Continue on the trail to the summit. Matterhorn and Sacajawea Peak are limestone and marble of the Wallowa Terrane. A scree slope of marble crystals on the southeast slope of the Matterhorn can be descended in minutes.

SACAJAWEA PEAK, 9838', 20 miles RT, 5300' gain (USGS Joseph, Aneroid Mountain, Eagle Cap). Hike as above to Ice Lake. Pass the lake on the north side and ascend west to the ridge. Turn north and follow the ridge to the summit.

US-395

Umatilla Bridge to Silvies

UMATILLA INFORMATION CENTER. From the west intersection of US-395 and US-730, turn west on US-730 to the first stop signal, then go north parallel to US-395. If entering from Washington State on I-82/US-395, exit to US-730 immediately after crossing the bridge and turn west on US-730. The information center, on the left at 0.3 miles from US-730, has information on the local Indians and early settlers and a large selection of free maps and brochures concerning local activities and facilities. Opens end of May and closes in October.

UMATILLA MARINA PARK AND CAMPGROUND. Drive as above for the Umatilla Information Center, turning left on 3rd St. before reaching the information center. Follow directions signs to the marina, 0.8 miles from US-730. Facilities and activities: boat launch, boat mooring, boat docks, picnicking, pull throughs and full hookups for recreational vehicles of any length, showers, water, parking for boat trailers, no tents. Telephone: 922-3939.

McNARY DAM-UMATILLA BRIDGE INFORMATION. West of the boat launch ramp in Umatilla Marina Park, look for examples of the three thousand 12 ton concrete tetrahedrons that were dropped into the Columbia River to form a coffer dam to divert the water of the river during construction of McNary Dam. Attached to two of these tetrahedrons are plaques telling the history of the dam and bridge construction.

UMATILLA BRIDGE, 291' (USGS Umatilla). From the Umatilla Information Center, drive south to the first cross street and turn east on 3rd St. under I-82/US-395. Park just east of the underpass. Walk north on the walkway to the bridge. The middle of the bridge gives a sweeping view of the Columbia River and the McNary Dam. Work on the bridge was completed in 1955. The approach overlooks the McNary Wildlife Area. **McNary Wildlife Area.** A road immediately east of the Umatilla bridge goes north into the Wildlife Area and gives access to the Columbia River.

UMATILLA, 280', population 3,085 (USGS Umatilla). On US-730 one mile west of US-395, this town has the following facilities and activities: stores, food, lodging, gas. Travel information: **Umatilla Chamber of Commerce**, 1300 Sixth St., Suite A, 97882, 922-4825. **Umatilla Park:** Drive one mile west of the Umatilla Bridge on US-730. Turn south into the park, situated on the Umatilla River. Facilities and activities: picnicking, playground, restrooms, boat launch, water.

Events: Landing Days, early September, tel. 922-4825.

Camping and RV Parks: Umatilla Trailer Court. From the Umatilla Bridge, drive west on US-730 for 0.5 mile. Facilities and activities: hookups, showers, laundry, no pets, open all year. Telephone: 922-4816. Shady Rest RV Park. From the Umatilla bridge, drive west 2.5 miles on US-730. Facilities and activities: pull throughs and full hookups for recreational vehicles of any length, showers, tent area, open all year. Telephone: 922-5041.

McNARY DAM OVERLOOK. At the intersection where US-395 turns south from US-730, turn north toward McNary Dam and stop at the overlook, which has an informative map and historical display.

McNARY DAM, 361' (USGS Umatilla). From the overlook above, continue north to the dam, which has several viewing and visiting areas: fish ladder, generator room, dam operation area, beach, boat launch, restrooms, no camping. Construction on the dam began in 1947 and first generated electricity in 1954.

WALLULA LAKE, 340' (USGS Umatilla, Hat Rock, Juniper, Juniper Canyon). The lake extends from McNary Dam into Washington State past the junction of the Snake River with the Columbia River.

SPILLWAY PARK. From the McNary Dam parking area, drive north to Spillway Park. Picnicking, restrooms, no camping.

McNARY WILDLIFE PARK. From the intersection at the entrance to the McNary Dam visitor area, drive west 0.2 miles to the wildlife area and nature trail. Another road 0.5 mile west gives access to the river in the Wildlife Park. Restrooms.

WEST McNARY PARK. Drive 0.5 mile from the entrance to the McNary Dam visitor Area. Facilities and activities: picnicking, restrooms, playfield, no camping.

BOAT LAUNCH RAMP. From the east intersection of US-730 and US-395, drive north to the first intersection. Turn east to the boat launch ramp.

McNARY, 400' (USGS). Drive one mile east from US-395 on US-730. The housing for the construction workers during construction of the dam is now private housing. Facilities and activities: lodging, golf.

McNARY BEACH PARK. From US-395 at the east intersection with US-730, drive east on US-730 for two miles. Turn left (north) 1.5 miles to the park at a beach on Wallula Lake. Facilities and activities: picnicking, swimming, restrooms.

HAT ROCK STATE PARK, 360' (USGS Hat Rock). Drive east eight miles on US-730 from US-395. Turn north to the park. Facilities and activities: Picnicking, launch ramp, moorage, docks, swimming, hiking trails. Lewis and Clark camped in this area on October 19, 1805. An informative sign tells the story. Hat Rock is a remnant of Columbia Basalt left by the floods from Lake Missoula, which scoured this area at the end of the glacial age. These floods were hundreds of feet deep at this point.

HAT ROCK CAMPGROUND, 360' (USGS Hat Rock). This private campground, west of Hat Rock State Park, has the following facilities and activities: pull throughs and full hookups for recreational vehicles of any length, tent area, swimming, store, showers, no dogs, open all year. Route 3, Box 3780, Hermiston, 97838, tel. 567-4188.

SAND STATION RECREATION AREA, 360' (USGS). Drive 18 miles east on US-730 from US-395. Facilities and activities: camping, swimming, fishing.

POWER CITY, 445' (USGS Umatilla). On US-395 beginning south of US-730, the town has the following facilities and activities: food, stores, gas.

HERMISTON, 457', population 10,040 (area 23,673) (USGS Hermiston). Facilities and activities: food, lodging, stores, gas, several city parks with fireplaces, restrooms, and water.

Chamber of Commerce, at 540 S. Highway 395, has maps and information. PO Box 185, 97838, tel. 567-6151.

Inland Empire Bank Museum, at 101 E street, has displays of clothing and artifacts from Indians of the Northwest and the early settlers of the region. A totem pole is part of the collection.

J. R. Simplot Company, at Hinkle, has tours of their production facility for making various potato products, including french fries for McDonalds. Telephone 567-9733.

Maxwell Siding Railroad Display, off US-395, near Hinkle. Call 567-6151 for tour.

Marlette Homes, 400 W. Elm St. A manufacturer of moveable homes has tours. Call 567-5546.

Events: Home & Garden Fair, mid-March, tel. 567-6151. **Cutting Horse Show**, Fair Grounds, early May, tel. 567-6151. **Armed Forces Day**, Umatilla Depot. **Gem & Mineral Show**, early June, tel. 567-6151. **Spud Fest**, downtown Hermiston, early July, tel. 567-6151. **4-H Horse Show**, early August, Fair Grounds, tel. 567-6151. **Umatilla County Fair**, early August, Fair Grounds, tel. 567-6151.

RV Parks: Umatilla County Fairgrounds, 425 W. Orchard St., 97838, tel. 567-6121. Hookups, showers. No tents.

Back Country Trips: Columbia River Guide Service, 735 NW 3rd St., 97838, tel. 800-821-2119. River trips. **Mid Columbia Outfitters**, Rt. 6, Box 6017,

97838, tel. 567-7107. Fishing, hunting, and pack trips.

COLD SPRING NATIONAL WILDLIFE REFUGE, 623' (USGS
Stanfield, Umatilla). From US-395 in Hermiston, drive four miles east on
SR-207. Where SR-207 bends north, continue three miles east. The refuge
has 3,000+ acres of land, marsh, and water for migrating and resident birds.
Fishing, hunting in season, and boating (no power boats) are allowed.

STANFIELD, 592', population 1,568, (USGS Stanfield). Facilities and
activities: food, stores, lodging, gas, Fourth of July celebration with parade.
Stanfield RV Park, 345 Main St., tel. 449-8784. Hookups for recreational
vehicles of any size. Showers, laundry. No tents.

From Stanfield, US-395 joins highway I-84 to Pendleton, then turns
south.

McKAY CREEK NATIONAL WILDLIFE REFUGE, 1152' (USGS
McKay Reservoir). At MP-7 on US-395, turn east to an information display.
Continue south two miles from US-395 to the McKay Reservoir dam. On
the 1,837 acres of the refuge, geese and other water birds feed and rest
during their migrations. Facilities and activities: hunting, fishing, boating,
no power boats, hiking. Open each day from one hour before sunrise to one
hour after sunset. No camping and no open fires. Closed from the end of
the State Waterfowl Season to the end of February.

PILOT ROCK, 1636', population 1,478 (area 2,642) (USGS Pilot
Rock). The town is named for the imposing cliff of Columbia Basalts to the
southwest that guided early travelers. The region grows wheat and cattle
and is the end of a Union Pacific Railroad branch line from Pendleton. Facilities and activities: food, stores, lodging, gas. A city park on Birch Creek
off US-395 at the south edge of town has picnicking, restrooms, water. **Back
Country Tours: Anderson Land & Livestock**, 49603 McKay Creek Road, 97801,
tel. 443-9213, 276-8546. Hunting trips.

INDIAN LAKE CAMPGROUND, 4173' (USGS Bally Mountain).
From Pilot Rock, drive south nineteen miles on East Birch Creek Road
to this recreation area. Facilities and activities: tents, trailers, picnicking,
swimming, fishing, hiking.

McCLELLAN MEADOW LOOP, high point 5000', 20 miles RT,
1200' gain (USGS Bally Mountain, Tamarack Gulch). **Mt. Bicycle Route.**
From Indian Lake Campground, ride south, taking left turns, on road FS-
275, joining road FS-21 from the left at two miles. Continue south 1.5 miles,
descending to McCoy Creek, 3870'. Turn right (northwest) for one-fourth
mile, then turn southwest, ascending a branch of McCoy Creek and staying
on the road in the bottom of the canyon, avoiding roads that ascend out
of the canyon. The road goes west just north of the Starkey Experimental

Forest (see p. 141). Where the road levels onto a plateau at the upper (west) end of the canyon, 4600', continue west and southwest to join a road that follows the south edge of the plateau. Continue west, ascending gradually to 5000', taking the west fork at road junctions to stay on the ridge between Meadow Creek to the south and McCoy Creek to the north. At ten miles from Indian Lake campground, leave road FS-21, turning right (northwest) on FS-2115, which curves north into McClellan Meadow, passing McClellan Spring at the site of an old cabin. Join road FS-5427, turning right (northeast). Continue northeast on road FS-5427 to return to East Birch Creek Road, which leads east to Indian Lake campground.

GRIEFY SUMMIT, 5219', 30 miles RT, 2500' gain (USGS Granite Meadows, Tamarack Gulch, Sevenmile Creek). **Mt. Bicycle Route.** From US-395 in Pilot Rock, drive 10 miles south on East Birch Creek Road (toward Indian Lake) to the junction with the Pearson Creek Road. Park and ride south on Pearson Creek Road, FS-54, ascending along Pearson Creek to the crest of a ridge and a road junction, ten miles from the starting point. Turn northeast on road FS-5411, following the ridge to the highest point in an open meadow. Avoid road forks that descend from the ridge or turn away from the northeast direction of the ridge.

GRANITE MEADOWS, high point 5129', 34 miles RT, 3000' gain (USGS Granite Meadows, Carney Butte). **Mt. Bicycle Route.** At MP-17 on US-395, one mile south of Pilot Rock, drive south on paved Yellow Jacket Road. Park at the junction of Bridge Creek and West Birch Creek, five miles from US-395. Ride south on Yellow Jacket Road, the right branch. Reach the site of Mountain Home, a supply center and stage stop during the days when mining was active in the region, eight miles from the starting point. From the Mountain Home site, continue south into road FS-5415, entering the Umatilla National Forest at 11 miles and meeting road FS-5412 at 13 miles on a forested plateau. Turn left (east) on road FS-5412 for three miles to a junction with road FS-54 at the high point near Granite Meadows. Several roads provide an opportunity to explore Granite Meadows and this plateau region. Return on road FS-5412 past the junction with road FS-5415 and continue west on the plateau until the road begins to descend steeply. Turn back east and north to the junction of FS-5415 to return to the starting point on Yellow Jacket road. Between one and two miles northwest of Mountain Home, garnet-bearing mica schist is exposed along the road and in the creek bottom north of the road. The sand in the creek bed is reported to be tinted pink by its content of garnet. The garnet here is not of gem quality. Continue northwest on Yellow Jacket Road to return to the starting point.

COLUMBIA PLATEAU OVERLOOK, MP-37. Before entering the forest while driving south on US-395, stop for a view to the north and west over hundreds of square miles of Columbia Basalt flows. Single eruptions covered this entire area, coming from vents most of which are now hidden.

BATTLE MOUNTAIN STATE PARK, 4167', 370 acres, MP-38 (USGS Gurdane, Carney Butte). On July 8, 1878, in the battle of Willow Springs, General O. O. Howard with a detachment of soldiers from the Army Post in Vancouver, Washington Territory, defeated a band of Paiute and Bannock Indians under Chief Egan who had come from Idaho. Facilities: restrooms, water, picnicking, hiking.

CARNEY BUTTE LOOKOUT, 4813', 5 miles RT, 1000' gain (USGS Carney Butte). From Battle Mountain State Park, cross US-395 ascend generally east on a branch road to the summit of Carney Butte. The lookout tower has a view of the battleground and the wide plains to the north.

JUNCTION SR-244, MP-49. Ukiah is one mile east.

UKIAH-DALE STATE PARK, 3300' (USGS Bridge Creek). On US-395 at MP-51, two miles south of the Ukiah junction, this state park has the following facilities and activities: tents, trailers of any size, showers, hiking in the Bridge Creek State Wildlife Area. No hookups. Fee.

NORTH FORK JOHN DAY RIVER, 2715' to 2200', 50 miles RT, 600' gain (USGS Bridge Creek, Deerhorn Creek, Meadowbrook Summit, Ritter, Slickear Mountain). **Mt. Bicycle Route.** Where US-395 from the north meets the North Fork John Day River near MP-61, park and ride west down the river to the junction with the Middle Fork John Day River. The road continues down the river to the town of Monument, touching the river at many places.

CAMAS PEAK, 3954', 3 miles RT, 1200' gain (USGS Bridge Creek). Where US-395 meets the North Fork John Day River, park, cross the fence, and hike to the summit in the Bridge Creek State Wildlife Area. The summit provides a view west over the North Fork John Day River valley. The Wildlife Area is closed to entry from the first of December to the end of April.

LATITUDE 45°, 2700' (USGS Bridge Creek). At the North Fork John Day River, US-395 crosses the 45th parallel, halfway between the North Pole and the Equator.

FLETCH, 3999', 3 miles RT, 1300' gain (USGS Bridge Creek). Park on the north side of the US-395 bridge over the North Fork John Day River. Cross the fence and hike north to the summit in the Bridge Creek State Wildlife Area. The summit gives a comprehensive view east into the North Fork John Day River valley. The Wildlife Area is closed to entry from the first of December to the end of April.

NORTH FORK JOHN DAY RIVER, high point 3400', 40 miles RT, 600' gain (USGS Bridge Creek, Ukiah SE, The Cockscomb, Kelsay Butte, NFJUW). **Mt. Bicycle Route.** Park on the north side of the US-395 bridge over the North Fork John Day River. Ride east on road FS-55, ascending along the river, passing evidence of old mining activity and ending at the North Fork John Day River Wilderness boundary where the the Big Creek trail begins. The Wilderness is closed to bicycles.

TOLL BRIDGE CAMPGROUND, 2800' (USGS Dale). For access to the campground, from the north end of North Fork John Day River bridge on US-395, drive east along the river to the next bridge. Turn right (south) across the bridge to find the campground between the road and the stream. Facilities and activities: tents, trailers to 25', water from stream, fishing, swimming, boating, bicycling. No fee.

DESOLATION BUTTE LOOP, 7028', 55 miles RT, 4500' gain (USGS Dale, The Cockscomb, Sharp Ridge, Desolation Butte, Kelsay Butte). **Mt. Bicycle Route.** From Toll Bridge Campground, ride east 10 miles on road FS-10, near or above Desolation Creek, to the junction of Desolation Creek and Spring Creek. Turn left (east) on road FS-1010, turning right (east) after two miles to continue on the ridge. Near the summit of Desolation Butte, turn north on road FS-300 to reach the summit. After returning from the summit on road FS-300 to road FS-1010, turn left (southeast) to road FS-10. Turn right on road FS-10 and descend along Desolation Creek to the starting point.

DALE, 2900', MP-66 (USGS Dale). Facilities and activities: store, gas.

PUTNEY MOUNTAIN LOOP, high point 5250', 25 miles RT, 1600' gain (USGS Dale, The Cockscomb, Wildcat Point, Meadow Brook Summit). **Mt. Bicycle Route.** Drive three miles south of the North Fork John Day River on US-395 to MP-66. Park and ride southeast on road FS-3969, then immediately go right on road FS-3974, 3140', which ascends Brush Creek. At the junction with road FS-3980, 4880', and eight miles from US-395, ride east one mile past Road Camp Spring. Turn southeast on road FS-160 to the summit of Putney Mountain, 5250'. From the summit of Putney Mountain, Desolation Butte Lookout is slightly south of directly east (100°) and 10 miles away. On returning to road FS-3980, ride west two miles, passing junctions with roads FS-3974 to the right and FS-3986 to the left after one mile. Continue southwest on road FS-3980. At three miles from road FS-3974, turn northwest. One-fourth mile after FS-3980 turns north, leave bicycle and hike southwest one-fourth mile to Point 4921', with a view southwest of the Middle Fork John Day River. On returning to bicycle, continue north and west on roads FS-3980 and CR-21 to US-395. Turn north to the starting point.

MEADOWBROOK RV PARK, 3800', MP-70 (USGS Meadowbrook Summit). Facilities and activities: store, LP gas, gas, pull throughs, partial hookups, showers, open all year, hiking, bicycling. Address: Box 37, Dale 97880. Telephone: 421-3104.

BONE POINT LOOKOUT, 4527', 16 miles RT, 800' gain (USGS Meadow Brook Summit). **Mt. Bicycle Route.** From Meadowbrook at MP-70, ride west and north on road FS-3963, ascending along Meadow Brook for the first two miles. After seven miles, turn left (north) on road FS-060 for one mile to the summit.

BONE POINT LOOP, high point 4527', 24 miles RT, 2000' gain (USGS Meadow Brook Summit, Dale, NFJDE). **Mt. Bicycle Route.** From Meadowbrook at MP-70, ride northeast on US-395, descending to the North Fork John Day River near Meadow Brook. After crossing the bridge over the North Fork John Day River, turn west down the river for three miles. At a junction, turn left (south), cross a bridge over the North Fork John Day River and ascend south on road FS-3963. At five miles from the North Fork John Day River, turn right (north) on FS-060 to the summit of Bone Point Lookout. Return from the lookout to road FS-3963 and continue south to return to the starting point at Meadowbrook.

RITTER HOT SPRINGS, 2500' (USGS Ritter). At MP-77, just before crossing the Middle Fork John Day River, drive right (west) down the river 10 miles to the hot springs. Facilities and activities: baths, swimming, showers, picnicking, open Memorial Day to Labor Day. Telephone: 421-3846. Zeolites have been found in the area.

GALENA–SUSANVILLE, 3766', 40 miles RT, 1000' gain (USGS Flowers Gulch, Wildcat Point, Sharp Ridge, Susanville). **Mt. Bicycle Route.** From the Middle Fork John Day River bridge on US-395 at MP-77, ride east up the river to the old mining community of Galena. From Galena, the mining town of Susanville is two miles northeast up Elk Creek. (See Ghost Towns of the Northwest by Norman D. Weis). This area is reported to have produced five pound gold nuggets as well as lead ore.

LONG CREEK, 3772', population 249 (area population 970), MP-90 (USGS Long Creek). Facilities and activities: food, stores, lodging, gas. **Hitchin' Post Trailer Court**, tents, trailers, showers, open all year. Telephone: 421-3043.

LONG CREEK MOUNTAIN–FOX VALLEY LOOP, high point 5102', 32 miles RT, 2000' gain (USGS Long Creek, Fox, NFJDW). **Mt. Bicycle Route.** From Long Creek, ride west on the road to Monument for eight miles. Turn left (south) on the Basin Road (CR-9) and ascend over Long Creek Mountain (high point 4866') into the Fox Valley to meet road CR-25. After joining CR-25, turn left (east) to the community of Fox on

US-395. Turn left (west) on US-395 over Long Creek Mountain summit (5102') to return to Long Creek.

TABLE ROCK, 4995', 12 miles RT, 1400' gain (USGS Hamilton). **Mt. Bicycle Route.** From Long Creek, drive west 12 miles on the road to Monument. At the junction with road CR-8 in the community of Hamilton, park and ride south on CR-8 along the east fork of Deer Creek for four miles. Turn west and ascend on road FS-165 to the summit for a commanding view of this semi-desert country.

KEENEY POINT, 5430', 20 miles RT, 1800' gain (USGS Long Creek, Keeney Point). **Mt. Bicycle Route.** From Long Creek, ride east on CR-18 for nine miles to the junction with CR-35, two miles east of the Forest Boundary. Turn north on roads CR-35 and FS-3514 for two miles. Leave bicycle and hike west one-half mile to the summit. Desolation Butte lookout tower is 20 miles distant to the northeast (54°).

FOX, 4300', MP-98 (USGS Fox). This area of cattle ranches was first settled in the 1870's. A church from this time still remains but other services are gone.

BEECH CREEK CAMPGROUND, 4687' (USGS Beech Creek Summit–Johnson Saddle). This minimum campground is near MP-105. Facilities and activities: tents, trailers to 25'. No fee.

BLACK BUTTE, 6235', 5 miles RT, 1600' gain (USGS Beech Creek Summit–Johnson Saddle, Belshaw Meadows). From Beech Creek Campground, hike southwest to the summit, using or crossing several roads.

COTTONWOOD CAMPGROUND, 4150', MP-106 (USGS Beech Creek Summit–Johnson Saddle). Facilities and activities: tents, trailers to 25'. No fee.

LONG CREEK MOUNTAIN–HUCKLEBERRY BUTTE LOOP, high point 6206', 30 miles RT, 1800' gain (USGS Fox, Long Creek, Beech Creek Summit–Johnson Saddle, Belshaw Meadows, Magone Lake). **Mt. Bicycle Route.** From Beech Creek campground or Cottonwood campground, ride north on US-395 three miles past the community of Fox to Long Creek Mountain summit. Turn east on road FS-3940 to the high point at the summit of Long Creek Mountain, five miles from US-395. Continue south on road FS-3940 along the ridge of Long Creek Mountain to the junction of FS-3945 ten miles from US-395, 5600'. Turn east 0.5 mile on road FS-3945 to Huckleberry Camp, a primitive camp site. Leave bicycle and hike north to the summit of Huckleberry Butte, 6084'. Return to FS-3945, ride west and southwest on road FS-3945 for three miles from Huckleberry Camp, crossing Day Creek. One mile west of Day Creek, turn south on roads FS-213 and FS-266 for two miles. Join road FS-131, turning west to pass Raddue Forest Service Station and return to US-395 at Cottonwood campground, two miles southeast of Beech Creek campground.

NIPPLE BUTTE, 6157', 20 miles RT, 2200' gain (USGS Beech Creek Summit–Johnson Saddle, Magone Lake). **Mt. Bicycle Route.** From Cottonwood Campground, ride south on US-395 for three miles. At Mountain Rest, MP-109, ride northeast from US-395 on road FS-3940, turning right (east) at a junction after three miles, staying on road FS-3940. The road bends north and, after another three miles, comes to a road junction. Turn right (east) on road FS-3947 for one mile. Leave bicycle and hike south 0.5 mile to the summit.

KEENEY MEADOWS LOOP, high point 5600', 30 miles RT, 1600' gain (USGS Beech Creek Summit–Johnson Saddle, Magone Lake). **Mt. Bicycle Route.** Ride as above toward Nipple Butte. At six miles from US-395, remain on road FS-3940, going north through Keeney Meadows to a junction with road FS-3945. Turn west on FS-3945 to return to US-395. Ride south to Cottonwood Campground.

MAGONE LAKE CAMPGROUND, 5000' (USGS Magone Lake). Near MP-110 on US-395, drive east on road FS-36 for seven miles. Turn left (north) on FS-3618 to the campground on Magone Lake, nine miles from US-395. Facilities and activities: tents, trailers to 25', water, hiking, fishing, boating, swimming, boat launch. Fee.

LAKE BUTTE, 6227', 4 miles RT, 1300' gain (USGS Magone Lake). From the Magone Lake campground, hike north cross-country to the summit.

BIG ROCK, 5990', 15 miles RT, 1000' gain (USGS Magone Lake). **Mt. Bicycle Route.** From Magone Lake Campground, ride north then east to join road FS-3620 after one mile. Turn left (north) toward the summit. A road spur left at five miles from Magone Lake Campground goes to the summit of Lake Butte. At seven miles, where the road turns sharply left (west) and begins to descend, leave bicycle and hike northeast to the summit.

EAGLE ROCK, 5160', 20 miles RT, 400' gain ((USGS Magone Lake, Cougar Rock). **Mt. Bicycle Route.** From Magone Lake Campground, ride south to road FS-36. Turn left (east), then north, staying on road FS-36 to its junction with road FS-3640. Leave bicycle and hike north to the summit.

MOUNT VERNON, 2871', population 538 (USGS Mt. Vernon). Lying at the junction of US-26 and US-395, the town has the following facilities and activities: food, stores, lodging, gas. **Events: Cinnabar Mountain Rendevous** on Memorial Day weekend: parade, bicycle races, sawing contest, archery contest, dance, games, potluck dinner. For information, call 932-4501, 932-4688.

CLYDE HOLLIDAY STATE PARK, 2900', MP-155 (USGS Mt. Vernon). This campground, 1.5 miles east of Mt. Vernon on US-26/US-395, has the following facilities and activities: electrical hookups for recreational vehicles, maximum site 60', showers, tent area, hiking. Fee.

ALDRITCH MOUNTAINS LOOP, high point 5500', 40 miles RT, 3000' gain (USGS Fall Mountain, Canyon Mountain, John Day, Mount Vernon). **Mt. Bicycle Route.** From Clyde Holliday State Park, ride east on US-26 for one mile. Turn south on CR-49 and ascend over the ridge of Aldritch Mountain to descend toward the Silvies River valley. At 4800', where CR-49 bends to the southwest at a junction, turn east on road FS-333 for three miles to meet US-395. Turn left and ride north to Canyon City and John Day. At John Day, turn left (west) on US-26 to return to Clyde Holliday State Park.

JOHN DAY, 3085', population 1,836 (area 4,919) (USGS John Day). Forest maps and information are available at the Malheur National Forest Supervisor's office at 139 NE Dayton St., and at the Bear Valley and Long Creek Ranger District Office at 528 E. Main St. For other information, visit the Grant County Chamber of Commerce, 281 West Main Street, 97845, tel. 575-0547, or the Bureau of Land Management office at 420 W. Main St., 97845, tel. 575-2632. Facilities and activities: food, stores, lodging, gas.

Kam Wah Chung & Company Museum, located near the central City Park, has many artifacts from the early Chinese immigrants of the region. The building dates from 1866 when it was built to house a trading post at the peak of the mining activity. For many years, the building served as a religious center and store for the Chinese, who, at one time, were the largest ethnic group in the area. Hours Mon–Thurs 9am-12pm, 1pm-5pm; Sat–Sun 1pm-5pm.

John Day Fossil Beds National Monument. The Headquarters, at 20 W Main St., has displays and information on weekdays all year.

Back Country Trips: Savage Creek Outfitters, PO Box 185, John Day, 97845, tel. 575-2857. Hunting and fishing trips. **John Day River Outfitters**, HCR56, Box 140, John Day 97845, tel. 575-2386. Raft rentals, shuttle service, guides.

Events–Grant County Fairgrounds: John Day Valley Draft Mule Classic, mid-June, a show and competition., tel. 575-0547. **Queen's Dance**, early August, tel. 575-1900, 575-1670. **Grant County Open Class Horse Show**, mid-August. Address: PO Box 7, John Day, 97845, tel. 575-1900. **Grant County Fair**, late August, 4-H exhibits, booths, games, livestock show, rodeo. Address: PO Box 7, John Day 97845, tel. 575-1900. **Grant County Jackpot Rodeo and Horse Races**, end of August, PO Box 7, John Day 97845, tel. 575-1900, 575-1670. **Arts and Crafts Bazaar**, early

December, local artists and craftsmen display and sell their work, tel. 575-1890.

CANYON CITY, 3199', population 648 (USGS John Day). Canyon City, the seat of Grant County (population 7,853, area 4,525 square miles), is the center of a mining region that was most productive before 1900. Buildings from 1877 still remain. The following mines contributed to the mineral production: Iron King, Great Northern, Golden West, Miller Mountain, Potato Patch, and Ward. Facilities and activities: food, stores, lodging, gas.

In the **Humboldt Diggings,** west of the Humboldt School, one mile north of the center of Canyon City, miners dug deep into the bed of Canyon Creek in cuts and tunnels to extract the gold. Cross Canyon Creek west on Nuggett Street and drive south on Humboldt Street to Portal Street to see the remaining evidences of mining.

Grant County Historical Museum, on US-395, has extensive rock collections, mining, Indian, and pioneer artifacts, the Greenhorn jail, and the Joaquin Miller cabin. Open June 1 to September 20, Monday-Saturday 9:30am to 4:30pm, Sunday 1pm-5pm.

Ox Bow Trading Co. & Museum, located on US-395, contains many artifacts of the early days. Open most days in summer and in winter by appointment. Call 575-2911.

Events: '62 Days Celebration, mid June. Celebrates the discovery of gold in 1862: exhibits, shows, booths, breakfast, dinner, games. Address: PO Box 263, Canyon City 97820, tel. 575-0801.

CANYON MOUNTAIN, 8007', 12 miles RT, 4000' gain (USGS John Day, Canyon Mountain). From Canyon City, drive east on CR-52 for two miles, then south on CR-77 to the trailhead five miles from US-395. Hike the trail to the ridge near the summit. Leave the trail and hike to the summit. The rocks of this area are part of the Canyon Mountain Complex: serpentine and gabbro from the earth's mantle that were mixed into the sea floor and brought here by tectonic forces.

J-BAR-L RANCH, 3900' (USGS Canyon Mountain). At MP-10 on US-395. This former Civilian Conservation Corps camp has the following facilities and activities: cabins, space for tents and trailers, showers, sanitary disposal, swimming. Address: Canyon City, 97820. Telephone: 575-1123.

PINE CREEK MOUNTAIN, 7390', 12 miles RT, 1700' gain (USGS Canyon Mountain, Pine Creek Mountain, SMMRW). At MP-10 on US-395, turn left (southeast) on paved road CR-65 and FS-15 for three miles then left on CR-6510 to the end of the road at Joaquin Miller Trailhead, 5800' and eight miles from US-395. Alder Spring is just southeast of the trailhead. Hike the trail (FS-219 and FS-218) north to the summit, keeping left at a junction after two miles from the trailhead.

WICKIUP CAMPGROUND, 4294' (USGS Big Canyon-Canyon Meadows Lake). From MP-10 on US-395, drive southeast on CR-65 and FS-15 for eight miles to the campground. Facilities and activities: tents, trailers to 25', water, hiking. No fee.

INDIAN CREEK BUTTE, 7889', 13 miles RT, 3000' gain (USGS Big Canyon-Canyon Meadows Lake, Pine Creek Mountain, SMMRW). From mile seven on road CR-65 and FS-15, 0.5 mile west of the Wickiup campground, drive north on road FS-651 for two mile to the Table Mountain trailhead. Hike the trail (FS-217) north to the summit.

TABLE MOUNTAIN, 5292', 4 miles RT, 1000' gain (USGS Big Canyon-Canyon Meadows Lake). From Wickiup Campground, hike northwest on FS-15 for one-half mile, then turn northeast on a road. At one mile from FS-15, turn southeast on a road which circles the south side of the mountain to the summit and a close view of the Strawberry Mountains. Table Mountain can also be reached from Wickiup Campground by going north directly across road FS-15 and hiking north cross country up a valley to the first road. Turn right (east) on the road to the summit.

SPION COPP, 5603', 4 miles RT, 1400' gain (USGS Big Canyon-Canyon Meadows Lake, Seneca). From Wickiup Campground, hike south on road FS-1516 until the road turns southeast after one mile. Leave the road and hike west cross country to the summit.

SUGARLOAF LOOP, 5612', 16 miles RT, 2000' gain (USGS Big Canyon-Canyon Meadows Lake, Seneca). **Mt. Bicycle Route.** From Wickiup Campground, ride south on road FS-1516, turning right (northwest) after two miles to ride the ridge over Spion Copp and Dry Soda, 5593', an abandoned lookout, to the summit of Sugarloaf. From the summit, descend north in Sugarloaf Gulch, taking the left branch at a "Y" two miles down from the summit, to return to road CR-65, FS-15. Turn right (east) to Wickiup Campground.

CANYON MEADOWS CAMPGROUND, 5100' (USGS Big Canyon-Canyon Meadows Lake). Drive on CR-65, FS-15 past Wickiup Campground (see above). At nine miles from US-395, and one mile past Wickiup campground, turn left (northeast) on road FS-1520 to the campground on Canyon Meadows Lake, 14 miles from US-395. Facilities and activities: tents, trailers to 25', hiking, fishing, boating, water. No fee.

INDIAN CREEK BUTTE, 7889', 11 miles RT, 2000' gain (USGS Strawberry Mountain, Pine Creek Mountain, SMMRW). From Canyon Meadows Campground, drive road FS-1520 east and north to the trailhead in Buckhorn Meadow, 6000'. Hike the trail northeast, turning left (northwest) at a trail junction in Wildcat Basin (6969'), three miles from the trailhead where a trail goes right (east) to Strawberry Mountain. At another trail junction near the summit, 7500', leave the trail and ascend westnorthwest cross country on the ridge to the summit.

STRAWBERRY MOUNTAIN, 9036', 12 miles RT, 3000' gain (USGS Strawberry Mountain, Pine Creek Mountain, SMMRW). Hike as above toward Indian Creek Butte, turning right at the trail junction after three miles to reach the summit.

PARISH CABIN CAMPGROUND, 4923' (USGS Big Canyon-Canyon Meadows Lake). Drive CR-65, FS-15 for 15 miles from US-395 at MP-10 to the campground 0.2 mile southwest on road FS-16 from the junction of FS-15 with FS-16. Facilities and activities: tents, trailers to 25', water, hiking.

POINT 5906, 5906', 5 miles RT, 1000' gain (USGS Big Canyon-Canyon Meadows Lake, Logan Valley West, SMMRW). From Parish Cabin Campground, hike north across road FS-15 into road FS-1530 for one-fourth mile. Turn right (east) on road FS-673 until the road begins to descend. Leave road and hike northwest to the summit for a close view of the Strawberry Mountains.

JUNCTION FS-16 (USGS Big Canyon-Canyon Meadows Lake). This junction is 15 miles east from US-395 on CR-65/FS-15 and 14 miles west on road FS-16 from the junction of CR-14 with FS-16. These roads are all paved.

FRASER POINT LOOKOUT LOOP, 6288', 30 miles RT, 1500' gain (USGS Magpie Table, Logan Valley East). **Mt. Bicycle Route.** From Parish Cabin Campground, ride east on FS-16 for 2.5 miles. Turn first south then southeast on FS-1630, taking the southeast fork at junctions until four miles from FS-16. Continue on the middle of three forks, going southeast to climb away from Frazier Creek. From this point on, keep left at all road junctions to the summit of Frazier Point. Returning south from the summit, turn first east then north on road FS-1540 to join road FS-1643. Continue north on road FS-1643 to paved FS-16. Turn left to return to Parish Cabin Campground.

INDIAN SPRINGS CAMPGROUND, 6900' (USGS Strawberry Mountain, SMMRW). From MP-10 on US-395, drive east 17 miles on CR-65/FS-15/FS-16, then north on road FS-1640 for eight miles on a narrow road to this minimum campground. Trailers not recommended. Facilities and activities: tents and small recreational vehicles, hiking. No fee.

STRAWBERRY MOUNTAIN, 9036', 8 miles RT, 3000' gain (USGS Strawberry Mountain, SMMRW). From MP-10 on US-395, drive east 17 miles on CR-65/FS-15/FS-16, then north on road FS-1640 for 10 miles past Indian Springs campground, to the trailhead, 7868'. From the trailhead, hike at first northwest on trail FS-201, then turn north on trail FS-368 to the summit.

INDIAN SPRINGS BUTTE, 8529', 3 miles RT, 600' (USGS Strawberry Mountain, SMMRW). Drive past the Strawberry Mountain trailhead for 0.5 mile (see above) to the Indian Rim trailhead, 7900'. From the trailhead, hike north cross country up the ridge to reach the summit.

SLIDE LAKE, 7222', 10 miles RT, 2000' gain (USGS Strawberry Mountain, SMMRW). From the Indian Rim trailhead (see above for Indian Springs Butte), hike trail FS-385 northeast, passing High Lake and the trail to Little Slide Lake.

LAKE CREEK YOUTH CAMP, 5200' (USGS Logan Valley West, SMMRW). The Jackman Youth and Natural Resources Center, a campground that is open to the public, is operated by the Lake Creek Recreation Association, a non-profit organization. From US-395 at MP-10, drive 21 miles east on road CR-65/FS-15/FS-16 and two miles north on road FS-924. Facilities and activities: cabins, tent area, trailer space, electrical hookups, showers, programs, hiking, fishing nearby. Information: Marti Boatman, 156 S. Quincy, PO Box 924, Hines 97738, tel. 573-7498.

MURRAY CAMPGROUND, 5240' (USGS Logan Valley West). From US-395 at MP-10, drive east on CR-65/FS-15/FS-16 for 21 miles. Turn left (north) on road FS-924 for three miles to a minimum campground. Facilities and activities: tents, trailers. No fee.

BIG CREEK CAMPGROUND, 5100' (USGS Logan Valley East). From US-395, drive east 23 miles on CR-65/FS-15/FS16 and two miles north on FS-924 to this minimum campground. Facilities and activities: tents, trailers to 25', fishing, water. No fee.

BIG CREEK HORSE CAMP, 5300' (USGS LOGAN VALLEY EAST, SMMRW). From US-395 at MP-10, drive 24 miles east on CR-65, FS-15, FS-16 or five miles west of CR-42/FS-14 at Summit Prairie. Drive three miles north on road FS-1648. Facilities and activities: horse loading ramp, fishing and hunting nearby.

VANCE CREEK STATE REST AREA, 4000' (USGS Canyon Mountain). On US-395 at MP-11. Facilities and activities: picnicking, water, bicycling.

FALL MOUNTAIN LOOKOUT LOOP, 5944', 10 miles RT, 2000' gain (USGS Canyon Mountain, Fall Mountain). **Mt. Bicycle Route.** From Vance Creek State Rest Area, ride west on road FS-3920 to the summit. Return south to US-395 on road FS-4920. Turn northeast on US-395 to starting point.

STARR CAMPGROUND AND WINTER SPORTS CENTER,

5100', MP-16 (USGS Fall Mountain). Facilities and activities: tents, trailers, hiking, skiing, snowmobiling, SnoPark.

COAL PIT MOUNTAIN, 6738', 20 miles RT, 1800' gain (USGS Fall Mountain, Scotty Creek). **Mt. Bicycle Route.** From Starr Campground, ride south on US-395 for one mile, then west on road FS-333 for three miles to the junction with road CR-49. Turn right (north) to the crest of the ridge. Turn west at a T-intersection on to road FS-844, then again north at another intersection on road FS-845 for two miles. Leave bicycle and hike west 0.5 mile to the summit.

LOGDELL, 4791' (USGS Logdell). From US-395 at MP-17, drive southwest five miles on CR-63. Many cattle feed here in the broad valley of the Silvies River. No services.

INGLE MOUNTAIN, 6788', 6 miles RT, 1600' gain (USGS Fall Mountain, McClellan Mountain). From US-395 at MP-17, drive five miles west and southwest on CR-63. Turn northwest on road FS-21 for 2.5 miles, then northeast on road FS-4955 for three miles. Where road FS-4955 turns east to cross Percival Creek, park and hike north cross country for three miles to the summit, passing west of Ingle Rock.

BEAR VALLEY FOREST SERVICE STATION, 4900' (USGS

Logdell). From US-395 at MP-17, drive southwest nine miles on CR-63. Maps and information are available at the station during the summer.

FLAGTAIL MOUNTAIN LOOKOUT, 6584', 5 miles RT, 1600' gain (USGS Big Weasel Springs, Logdell). At MP-17 on US-395, drive west on CR-63 for 10 miles. Park at the junction of roads CR-63 and FS-24. Hike at first west and then northwest, beginning on the north side of the Silvies River (road FS-645), to the summit, either cross country or using the network of roads in the area.

IZEE, 4100' (USGS Izee). From MP-17 on US-395, drive west on CR-63, CR-67 for 24 miles to the site of Izee, a supply center for early settlers and now cattle ranches. No services.

GRAYLOCK BUTTE LOOP, 5594', 40 miles RT, 2300' gain (USGS Logdell, Flagtail Mountain, Graylock Butte). **Mt. Bicycle Route.** From US-395 at MP-17, drive west and southwest on road Cr-63 for 24 miles. Park at the junction with road FS-24, where Wickiup Creek joins the Silvies River. Ride northwest and north on FS-24, following Wickiup Creek, turning west after three miles to descend gradually along the North Fork of Deer Creek. The South Fork of Deer Creek joins the North Fork ten miles from CR-63 and one mile past the turnoff to the Deer Creek Forest Service Station.

Continue west on FS-24 for six miles after passing the junction to the Deer Creek Forest Service Station. Turn south on road FS-338 for four miles to road FS-6370. Turn left (west) on FS-6370 for one-half mile. Leave bicycle and hike southwest one-half mile to the summit of Graylock Butte. Return to bicycle and ride east on FS-6370, following the crest of the ridge between the South Fork of the John Day River to the south and Deer Creek to the north. On reaching paved CR-63, turn left (north and northeast) to return to the starting point.

SENECA, 4700', population 191 (area population 352) (USGS Seneca). Facilities and activities: food, stores, lodging, gas.

WOLF MOUNTAIN, 6411', 24 miles RT, 1700' gain (USGS Jump-off Joe Mountain, Big Canyon-Canyon Meadows Lake). **Mt. Bicycle Route.** From Seneca on US-395 at MP-25, drive east on road FS-16 for nine miles from US-395 to the junction with FS-1619. Park and ride south on FS-1619. After six miles, turn southeast on road FS-1710, crossing Wolf Creek Meadow after four miles from FS-1619. Jump-off Joe Mountain is the summit to the west of Wolf Creek Meadow. At a junction, 6127', one mile past Jump-off Joe Mountain, turn left (northeast) into a spur road that rounds south to the summit of Wolf Mountain. On the return, take road FS-805 north at the road junction in Wolf Creek Meadow to go past Kirkwood Spring. After two miles on FS-805, go right (northest) on road FS-750 for a mile, then northwest and west on road FS-655 to reach the outgoing route (FS-1619). Turn north to road FS-16 and the starting point.

PONDEROSA GUEST RANCH, 4600', MP-31 (USGS Silvies). This 120,000 acre working cattle ranch located in the Silvies River valley begins near the junction of road FS-37 with US-395. Guests can participate in the work of the ranch. Facilities and activities: lodge, riding, fishing, hunting. Address: PO Box 190, Seneca 97873, tel. 800-331-1012, 542-2403.

RAIL CREEK BUTTE, 6020', 6 miles RT, 1000' gain (USGS Rail Creek Butte). Drive six miles west on FS-37 from US-395 at MP-31. Park at a side road turning north. Hike north on the road for one mile. Turn north and ascend cross country to the summit.

WEST MYRTLE BUTTE LOOP, high point 6384', 30 miles RT, 1600' gain (USGS West Myrtle Butte, Five Hundred Flat, Rail Creek Butte). **Mt. Bicycle Route.** At MP-31 on US-395, six miles south of Seneca, drive west on road FS-37 for seven miles to a junction with roads FS-3780 and FS-3770. Park and ride south on road FS-37 for six miles, passing a junction with road FS-3765 at 2.5 miles. Continue south on road FS-37 for two miles. Turn east to the summit of West Myrtle Butte. Return north on road FS-37 to the junction with road FS-31 in Cheatem Holler, 5593'. Turn northwest for six miles on road FS-31 through Five Hundred Flat, then ride east on road FS-3770 for eight miles, passing Elkhorn Cow

Camp, to return to the starting point.

MYRTLE PARK MEADOWS, high point 5600', 15 miles RT, 600' gain (USGS Rail Creek Butte, Myrtle Park Meadows). **Mt. Bicycle Route.** After parking at the junction of roads FS-3780 and FS-3770 on FS-37, seven miles from US-395 at MP-31, ride south on FS-37 for 2.5 miles. Turn south on FS-3765 where FS-37 turns west. Where FS-3765 turns east after one mile, continue south on road FS-864, taking the first left fork (FS-895) into the meadows, seven miles from the starting point. Opalized wood has been found in this area.

ICE CAVES, 5400', 20 mile RT, 500' gain (USGS Myrtle Park Meadows, Rail Creek Butte). **Mt. Bicycle Route.** From the starting point for West Myrtle Butte (see above) seven miles from US-395 at MP-31 on FS-37, ride south on FS-37 for 2.5 miles, then turn south on road FS-3765, which, after one mile, turns northeast for a mile, then turns again to the south. After seven miles from the starting point, pass two roads turning off to the southwest, then turn right (southwest) on road FS-570. Ride 0.5 mile to the caves. Return to road FS-3765 and turn south then southwest to join road FS-31 four miles from the Ice Caves. Turn north on FS-31 for six miles to a junction with road FS-37. Turn right (northeast) on road FS-37 to return to the starting point.

POTHOLES LOOP, high point 6000', 30 miles RT, 2000' gain (USGS Rail Creek Butte, Scotty Creek, Five Hundred Flat, Logdell). **Mt. Bicycle Route.** From the junction of road FS-37 with roads FS-3770 and FS-3780, seven miles from US-395 at MP-31, ride north up Burnt Cabin Creek on road FS-3780 to pass over a saddle at 5811', taking the north or northwest fork at road junctions for 10 miles to join road FS-24. Continue northwest on FS-24 to reach paved CR-63. Turn left (west) on the paved road. After one mile on CR-63, turn south (left) on FS-31. This roads jogs west for a mile where it crosses the south fork of Scotty Creek, five miles from CR-63. Seven miles from CR-63 pass The Potholes, several depressions that are filled with water in the spring. After passing The Potholes, continue southeast three miles, then turn left (east) on FS-3770, 10 miles from CR-63 and descend along Camp Creek to meet FS-37 at the starting point.

SILVIES, 4586', MP-35 (USGS Silvies). In the past this was a station on the railroad from Burns and a busy logging area. Now nothing remains.

ROCK SPRINGS CAMPGROUND, 5200' (USGS Jump-Off Joe Mountain). At MP-36 on US-395, drive east on CR-73/FS-17 five miles to a multiple road intersection. Turn right and drive east 0.5 miles to this minimum campground on the gravel road that at first parallels FS-17. Facilities and activities: tents, trailers to 25'.

SR–74, FS–52, FS–53

Blue Mountain Scenic Byway:
Heppner Junction to Granite Junction

From Interstate-84 at Heppner Junction, Exit 147, drive south on SR-74, ascending in the fertile Willow Creek valley, passing hay fields in the valley and wheat fields on the plateau above.

CECIL, 650', MP-14 (USGS Cecil, Hickland Butte, Horn Butte). Facilities: store.

The Oregon Trail crossed Willow Creek near Cecil then turned north for 0.5 mile before ascending near the first canyon to reach the plateau to the west. After crossing the plateau, the route descended into Four-Mile Canyon two miles southeast of the junction of Four-Mile Canyon with Eight-Mile Canyon. On reaching the junction of these two canyons, the Oregon Trail route continued on to the west.

From SR-74 in Cecil, drive west across the railroad tracks, then turn north and follow the road west four miles to Four Mile Canyon. Turn right 0.7 mile to the Bureau of Land Management display where Oregon Trail ruts are visible to the west. This display is at mile 1755 of the Oregon Trail.

WELL SPRING, 850' (USGS Cecil, Dalreed Butte, Ella, Well Spring). At Cecil, turn east for 14 miles on Immigrant Road, a gravel road that passes through Ella crossroad. The Oregon Trail route is under this road to the place where the road jogs to the north after three miles at a road junction. After Immigrant Road turns east again, the Oregon Trail is up to one-third mile north of Immigrant road. For example, at Ella Crossroads, nine miles east of SR-74, the Oregon Trail is 1600' north, coming down a minor gully from the east to cross Six Mile Canyon and continue west. The road in Six Mile Canyon is three miles west of the Boardman Bombing Range. At Well Spring, where the BLM maintains an information kiosk, the trail is inside the Boardman Bombing Range, travelling southeast after it crossed Butter Creek west of Echo. The cemetery at Well Spring, including a memorial to Robert Evan Williams who died in 1852, is one-half mile west of the well. The information display on the road near the spring tells of this popular resting place where the Oregon Trail travelers could feed and water their animals. Facilities: a gate allows access to Well Spring, north of the road, and a well-marked seven mile hiking segment on the Oregon Trail extends from north of Ella Crossroad east to Butter Creek.

IONE, 1093', population 255 (area population 1,054), MP-28 (USGS Ione North, Ione South). Ione is an agricultural center and shipping point. An Oregon Trail site at Well Spring is accessible from here by driving north to Ella Crossroad, then east a total of 15 miles. Facilities and activities: food, lodging, stores, gas. For information, call 422-7122.

LEXINGTON, 1468', population 286, MP-36 (USGS Lexington). This town lies at the junction of SR-74 and SR-207. The Oregon Trail crossed the line of SR-207 at Butter Creek, 25 miles north. Facilities: store, gas, park.

HEPPNER, 1905', population 1,412 (area population 2,127), MP-45 (USGS Heppner). The seat of Morrow County (population 7,625, area 2,094 square miles), Heppner is the agricultural and commercial center for the county and the terminus for a Union Pacific Railroad branch line from the Columbia River. The town is named for Henry Heppner who, with a partner, opened the first store in 1872 and was instrumental in establishing the first school. For information, call 676-5536. Facilities: food, lodging, stores, gas. The Heppner Museum is open Saturday through Wednesday from 1pm to 5pm. Closed in January. **Events: Morrow County Fair**, mid-August, tel. 676-5536. **RV Parks: Northwestern Motel**, 389 N. Main St., tel. 676-9167. Hookups. **Fairgrounds**, 0.5 mile east of Heppner center and north of SR-74. Hookups, restrooms, PO Box 464, 97836, tel. 676-7494.

SR-206/SR-207. From Heppner, continue south for one mile. Turn right on SR-206/SR-207, leaving the Blue Mountain Scenic Byway.

DONALDSON SUMMIT, 2900', MP-80 ((USGS Ruggs, Heppner). SR-206/SR-207 ascends Donaldson Canyon to a plateau with commanding views of Madison Butte (154°) fifteen miles to the southwest at the head of Rhea Creek valley and Black Butte to the east (114°). The highway then descends southwest in Cason Canyon.

RUGGS, 2115' (USGS Ruggs). This agricultural center, where SR-207 leaves SR-206, lies 11 miles south of Heppner on SR-206/SR-207. No services.

HARDMAN, 3590', population 15 (USGS Hardman). Situated twenty miles south of Heppner on SR-207, a once important stage coach stop is being restored by private owners. Many of the buildings that were built around 1900 still remain standing. For example, a dance hall from the early days is in use as a community center. Originally known as Rawdog, later Dogtown, the town derives its name from Dan Hardman, an early settler. South of Hardman the land changes from wheat growing to grazing land for cattle and sheep. No services.

ANSON WRIGHT MEMORIAL PARK, 3404' (USGS Chapin Creek,

Big Rock Flat). Drive 25 miles south of Heppner on SR-207. Facilities and activities: pull throughs and full hookups for recreational vehicles of any size, tent area, showers, water, hiking, mineral collecting. May 15 to Nov. 15. tel. 676-9061.

MADISON BUTTE LOOKOUT, 5707', 12 miles RT, 2400' gain (USGS Big Rock Flat, Madison Butte). From Anson Wright Memorial Park, drive south one mile on SR-207 (near MP-14), then three miles east on Rock Creek Road, passing the site of Reed's Mill, to Parker's Mill, a T-intersection at 3577', now a stock ranch. Park and hike east on a minimum road, going to the left (north) of the corrals and buildings into the valley of Tupper Creek to ascend the road up Tupper Creek through Tupper Meadow, staying to the north side of Tupper and Hollywood Creeks. The two creeks join at 3918'. Pass the outlet from Hollywood Springs at 4500' and join road FS-033 to go east and north to the summit. Mountain finder: see below under Tupper Butte–Madison Butte.

MADISON BUTTE LOOKOUT, 5707', 22 miles RT, 2200' gain (USGS Big Rock Flat, Madison Butte, HRDMA). **Mt. Bicycle Route.** Drive as above to the starting point at Parker's Mill or ride from Anson Wright Memorial Park to add seven miles and 200' of elevation gain. Park and ride northeast on the road ascending along Board Creek for seven miles. Turn at first south on road FS-033 then ascend east and north to the summit, passing Bottle Spring one mile below the lookout.

OPAL BUTTE, 5015', 8 miles RT, 1100' gain (USGS Chapin Creek, Big Rock Flat). South of MP-21 on SR-207 and seven miles after leaving Rock Creek, drive northeast on road FS-21 for four miles to French Pass, 4000'. If coming from the south on SR-207, turn northeast on FS-21 at MP-24. Park at the junction of roads FS-21 and FS-2128 and hike west 0.3 mile to a road at the west end of the saddle. Hike this minimum road, at first northeast, then bending southeast to pass south of a minor knob. Take a left fork one-half mile after leaving the road in French Pass and continue northeast, passing a prospect (opal digging?) at 4500', to the tree-covered summit with keyhole views of Madison Butte to the northeast. Allen Spring is one-fourth mile northwest of the summit, just below a road that crosses to the north side of Opal Butte. This area is noted for opals and many prospects are visible on the slopes.

TUPPER BUTTE–MADISON BUTTE, 5184', 5707', 8 miles RT, 2000' gain (USGS Madison Butte, Big Rock Flat, HRDMA). Drive as above for Opal Butte to French Pass. Continue north on road FS-21 to the Madison Butte Trailhead near the Tupper Forest Service Station, 17 miles from SR-207. Park near the trailhead, one-fourth mile south of the Station. Hike northwest on the trail to a road junction, one mile from FS-21 and 5000'. The left branch goes to the west shoulder near the summit of Tupper Butte from which Mt. Hood can be seen (280°). The right branch continues across the east side of Tupper Butte and soon becomes a trail that drops into the saddle between Tupper Butte and Madison Butte. Ascend north to pass Bottle Spring with old cattle watering troughs and join road FS-033. Continue to the summit on the road. From the summit, Mt. Hood is 280° and 109 miles, Mt. Adams is 308° and 122 miles and Mt. Rainier is 318° and 160 miles.

BULL PRAIRIE LAKE CAMPGROUND, 4040' (USGS Whitetail Butte). At MP-28 on SR-207, turn east on a paved road (FS-2039) to Bull Prairie Lake and campgrounds on the west and south side of the lake. Facilities and activities: swimming, boating, boat ramp, tents, trailers, piped water, and a trail around the lake. Fee.

WHITETAIL BUTTE, 4588', 3 miles RT, 600' gain (USGS Whitetail Butte). From the campground on Bull Prairie Lake, walk south on the road toward SR-207 across the cattle guard and fence line west of the campground. Leave the road immediately after passing the cattle guard and hike west cross country to the summit.

TAMARACK MOUNTAIN LOOKOUT, 4970', 30 miles RT, 2200' gain (USGS Whitetail Butte, Kimberley). **Mt. Bicycle Route**. From Bull Prairie Lake, ride southwest on road FS-2039 for three miles to road SR-207. Turn south on SR-207 for one-fourth mile then go southeast on road FS-24 for seven miles, passing a junction on the right with road FS-2406. Turn right on road FS-2407, going southwest and crossing road FS-2408. After one mile on FS-2407, at the saddle between Tamarack Mountain and Little Tamarack Mountain, continue northwest on road FS-040 to the lookout on the summit of Tamarack Mountain. On the return from the summit, follow roads FS-040 and FS-2407 to FS-24. Turn left and again left on road FS-2406 to go at first south then northwest to reached paved SR-207. Turn right on SR-207 for four miles, passing Fairview Campground (spring), then continue to the right on road FS-2309 to Bull Prairie Lake.

LITTLE TAMARACK MOUNTAIN, 5013', 30 miles RT, 2300' gain (USGS Whitetail Butte, Kimberley). **Mt. Bicycle Route**. Ride as above to the saddle southeast of Tamarack Mountain at the junction of roads FS-2407 and FS-040 (see above). Turn east to the summit of Little Tamarack Mountain.

WILSON CREEK LOOP, high point 4450, 30 miles RT, 1400' gain (USGS Whitetail Butte, Turner Mountain, HRDMA). **Mt. Bicycle Route**. From Bull Prairie Lake, ride northeast on road FS-2039 down the valley of Wilson Creek to the broad meadow of Wilson Prairie. After three miles, turn right (east) on road FS-2128 through Wilson Prairie to continue descending along Wilson Creek to Big Wall Creek and a junction with road FS-23 eleven miles from Bull Prairie Lake. Turn left (west) and ascend along Big Wall Creek on road FS-23 to rejoin road FS-24, one-half mile before reaching SR-207. Turn right on SR-207 and again right on road FS-2039 to return to Bull Prairie Lake.

ANT HILL-TURNER MOUNTAIN LOOP, high point 4600', 60 miles RT, 3300' gain (USGS Whitetail Butte, Turner Mountain, Big Rock Flat, Chapin Creek, HRDMA). **Mt. Bicycle Route.** From Bull Prairie Lake, ride southwest on road FS-2039 to SR-207. Turn left and again left on road FS-24, to reach Ant Hill, 4600', 15 miles from Bull Prairie Lake. Continue east on road FS-24 down Indian Creek to road FS-22 on Wall Creek. Turn west on road FS-22/CR-670 along Wall Creek for two miles, then generally northwest for 12 miles to reach road FS-21, passing over the northeast shoulder of Turner Mountain and passing through Sunflower Flat. On reaching road FS-21, turn left (west) past French Pass to reach SR-207. Go southwest and south on SR-207 to road FS-2039. Turn left to Bull Prairie Lake.

FAIRVIEW CAMPGROUND, 4290' (USGS Whitetail Butte). This minimum campground is located near MP-29 on the west side of SR-207. Water is available from Fairview Spring, 0.1 mile west of SR-207 and just west of the restrooms at the first camp site. Facilities and activities: tents, trailers, hiking.

FS-53. From Heppner, turn east on the Blue Mountain Scenic Byway, now CR-678 and becoming FS-53 at the Umatilla National Forest boundary.

WILLOW CREEK RESERVOIR, 2000' (USGS Heppner). Two miles east of Heppner on the Blue Mountain Scenic Byway, a reservoir of 125 acres is contained by a roller compacted concrete dam. The area has the following facilities and activities: fishing, swimming, boat launch, dock, restrooms, no camping.

CUTSFORTH PARK, 4200' (USGS Arbuckle Mountain). The park on Willow Creek, located 20 miles southeast of Heppner on FS-53, has the following facilities and activities: hiking, tents, trailers, showers, water. May 15 to Nov 15. tel. 676-9061. Fee.

COAL MINE HILL, 5272', 4 miles RT, 1300' gain (USGS Arbuckle Mountain). From Cutsforth Park (see above), hike west to the ridge, using roads where possible, then turn south to the summit.

BALD MOUNTAIN, 5775', 6 miles RT, 1800' gain (USGS Arbuckle Mountain). The trail begins 0.3 mile south on road FS-53 from Cutsforth Park on the south side of a cattle guard and fence line. Ascend to the east. At the saddle between Little Bald Mountain and Bald Mountain, turn north to the summit.

KELLY MOUNTAIN, 5727', 8 miles RT, 2200' gain (USGS Arbuckle

Mountain). Hike as above to Bald Mountain, then continue north cross country along the ridge to the summit.

ARBUCKLE MOUNTAIN, 5847', 14 miles RT, 1900' gain (USGS Arbuckle Mountain, Matlock Prairie). **Mt. Bicycle Route.** From Cutsforth Park (see above), ride north on road FS-53 for one mile. Turn east on road FS-5326, the Shaw Creek Road, for six miles, passing two roads left (north) at four miles. Where the road turns east again after bending south, continue south at a road junction to a saddle, passing Arbuckle Spring. At saddle southwest of the summit, leave bicycle and ascend northeast cross country to the summit.

BLACK MOUNTAIN, 5932', 8 miles RT, 2000' gain (USGS Arbuckle Mountain). **Mt. Bicycle Route.** From Cutsforth Park, ride north on road FS-53 for one mile, then two miles east on road FS-5326. Turn north and ascend a switchback road for two miles to the summit.

LITTLE BALD MOUNTAIN, 5678', 6 miles RT, 1100' gain (USGS Arbuckle Mountain). From the trailhead at the northeast corner of a SnoPark north off road FS-53, 2.5 miles south of Cutsforth Park, hike east on the trail to the summit.

PENLAND LAKE CAMPGROUND, 4940' (USGS Arbuckle Mountain, Lake Penland). Three miles south of Cutsforth Park on road FS-53 and 23 miles from either Heppner or Ukiah, turn south on road FS-21 for three miles then east for three miles on road FS-2103 to Penland Lake. The roads off FS-53 are not recommended for trailers. Facilities and activities: swimming, fishing, boating (electric motors only), camping for tents and small recreational vehicles (no trailers). No fee.

DITCH CREEK FOREST SERVICE STATION, 4400' (USGS Lake Penland). From FS-53, three miles south of Cutsforth Park (see above), drive south on FS-21 four miles. Maps and information are available here during the summer.

COPPLE BUTTE, 5438', 9 miles RT, 1000' gain (USGS Lake Penland, Madison Butte, Summerfield Ridge). Drive as above to Ditch Creek Forest Service Station, four miles from road FS-53. Park near road FS-21 and hike northwest up the road along Martin Creek for one mile. Where the road along Martin Creek enters a wide, open, flat valley, leave the road to the left (west) on a minor logging track, crossing Martin Creek and two fence lines. Ascend west on the logging track for one-half mile. On entering the east edge of a clear cut, cross the small stream toward the west to find an open passage in the forest continuing to the west. Follow a minor track, climbing over downed trees to the gentle saddle between Martin Creek on the east and the Rhea Creek drainage to the west. On reaching the crest of the ridge, turn southwest one mile along the ridge on a track to the summit of Copple Butte.

TEXAS BUTTE, 5370', 12 miles RT, 1400' gain (USGS Lake Penland, Madison Butte, Summerfield Ridge). Hike as above to Copple Butte. Follow the trail southwest to the summit of Texas Butte.

POTAMUS POINT, 4480', 32 miles RT, 600' gain (USGS Matlock Prairie, Thompson Flat). **Mt. Bicycle Route.** At Four Corners on road FS-53, seven miles east of road FS-21 junction, 30 miles east of Heppner, and 15 miles west of US-395, ride southeast on road FS-5327 for four miles then south on road FS-5315 to Potamus Point, 16 miles from road FS-53 and 2000' above the North Fork John Day River. The rocky points of Devils Backbone below to the southeast are remaining fragments of Columbia Basalts. Hike or ride down the road northeast to Thompson Spring and a view of Thompson Falls.

JUNCTION US-395/SR-244, 90 miles from I-84 at Heppner Junction. Continue east on SR-244 for one mile to Ukiah.

UKIAH, 3353', population 250 (USGS Ukiah). This area supports many beef cattle. Facilities and activities: food, lodging, stores, gas. The North Fork John Day River Forest Service Station at the west edge of town on SR-244 has maps and information and is open weekdays all year. **Camping: C & D Motel**, on SR-244 east of the road FS-52 junction, has space for overnight recreational vehicles. Telephone: 427-3352.

LANE CREEK CAMPGROUND, 3800', MP-12 (USGS Owens Butte). From Ukiah, turn east on SR-244 for 11 miles to the campground or drive 44 miles from I-84 at Exit 252. Facilities and activities: tents, trailers, hiking. No fee.

OWEN BUTTE, 4576', 4 miles RT, 800' gain (USGS Owens Butte). From Lane Creek Campground, cross the fence line northwest of the campground and hike west cross country to the summit.

BEAR WALLOW CAMPGROUND, 3900' (USGS Owens Butte, Lehman Springs). Located at MP-12 on SR-244, 43 miles from I-84 at Exit 252, the campground has the following facilities and activities: tents, trailers, hiking, picnicking, water from stream. No fee.

BEAR WALLOW INTERPRETIVE TRAIL, 3900', 2 miles RT, no gain (USGS Owens Butte, Lehman Springs). On SR-244 at Bear Wallow Campground, this trail is partly wheelchair accessible. The Forest Service and others have prepared informative signs for the trail that present the many factors contributing to maintaining a healthy population of fish and wildlife.

LEHMAN SPRINGS, 4400' (USGS Lehman Springs). At MP-17, 38 miles southeast of I-84 at Exit 252, drive one mile south of SR-244 on road

FS-390. Facilities and activities: hookups for recreational vehicles, tents, showers, swimming in a natural hot water pool, hiking, horseback riding, skiing, fishing nearby, cabins, dormitory, open all year. Fee. Address: PO Box 187, Ukiah 97880, telephone 427-3015.

FRAZIER CAMPGROUND, 4300' (USGS Lehman Springs).
Near MP-18, 37 miles from I-84 at Exit 252, drive south of SR-244 on road FS-5226 for 0.5 mile. This campground has the following facilities and activities: tents, trailers, hiking, shelter, water from stream, bicycling. No fee.

FRAZIER FOREST SERVICE STATION, 4300' (USGS Lehman
Springs). The station is beyond the Frazier Campground one mile from SR-244. The station has maps and information during the summer months.

TOWER MOUNTAIN, 6850', 20 miles RT, 2600' gain (USGS
Lehman Springs, Tower Mountain). **Mt. Bicycle Route.** From Frazier Campground, ride south on road FS-5226 along the ridge to the lookout tower (see p. 142).

FOUR CORNERS WINTER RECREATION AREA AND CAMP-
GROUND, 4350' (USGS Lehman Springs, Sullivan Gulch). Located at MP-20 on SR-244, 35 miles from I-84 at Exit 252, the recreation area has the following facilities and activities: tent and vehicle camping, cross-country skiing, snowmobiling, SnoPark, restrooms.

STARKEY EXPERIMENTAL FOREST, 4100' to 4923', 25,000 acres
(USGS Sullivan Gulch, Bally Mountain, Marley Creek). The Starkey Project, at MP-26 on SR-244, 28 miles from I-84 at Exit 252, is a long-term research area for studies of wildlife, watershed, soils, forest diseases, and other forestry topics. The study area is surrounded by 27 miles of fence eight feet high with an additional 11 miles of fencing to separate study areas within the project. The area is open to the public for day hiking but vehicle use may be restricted at times and in some areas. The study area contains a resident population of about 250 deer and 400 elk. Hunting is allowed in season.

BALLY MOUNTAIN, 4716', 20 miles RT, 1000' gain. (USGS Sullivan
Gulch, Bally Mountain). **Mt. Bicycle Route.** Park at the headquarters of the Starkey Experimental Forest, one mile from SR-244. Ride north on road FS-2120 to the summit of Bally Mountain at the north end of the Starkey Experimental Forest. The road crosses many branches of Meadow Creek.

FS-52 From Ukiah, turn south on road FS-52. Mileages for this section of the Blue Mountain Scenic Byway road log are given as distances from Ukiah.

BRIDGE CREEK WILDLIFE AREA, mile 4-8. The Oregon Depart-

ment of Fish and Wildlife provides a winter feeding ground for elk and deer. Early morning is the best time to view animals.

DRIFTFENCE CAMPGROUND, 4650', mile 8 (USGS Bridge Creek, Ukiah SE). From the campground, Twin Tank Spring is one mile southwest and Skull Spring is one mile south. To see elk and deer, hike west into the Bridge Creek Wildlife Area in the early morning. The wildlife area is closed to entry from 1 December to the end of April. No fee. Facilities and activities: tents, trailers, hiking. No fee.

NORTH FORK JOHN DAY RIVER OVERLOOK, mile 14 (USGS Bridge Creek, Ukiah SE). Spectacular view of the steep canyon of Camas Creek dropping from Ukiah to the North Fork John Day River 600' below. The Strawberry Mountains are 50 miles directly south from the viewpoint. The tower of Desolation Butte Lookout is 15 miles south at 158°.

PEARSON FOREST SERVICE STATION, 5400', mile 15.5, (USGS Pearson Ridge). A flowery meadow next to the station is ideal for a picnic. A former campground is now closed.

ROUND MEADOWS TRAIL, high point 5700', mile 16, 12 miles RT, 300' gain (USGS Pearson Ridge). Park at the trailhead 0.4 mile east of the Pearson Forest Service Station. Hike east to the meadows, then north across several branches of Cable Creek to a trailhead on the north fork of Cable Creek.

PEARSON RIDGE, 5726', 2 miles RT, 400' gain (USGS Pearson Ridge). Park at the Round Meadows trailhead. Cross FS-52 to the west and continue on an overgrown track to the west and southwest for keyhole views over the John Day River valley.

ORIENTAL CREEK, 5300' to 3400', mile 19, 20 miles RT, 2000' gain (USGS Pearson Ridge, Kelsay Butte, NFJDW). **Mt. Bicycle Route.** Ride south on road FS-5507. A network of roads south of FS-52 gives views of and access to the North Fork John Day River at Oriental Creek and Texas Bar.

WINOM CREEK CAMPGROUND, 4938' (USGS Pearson Ridge, Kelsay Butte). At mile 23, drive southwest one mile to the campground. Facilities and activities: tents only, no trailers, hiking. No fee.

WINOM CREEK TRAIL, 4938' to 3400', 12 miles RT, 1600' gain (USGS Kelsay Butte, Pearson Ridge). From the lower end of the Winom Creek Campground, descend along Winom Creek to the North Fork John Day River, joining the Big Creek Trail after four miles.

BIG CREEK MEADOWS, 5100', mile 24 (USGS Tower Mt.). More than one thousand acres of meadow along meandering Big Creek provide feed for deer and elk.

TOWER MOUNTAIN LOOKOUT, 6850', 11 miles RT, 2000' gain (USGS Tower Mt.). Park on the south side of FS-52, mile 24 at the crossing of Big Creek. Find trail on the north side of FS-52 and the west side of Big Creek. Hike north in the grassy meadows surrounding Big Creek for 2.5 miles, then turn west (left) on a less distinct trail into the North Fork John Day River Wilderness (sign) away from the vehicle track. The trail follows the creek for another half mile, then begins to ascend in open woods. On reaching an old road, turn right (east) to reach a heavily travelled gravel road near the summit. Turn left (northwest) uphill 600', then leave the road to the right, ascending northeast to the 88' summit tower and a lookout that is staffed into October. The view to the west and northwest extends from Mt. Hood, 152 miles away at 278°, to Mt. Adams, 161 miles at 298° and Mt. Rainier, 196 miles at 308°.

BIG CREEK CAMPGROUND, 5100' (USGS Tower Mt.). At mile 24.5, turn south then immediately west to cross a bridge over Big Creek and find a primitive campsite.

BIG CREEK TRAIL, 5100' to 3400', 14 miles RT, 1800' gain (USGS Tower Mountain, Kelsay Butte). At mile 24.5, turn south from FS-52 then west across Big Creek. Drive south downstream to the trailhead, one mile from FS-52. Hike down Big Creek in the North Fork John Day Wilderness to the North Fork John Day River (no vehicles).

BIG CREEK CAMPGROUND, 5100'. Other primitive campgrounds are accessible north of road FS-52 between the crossing of Big Creek and the Tower Mountain Road 0.3 miles east.

TOWER MOUNTAIN, 6850', 20 miles RT, 2000' gain (USGS Tower Mt.). **Mt. Bicycle Route.** At mile 24.5, park at the beginning of Tower Mountain Road, across from the turnoff to Big Creek Campground. Ride north on the road to the summit and lookout tower.

FLY SUMMIT, 6433', 6 miles RT, 1400' gain (USGS Tower Mountain, Silver Butte). At mile 28.5, park and hike the Squaw Creek Trail northeast in open woods for one mile then turn north and ascend on the ridge. Where the trail begins to descend to the east, continue north to the summit.

PACK SADDLE SUMMIT, 6400', 10 miles RT, 1100' gain (USGS Silver Butte, Trout Meadow). At mile 31, trail FS-3029 goes south through the upper (western) part of Trout Meadows, passing a trail at two miles that goes north to Log Table Camp. Continue southwest on the plateau between Martin Creek and Wagner Gulch. Find Pack Saddle Spring four miles from FS-52. From the spring, continue southwest one mile to the 6400' summit, which is one-fourth mile west of the trail just before the trail begins to descend into Wagner Gulch. The summit overlooks Silver Butte and some of the North Fork John Day River Canyon.

JUNCTION ROAD FS-51, mile 39 from Ukiah. Road FS-51 goes 28 miles north to a junction with SR-244, 13 miles from I-84 at Exit 252.

WOODLEY CAMPGROUND, 4500' (USGS Limber Jim Creek). Drive 15 miles north on road FS-51 from road FS-52 or 27 miles from I-84 at Exit 252. Turn south on Rainbow Road (FS-5125) six miles along the Grande Ronde River to the campground. Facilities and activities: tents, trailers, water, fishing, bicycling.

ANTHONY BUTTE, 6805', 30 miles RT, 2500' gain (USGS Limber Jim Creek, Anthony Butte, WWLGT). **Mt. Bicycle Route.** From Woodley campground, ride southeast on road FS-5125, keeping left at the first two road junctions, then right (SW) at the next two junctions. Twelve miles from the campground, turn right on Ladd Canyon Road, FS-43, to the summit.

LIMBER JIM LOOP, high point 6270', 20 miles RT, 1400' gain (USGS Limber Jim Creek, Anthony Butte, Little Beaver Creek, WWLGT). **Mt. Bicycle Route.** From Woodley campground, ride southeast on road FS-5125, keeping left at the first two road junctions. At the second road junction, FS-5125 turns away from the Grande Ronde River. Turn left on road FS-5140 at the second "Y" after leaving the Grande Ronde River. Continue to ascend northeast. On reaching the La Grande watershed at the summit of the ridge, turn northwest along the ridge to Limber Jim summit, 6270'. Turn west and southwest on road FS-5140 and FS-5130 to return to road FS-5125. Turn left (southeast) to Woodley Campground.

GRANDE RONDE FOREST SERVICE STATION, 3800' (USGS Little Beaver Creek). The station is 17 miles from FS-52 on road FS-51, or 25 miles from I-84 at Exit 252. Maps and information are available here during the summer months.

RIVER CAMPGROUND, 3800' (USGS Little Beaver Creek). The campground is 17 miles from FS-52 on FS-51 or 25 miles from I-84 at Exit 252. Facilities and activities: tents, trailers, water, fishing. No fee.

JOHNSON ROCK, 5714', 7 miles RT, 2000' gain (USGS Little Beaver Creek, Marley Creek). From River Campground, hike west on roads FS-136/FS-137 to road FS-120. Follow this road south one mile and west for one mile. Turn north one mile to the summit.

PARK SADDLE LOOP, high point 5400', 25 miles RT, 2000' gain (USGS Little Beaver Creek, WWLGT). **Mt. Bicycle Route.** From River Campground, ride east on road FS-4305, keeping left at road junctions to Park Saddle, six miles and 5400'. Park Saddle Spring is east of the road junction. From the road junction in Park Saddle, continue north on road FS-5110 along Dry Beaver Ridge. At the north end of the ridge, descend west on Dry Beaver Road to join paved FS-51. Turn south to return to River Campground.

TIME-AND-A-HALF CAMPGROUND, 3700' (USGS Little Beaver Creek). Drive north on FS-51 for 20 miles from road FS-52 or 22 miles from I-84 at Exit 252. Facilities and activities: tents, trailers, hiking, fishing. No fee.

FLY RIDGE VIEWPOINT, 5186', 8 miles RT, 1500' gain (USGS Little Beaver Creek, Marley Creek, WWLGT). From Time-and-a-Half Campground, hike west on road FS-5115, which goes southwest from road FS-51 near the campground.

SPOOL CART CAMPGROUND, 3500' (USGS Marley Creek). Drive 25 miles north on road FS-51 from road FS-52 or 19 miles from I-84 at Exit 252. Facilities and activities: fishing, tents, trailers, hiking. No fee.

FS-52

NORTH FORK JOHN DAY RIVER TRAIL, 5200' to 3400', mile 41 (USGS Trout Meadows, Silver Butte, Olive Lake, Kelsay Butte, NFJDW). Destinations and junctions on this trail include: Trout Creek Trail, 4900', 2.5 miles one way; Crane Creek Trail, 4500', 6 miles one way; Granite Creek Trail and campground, 4300', 13 miles one way; Dixson Bar and campground, 3800', 17 miles one way; Big Creek Trail and end of road FS-5506, 3400', 25 miles one way. Bicycles are not allowed in the Wilderness.

NORTH FORK JOHN DAY RIVER CAMPGROUND, 5200', mile 41 (USGS Trout Meadow). Facilities and activities: fishing, hiking, tents, trailers, piped water. No fee.

BLACK BUTTE LOOP, high point 7076', 28 miles RT, 2600' (USGS Crawfish Lake, Trout Meadows, NFJUW). **Mt. Bicycle Route.** From the North Fork John Day River Campground, ride east on road FS-73 for 12 miles to the Black Butte road. Turn north on Black Butte road (FS-7325). After crossing the Middle Fork of Trail Creek, three miles from FS-73, leave bicycle and hike north to the summit of Black Butte, the high point. Return to Black Butte Road and ride west to a junction with paved FS-51. Turn left (south) on the paved road to return to the campground.

CHICKEN HILL LOOP, high point 7270', 30 miles RT, 2800' gain (USGS Crawfish Lake, Trout Meadows, NFJUW). **Mt. Bicycle Route.** From the North Fork John Day River Campground, ride east on road FS-73 for 14 miles to a junction with the Chicken Hill Road, FS-5185 and the high point of the trip. Turn left on FS-5185 (west) and ride along the divide between the Grande Ronde watershed to the north and the John Day River watershed to the south. At a road junction, six miles from FS-73, turn left on a branch road and ascend to the summit of Chicken Hill, 6989'. Return to road FS-5185 and continue west to a junction with road FS-51. Ride south on the pavement to the starting point.

JUNCTION ROAD FS-73, mile 41. From this junction, the community of Granite is nine miles south and Anthony Lakes are 17 miles east (see road log FS-73).

History

1579   Francis Drake from England in the *Golden Hind* sailed as far north as southern Oregon, but, as far as known, made no landings.

1602   Sebastian Viscaino of Spain sailed north to southern Oregon but didn't land in Oregon.

1774   Juan Perez of Spain sailed past the Oregon coast but didn't land in Oregon.

1776   Bruno Heceta of Spain landed on the mainland near the Strait of Juan de Fuca and spent time near the mouth of the Columbia, concluding that a great river drained nearby.

1776   James Cook passed by the Oregon coast and landed on Vancouver Island.

1788   Robert Gray landed at Tillamook Bay.

1792   On the basis of information derived from Heceta, Robert Gray found the Columbia River and traveled up the river some miles. The river is named after his ship.

1793   Alexander Mackenzie made the first crossing of the continent, reaching the shore north of what is now Vancouver, Canada.

1805   Meriwether Lewis and William Clark in a party totaling 31 people, including Sacajawea with her infant son, reached the Columbia River and camped near Hat Rock.

1811   A party organized by John Jacob Astor and led by Wilson Price Hunt reached Eastern Oregon in the late fall. The party included Pierre Dorion, his wife Marie and their two children, and John Day.

1833   Benjamin L. E. Bonneville with a small party traveled from the Snake River near Farewell Bend across the mountains near the Snake River to the Wallowa valley.

1836   Marcus Whitman and party traveled as far as the Grande Ronde valley on what became the Oregon Trail emigrant route, then directly across the Blue Mountains to what is now Walla Walla.

1842   Beginning of the Oregon Trail migration. Elijah White led a party of 112 people to Oregon.

1843   The Great Migration began. The emigrants in this year, nearly one thousand people, included Peter Burnett as leader, James Nesmith, and the Applegate brothers.

1843   John Charles Fremont explored, surveyed, and described the route of the Oregon Trail that was used by subsequent travellers.

1846   In a treaty with England, the United States acquired rights to the Oregon Territory, now Washington, Oregon, and Idaho.

1851   Utilla Indian Agency was established on the Umatilla River near what is now Echo. It also served as a trading post for the Oregon Trail emigrants.

1855   Fort Henrietta was built on the site of the Utilla Indian Agency near what is now Echo.

1859 Oregon admitted to statehood.

1861 Gold discovered at Auburn, near Baker City.

1862 Baker County established by the State Legislature.

1862 Umatilla County formed out of Wasco County.

1864 Grant County established, taking parts of Wasco and Umatilla counties.

1864 Union County was formed out of Baker County.

1869 The transcontinental railway reached California, effectively ending the Oregon Trail emigration.

1884 The railroad from Portland to Ogden was completed through Eastern Oregon.

1885 Morrow County established from Umatilla County.

1887 Malheur County was taken from Baker County.

1887 Chief Joseph flight from Wallowa Valley to Montana.

1887 Wallowa County was taken out of Union County.

1890 Construction started on the Sumpter Valley Railroad. The railroad was completed to Prairie City in 1910.

1908 Umatilla, Malheur, Whitman, and Wallowa National Forests established. Wallowa and Whitman were combined in 1945.

Sources:

Corning HM, ed.: *Dictionary of Oregon History*. Portland: Binfords & Mort, 1956. Clark RC, Down RH, Blue GV: *A History of Oregon*. New York: Row Peterson, 1925. *An Illustrated History of Baker, Grant, Malheur, and Harney Counties*. Western Historical Publishing, 1902. Evans JW: *Powerful Rockey–The Blue Mountains and the Oregon Trail*. La Grande: Eastern Oregon State College, 1991.

Geology

Northeast Oregon is made up of several different fragments of volcanic islands and ocean floor sediments that originated in the Pacific Ocean. Some of these fragments are identified by their fossil content as originating possibly as far south as the latitude of present Mexico City. These fragments were rafted by plate movements into contact with the pre-existing North American continent beginning about 130 million years ago. Geologists call these fragments "terranes". Many of the rocks we see exposed in northeast Oregon are the result of events that took place up to 300 million years ago far from what was then the edge of the continent.

The following different terranes are recognized in northeast Oregon: (1) The Olds Ferry terrane to the south and west beginning at Huntington is made up of 170- to 240-million-year-old volcanic islands that are exposed from around Ironside Mountain through Huntington and on into Idaho. The Connor Creek fault (see p. 6) separates the Olds Ferry terrane from the Baker terrane to the north.

(2) The Baker terrane, consisting of 220- to 300-million-year-old pieces of ocean floor, ranges from oceanic crust as formed at the mid-ocean ridge where plates are separating to allow the underlying mantle to emerge, through sediments collected in a deep ocean environment far from shore, to calcareous fossil-rich sediments deposited near shore. The oceanic crust is exposed in the peridotite, gabbro, and serpentine of the Canyon Mountain complex near Canyon City (see p. 127). The deep-ocean muds have been altered to the argillite of the Elkhorn Range west of Baker City (see p. 58) and to the schists along the Burnt River. The calcareous sediments are exposed in the limestone and marble quarries in the southern part of the Elkhorn Ridge near Marble Point (see p. 58) and in the Nelson Marble formation near Weatherby (see p. 6) where Ash Grove Cement West makes cement and other industrial products.

(3) The Wallowa terrane, as much as five miles thick, of rocks 220- to 280-million-years-old, and bounded on the south by a fault near the Powder river, includes fragments of volcanic islands and fossil-rich sediments accumulated in a near-shore environment. The remnants of the volcanic islands are represented by the Clover Creek greenstone exposed north of the Powder River near Keating and extending into the foothills near Eagle Creek and by the volcanic rocks found along the Snake River from Oxbow to the mouth of the Grande Ronde River. The compression forces produced as this terrane was pushed against the continental mass folded the layers until in places the older member is above a younger member. The Martin Bridge limestone and the Hurwal shales, both deposited in a shallow, warm water environment, contain many fossils. For example, an ichthyosaur from the Triassic age was found near Eagle Creek.

(4) The Izee terrane, near Izee and separated by a fault from the Olds Ferry terrane to the east and by the John Day fault from the Baker terrane to the north, contains deposits of limestone, mudstone, silt, and sandstone formed 140- to 240-million-years-ago in a shallow near-shore marine environment. The Izee terrane contains many fossils.

About the time that these terranes began to be joined to the North American continent, magma rose beneath the areas that are now the Elkhorn Range and the Wallowa Mountains and crystallized as granitic batholiths. Erosion has exposed these batholiths around Eagle Cap in the Wallowa Mountains and around the Anthony Lake Region in the Elkhorn Range. The lode gold deposits that have been mined around Bourne and Cornucopia are associated with the intrusion of these batholiths.

After these oceanic terranes became part of the continent, volcanic activity continued sporadically. In the western part of Northeast Oregon, the Clarno volcanic eruptions occurred from 50 to 35 million years ago and the John Day volcanic eruptions 37 to 20 million years ago. Many animals and plants have been preserved in the material from these predominantly ash eruptions. The remains of these plants and animals are now found in various fossil beds.

Beginning about 17 million years ago and continuing for about ten million years in northeast Oregon, the Columbia River Basalt Group of volcanic eruptions poured out from vents centered in the northeast corner of the state around the lower Grande Ronde river, in the western part of Grant county, and in other places in the area. These eruptions covered thousands of square miles thousands of feet deep with rapidly flowing basalt. During the same interval that saw the eruptions of the Columbia River Basalt Group, volcanic eruptions of much less fluid andesite lava erupted from vents near Strawberry Mountain (see p. 44) and at the Sawtooth volcano east of Baker City (see p. 63). The Strawberry volcanic eruptions covered an area of 1,500 square miles, including Lookout Mountain and much of the Monument Rock wilderness. From 15 to 12 million years ago, eruptions of volcanic ash and weathering of the basaltic lavas left strata rich in fossils that are now called the Mascall Formation. Then from eight to six million years ago, ash eruptions and erosion left layers with fewer fossils now called the Rattlesnake Formation.

Lake Idaho, which existed from seven to two million years ago, covered many of the valleys of northeast Oregon and into Idaho. The water from this lake may have drained into the Grande Ronde river before the drainage was captured by the Snake River at Oxbow to form Hells Canyon.

Uplifting and down faulting of blocks created the Baker and the Grande Ronde valleys in the last few million years and the soil in these valleys was deposited at least in part from lakes.

Glaciation of the region began about two million years ago and continued to about 15,000 years ago. Glacier carved valleys are common in the Elkhorn Range and in the Wallowa Mountains. Wallowa Lake was dug by one of these glaciers and the lateral and terminal moraines surrounding this lake are classic examples. Flooding at the end of the glacial age left its mark in the sand dunes near Farewell Bend and the erratic boulders along the Columbia River that were brought there by repeated floods from Lake Missoula in Montana. Lake Missoula was impounded by a glacier dam that repeatedly failed, allowing huge floods to travel across Washington State and down the Columbia River.

Some geologic features in the area have yet to be explained. The Olympic-Wallowa Lineament, a nearly straight line of topographic features extending from the Olympic Mountains in Washington State through Wallula Gap at the Oregon-Washington border and across the northern flank of the Wallowa Mountains, possibly represents the original continental margin before the island terranes were accreted. The most damaging earthquake in Oregon history occurred on this Lineament in Umapine in 1936.

Sources:

Alt DD, Hyndman DW: *Roadside Geology of Oregon.* Missoula: Mountain Press, 1981. Aylesworth TG: *Moving Continents.* Hillside: Enslow, 1990. Brooks HC: Plate tectonics and the geologic history of the Blue Mountains. *Oregon Geology* 41:71-80, 1979. Cloud P: *Oasis in Space.* New York: Norton, 1988. Kearey P, Vine FJ: *Global Tectonics.* Boston: Blackwell, 1990. Orr EL, Orr WN, Baldwin EM: *Geology of Oregon.* Dubuque: Kendall-Hunt, 1992. Thayer TP: *Geologic Setting of the John Day Country, Grant County OR.* USGS Publication. Reprinted by Northwest Interpretive Association, 909 First Ave. #630, Seattle WA 98104-1060. Vallier TL, Brooks HC: Geology of the Blue Mountains region of Oregon, Idaho, and Washington. *USGS Professional Paper 1435*, 93 pages, 1986. Oregon Dept. of Geology and Mineral Industries Publications, State Office Bld. #965, 800 NE Oregon St., Portland OR 97232. Free catalog. Roadside Geologic Markers Program, Grant County. Prepared by: Grant County Planning Commission, Oregon Dept. of Geology and Mineral Industries, State Highway Dept., Univ. Oregon Geology Dept., Oregon State Univ. Geology Dept., U.S. Geological Survey.

Woody Plant Communities

Juniperus Occidentalis Zone (2500'–4600')

Artemisia spp. (sagebrush), Chrysothamnus nauseosus (gray rabbitbrush), Chrysothamnus viscidiflorus (green rabbitbrush), Grayia spinosa (spiney hopsage), Juniperus occidentalis (western juniper), Pinus ponderosa (yellow pine), Purshia tridentata (bitterbrush), Ribes cereum (wax currant), Ribes velutinum (desert gooseberry), Tetradymia canescens (gray horsebush).

Pinus Ponderosa Zone (3000'–5000')

Abies concolor (white fir), Abies grandis (grand fir), Amelanchier alnifolia (serviceberry), Apocynum androsaemifolium (dogbane), Arctostaphylos patula (green manzanita), Artemisia arbuscula (low sagebrush), Artemisia rigida (stiff sagebrush), Artemisia tridentata (big sagebrush), Berberis repens (creeping western barberry), Betula spp. (birch), Ceanothus sp. (ceanothus), Clematis ligusticifolia (clematis), Crataegus douglasii (blackhawthorn), Holodiscus discolor (oceanspray), Juniperus occidentalis (common juniper), Physocarpus malvaceus (ninebark), Pinus contorta (lodgepole pine), Pinus ponderosa (yellow pine), Populus tremuloides (quaking aspen), Prunus virginiana melanocarpa (chokecherry), Pseudotsuga Menziesii (Douglas fir), Purshia tridentata (bitterbrush), Rosa nutkana (Nootka rose), Rosa woodsii (wood rose), Spiraea betulifolia lucida (spirea), Symphoricarpos albus (snowberry).

Pinus contorta zone (4000'–5000')

Arctostaphylos uva-ursi (kinnikinnick), Danthonia californica (danthonia), Danthonia intermedia (timber danthonia), Purshia tridentata (bitterbrush), Ribes cereum (currant), Ribes viscosissimum (sticky currant), Spiraea douglasii (spirea), Vaccinium sp.(huckleberry).

Pseudostuga menziesii Zone (2000'–4300')

Holodiscus discolor (oceanspray), Juniperus occidentalis (western juniper), Larix occidentalis (western larch), Physocarpus malvaceus (ninebark), Pinus contorta (Pinus contorta), Pinus ponderosa (yellow pine), Populus tremuloides (quaking aspen), Pseudotsuga menziesii (Douglas fir), Rosa nutkana (Nootka rose), Rosa woodsii (wood rose), Spiraea betulifolia (spirea), Symphoricarpos albus (snowberry).

Abies grandis Zone (5000'–6500')

Abies amabilis (silver fir), Abies concolor (white fir), Abies grandis (grand fir), Abies lasiocarpa (subalpine fir), Alnus spp. (alder), Amelanchier alnifolia (serviceberry), Ceanothus sanguineus (redstem ceanothus), Ceanothus velutinus (snowbrush ceanothus), Larix occidentalis (western larch), Libocedrus decurrens (incense cedar), Pachistima myrsinites (Oregon boxwood), Physocarpus malvaceus (ninebark), Picea engelmanii (spruce), Pinus contorta (lodgepole pine), Pinus lambertiana (sugar pine), Pinus monticola (western white pine), Pinus ponderosa (yellow pine), Pseudostuga menziesii (Douglas fir), Ribes lacustre (prickly currant), Rosa gymnocarpa (baldhip rose), Salix sp. (willow), Sambucus spp. (elderberry), Spirea betulifolia (spirea), Tsuga mertensiana (mountain hemlock), Vaccinium sp. (huckleberry).

Abies lasiocarpa Zone (4300'–8000')

Abies amabilis (silver fir), Abies grandis (grand fir), Abies lasiocarpa (subalpine fir), Abies procera (noble fir), Acer glabrum (Rocky Mountain maple), Alnus spp. (alder), Amelanchier alnifolia (serviceberry), Artemisia tridentata (big sagebrush), Juniperus communis (juniper), Larix lyallii (subalpine larch), Larix occidentalis (western larch), Ledum glandulosum (Labrador tea), Linnaea borealis (twin-flower), Lonicera spp. (twinberry), Menziesia ferruginea (false azalea), Pachistima myrsinites (Oregon boxwood), Picea engelmannii (spruce), Pinus albicaulis (whitebark pine), Pinus contorta (lodgepole pine), Pinus monticola (western white pine), Pinus ponderosa (yellow pine), Populus tremuloides (quaking aspen), Pseudotsuga menziesii (Douglas fir), Rhododendron albiflorum (azalea), Rubus spp. (raspberry, thimbleberry), Sorbus sitchensis (mountain ash), Spiraea betulifolia (spirea), Tsuga mertensiana (mountain hemlock), Vaccinium (huckleberry).

Timberline Zone (7000'–9000')

Abies lasiocarpus (subalpine fir), Cassiope Mertensiana (white mossheather), Phyllodoce spp. (heather), Picea engelmannii (spruce), Pinus albicaulis (white bark pine), Pinus contorta (lodgepole pine), Vaccinium spp. (huckleberry).

Shrub-steppe Zone

Alnus rhombifolia (white alder), Amelanchier alnifolia (serviceberry), Artemisia spp. (sagebrush), Atriplex confertifolia (shadscale), Celtis douglasii (hackberry), Cercocarpus ledifolius (mountain mahogany), Chrysothamnus nauseosus (gray rabbitbrush), Chrysothamnus viscidifloris (green rabbitbrush), Crataegus columbiana (Columbia hawthorn), Crataegus douglasii (black hawthorn), Grayia spinosa (spiney hopsage), Juniperus occidentalis (western juniper), Juniperus scopulorum (Rocky Mountain juniper), Philadelphus lewisii (mockorange), Populus trichocarpa (black cottonwood), Prunus virginiana (chokecherry), Purshia tridentata (bitterbrush), Rhus glabra (sumac), Ribes cereum (currant), Rosa spp. (rose), Sarcobatus vermiculatus (black greasewood), Spiraea betulifolia (spirea), Symphoricarpos albus (snowberry), Tetradymia canescens (gray horsebush).

Salt Desert Shrub Zone

Artemisia spp. (sagebrush) Atriplex confertifolia (shadscale), Atriplex Nuttalli (saltbush), Eurotia lanata (winter fat), Grayia spinosa (spiney horsebush), Sarcobatus vermiculatus (black greasewood).

Riparian Zone

Celtis reticulata (hackberry), Cratageus spp. (hawthorn), Populus tremuloides (quaking aspen), Prunus virginiana (chokecherry), Rhamnus purshiana (cascara), Salix spp. (willow).

Source:

Franklin JF, Dyrness CT: *Natural Vegetation of Oregon and Washington.* Forest Service Tech. Rep. PNW-8, USDA 1973. Corvallis: Oregon State Univ., 1988.

154

Weather

(ma=normal maximum temperature, mi=normal minimum temperature)
(pr=normal precipitation in inches)

	Jan	Feb	Mar	Apr	May	Jun	Jul	Aug	Sep	Oct	Nov	Dec
Baker City (annual pr=10.87)												
ma	34	41	50	59	67	76	85	84	75	62	46	35
mi	17	22	27	31	38	45	48	48	39	31	25	18
pr	1.03	.62	.84	.82	1.26	1.38	.58	.94	.74	.63	.96	1.07
La Grande (annual pr=17.44)												
ma	37	43	50	58	67	76	87	86	76	63	47	38
mi	23	27	30	35	42	49	53	52	44	35	30	24
pr	2.16	1.48	1.54	1.47	1.58	1.43	.60	.92	.95	1.30	2.04	1.97
Milton-Freewater (annual pr=14.33)												
ma	41	48	56	63	72	80	88	87	77	65	51	42
mi	27	32	37	42	48	54	59	58	50	41	34	28
pr	1.71	1.17	1.52	1.20	1.28	.94	.47	.65	.76	1.08	1.84	1.71
Ontario (annual pr=9.68)												
ma	35	45	56	66	76	86	95	93	82	67	49	37
mi	19	25	31	36	44	52	57	54	44	34	28	21
pr	1.33	.87	.82	.63	.73	.72	.20	.41	.53	.61	1.30	1.50
Pendleton (annual pr=12.02)												
ma	40	47	54	61	70	80	88	86	76	64	49	41
mi	27	32	35	39	46	53	58	58	50	41	34	28
pr	1.51	1.14	1.16	1.04	.99	.64	.35	.53	.59	.86	1.58	1.63
Richland (annual pr=13.16)												
ma	38	46	56	66	75	83	91	90	81	68	52	39
mi	19	23	29	35	41	48	53	52	43	33	26	20
pr	1.65	1.16	1.07	.94	1.22	1.03	.61	.80	.63	.78	1.65	1.62
Seneca (annual pr=13.15)												
ma	33	39	44	53	61	71	80	80	70	60	44	35
mi	9	14	20	25	31	36	38	37	28	21	19	12
pr	1.36	1.02	1.18	.99	1.34	1.11	.58	.87	.66	.91	1.49	1.64
Wallowa (annual pr=17.35)												
ma	34	42	50	59	67	76	85	84	75	62	45	35
mi	18	23	26	31	37	43	45	44	37	30	26	19
pr	1.94	1.34	1.40	1.25	1.68	1.43	.86	.90	1.24	1.43	1.88	2.00

Source:

Owenby JR: *Monthly Station normals of temperature, precipitation, etc. 1961-1990: Oregon.* Climatography of the U.S., No.81. Asheville: US Dept. Commerce, NOAA, National Climatic Data Center, 1992.

Oregon Trail
(Sites and Information)

Baker County: 5, 6, 8, 12, 63, 67.

Malheur County: 1, 3, 30, 31, 33.

Morrow County: 134.

Umatilla County: 21, 22, 27.

Union County: 13, 14, 19, 20.

Guided Tours
Backcountry Lodges and Guides

Baker County: 8, 9, 70, 71, 77.

Grant County: 41, 126, 132.

Malheur County: 30, 31, 32.

Morrow County: 29.

Umatilla County: 22, 23, 24, 26, 28, 118, 119.

Union County: 14, 15, 16, 95.

Wallowa County: 100, 102, 105, 106.

Geologic Sites

Baker County: 4-7, 9, 11, 35, 38, 39, 54-56, 58-60
63, 68-70, 73, 81, 83-85, 94.

Grant County: 44-46, 48-53, 127, 132.

Malheur County: 2, 3, 31, 32.

Morrow County: 136.

Umatilla County: 120, 121, 140.

Union County: 20, 98.

Wallowa County: 102, 104, 108, 115.

The supplementary maps listed by a five letter designation and included in parenthesis with the USGS maps are available from Forest Service and National Recreation Area offices:

HCNRA: Hells Canyon National Recreation Area.

Malheur National Forest:
MFPCR: Prairie City Ranger District.

Malheur and Wallowa–Whitman National Forests:
SMMRW: Strawberry Mountain Wilderness and Monument Rock Wilderness.

Umatilla National Forest:
HRDMA: Heppner Ranger District Motorized Access and Travel Management Plan (free).
NFJDE: North Fork John Day Ranger District East Half.
NFJDW: North Fork John Day Ranger District West Half.
NFJUW: North Fork John Day and North Fork Umatilla Wilderness.

Wallowa–Whitman National Forest.
WWBRD: Baker Ranger District Travel Opportunity Guide.
WWECW: Eagle Cap Wilderness & Travel Opportunity Guide.
WWLGT: La Grande Ranger District Travel Opportunity Guide.
WWURD: Unity Ranger District Travel Opportunity Guide.